SEEING PITTSBURGH

SEEING

Pittsburgh

Barringer Fifield

Photographs by Michael Eastman

University of Pittsburgh Press

Published by the University of Pittsburgh Press, Pittsburgh, Pa. 15260
Copyright © 1996, Barringer Fifield
Photographs copyright © 1996, Michael Eastman
All rights reserved
Manufactured in the United States of America
Printed on acid-free paper
10 9 8 7 6 5 4 3 2 1

Photographs for this book were made possible by a generous grant
from the Fisher Foundation.

Library of Congress Cataloging-in-Publication Data
Fifield, Barringer.
   Seeing Pittsburgh / Barringer Fifield ; photographs by Michael
Eastman.
     p. cm.
   Includes bibliographical references (p.   ) and index.
   ISBN 0-8229-3859-6 (cloth). — ISBN 0-8229-5542-3 (pbk.)
   1. Pittsburgh (Pa.)—Tours. 2. Pittsburgh (Pa.)—Pictorial works. I. Title.
F159.P63F54   1996
917.48'86—dc20   96-10111

A CIP catalog record for this book is available from
the British Library.

for my mother, Esther Fifield

CONTENTS

INTRODUCTION

Great cities don't need boosters, but they spawn urban critics. Pittsburgh has long been the object of acute analysis by writers like Franklin Toker, James Van Trump, Patricia Lowry, Walter Kidney, and Samuel Hays. Yet is Pittsburgh a great city? Pittsburghers display two peculiarities that make you wonder.

When I was doing research for this book, it seemed that Pittsburgh acquaintances took even neutral comments about their city as personal criticism. One normally savvy individual, for instance, objected to my calling a statue in Schenley Park "frightful." When asked if he honestly thought that it was good sculpture, he said, "No, but you should have at least mentioned the flowers we've planted around it."

Pittsburgh is not about flowers.

But what is it about? For all the scholarly studies written on their city, Pittsburghers entertain a quirky notion of their hometown. When they describe the place, they talk not about what's there, but about what's not there: smoke. They are dazzled by an absence.

One might understand their excitement if clean air were news, instead of dating back a generation, or if the city's formerly dingy skies were now blue. But Pittsburgh's heavens, though smoke free, remain mostly opaque; in the sunny day count, Pittsburgh ranks forty-sixth among the fifty largest American cities.

I was ill-suited to understand these peculiarities of the local temperament. As a Midwesterner, used to wide and mostly vacant expanses, what struck me about Pittsburgh was its fullness, not its

emptiness. The city has such visual density that to characterize it by
something that wasn't there seemed perverse.

The dangers of criticism also eluded me. Since leaving Indiana, I
have spent most of my adult life in Rome. Romans show their feeling
for Rome by criticizing it; it's as though they can't forgive their city for
no longer being the capital of an empire. Praising Rome, even faintly,
is for rubes.

Pittsburghers' touchiness, and their reluctance to see what the
city has become, rather than what it has been, made me wonder if the
place wasn't simply provincial. Yet, oddly enough, when I began commuting between Rome and Pittsburgh while writing this book, my view
changed. Each time I returned to Pittsburgh, I expected to be
disappointed—to find that my sojourns in sunny baroque Rome would
cast a definitive gloom over cloudy Gothic Pittsburgh. Instead, I discovered that Pittsburgh held up just fine. The churches were the best
test; I feared that those that most impressed me while living in Pittsburgh would seem pokey after months among Rome's splendors. But
they continued to affect me as they had at the outset.

It wasn't just the churches that continued to impress me; it was
the city as a whole. However provincial Pittsburgh may be from a
strictly geographical point of view, its history is that of a great city—
dense, violent, meaningful. As I worked on this book, I found that the
Pittsburgh experience resonated as deeply as that of any capital.

After a long time, I came to understand Pittsburghers' touchiness
about criticism, and I also began to figure out why they seem so
focused on what's not there, rather than on what is there. Pittsburghers' ongoing celebration of smoke's disappearance shows, paradoxically, how important heavy industry was in giving the city its
identity. It's not just smoke that has disappeared; so have the moun-
tainlike factories and mills, which until very recently lined and hid
and polluted the rivers, making them unusable as well as invisible. No
town has so quickly undergone such a radical visual transformation, a
reflection of the sometimes painful change from a manufacturing to a

service economy. Pittsburghers' touchiness comes from a well-founded concern that the activity that made their city great is no more.

Fortunately, the visual transformation suggests that a new civic identity is in the making. The Pittsburgh of clean rivers and green slopes is going to be at least as spectacular as the old city, and far healthier.

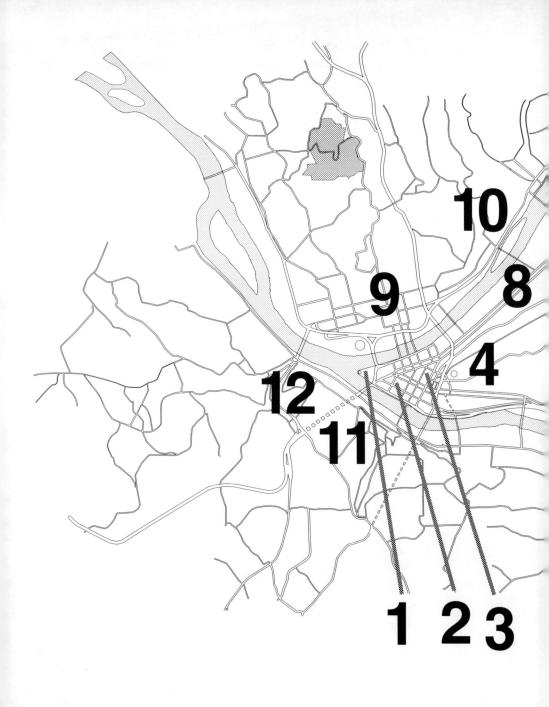

Numbers indicate areas where tours begin.

HOW TO USE THIS GUIDE

Pittsburgh is an emphatic place; its history and topography both exude drama. This guide's purpose is to make the drama easier to experience.

The city's pleasures have less to do with particular sights or attractions, plenteous though they are, than with Pittsburgh's overall textures and patterns. You can enjoy the place even if you choose not to spend time visiting a specific church or museum, which, in turn, means that you have a certain freedom in timing your tours.

But you may find it rewarding to follow the order of the tours as presented here. A rough narrative logic governs the itineraries; they begin where historical Pittsburgh did, and end with its future. The tours also alternate the agreeable with the grievous, the pretty with the potent. Each tour works independently of the others, but the story unfolds best if its beginning precedes its middle and the end follows both.

Read or skim through each tour before you set out. This will also enable you to telephone ahead to make sure any particular place you're interested in is going to be open. The telephone numbers of churches, museums, and other attractions appear as an appendix at the end of this book.

Part of the lure of Pittsburgh lies in the fact that it's not yet laid out for mass tourism, which means you get to make discoveries of your own. It also means that the logistics of touring require more patience than a visit to Disneyland would. The city's extraordinary collection of churches, for instance, merits attention, but you may have to seek out the church office in order to see them on weekdays.

Generally speaking, however, the tours do work best on weekdays during office hours. Two big exceptions would be open air attractions and museums, usually visible on weekend days. Churches, of course, are open on Sunday mornings, but they cannot be toured during services.

Pittsburgh invites walking far more than most American cities, and, in fact, downtown is organized into walking tours. For the other itineraries, you will need a car—at least for the long stretches—but sections of each tour can be walked. The driving portion of the itineraries is easier to follow if the driver has a navigator next to him or her. Pittsburgh's roads are difficult as it is; you won't want to be reading a book as you negotiate the Fort Duquesne Bridge. Neighborhood maps are included here, but a current city street map is an essential tool.

SEEING PITTSBURGH

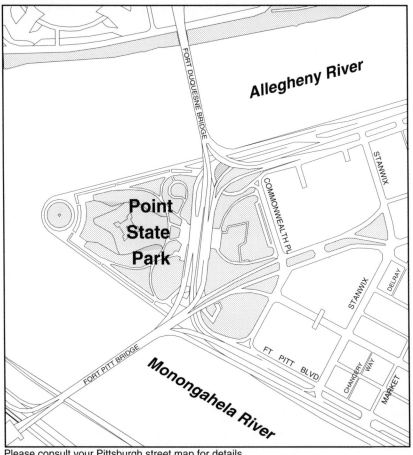

Allegheny River

FORT DUQUESNE BRIDGE

Point
State
Park

COMMONWEALTH PL

STANWIX

STANWIX

DELRAY

FORT PITT BRIDGE

Monongahela River

FT PITT BLVD

CHANCERY WAY

MARKET

Please consult your Pittsburgh street map for details.

POINT STATE PARK AND GATEWAY CENTER
This walking tour begins at the entrance to Point State Park at Liberty
Avenue and Commonwealth Place. Parking is available at garages on
Stanwix, Liberty, Penn, and Commonwealth.

1

What's the Point?

Pittsburghers love Point State Park, but for outsiders it is an acquired taste. The landscaping is ordinary, the views are limited, and the buildings look insignificant. One critic, insensitive to Pittsburgh's peculiarities, dubbed the empty space at the Forks of the Ohio "Pointless Park." It's not so poor as that, but, aside from a big fountain, it is pretty spare.

What's the reason for Pittsburghers' enthusiasm? A little observation suggests it may be akin to their persistent joy in smoke's absence. Compressed in space between rivers and hills, weighed down in time by overwhelming social dramas, the city has had too much stuff cluttering its ground and burdening its history, just as too much smoke once poisoned its air. Pittsburghers value unencumbered flat land the same way they celebrate the clear atmosphere—emptiness as event.

Though it appears innocent both of history and of aesthetic interest, this ground witnessed two of Pittsburgh's three defining moments: its birth in the mid eighteenth century and its rebirth in the middle of the twentieth century. Reminders of nineteenth-century industrialization are significantly missing.

Few cities can boast as vivid a beginning. Anyone acquainted with latter-day Pittsburgh's aggressive spirit will not be surprised to

Point State Park

learn that the town was born a warrior. Its site alone did not dictate this result. The wedding of the rivers might have produced a simple backwoods trader; instead, the place had a direct, even brutal, relation to power from the outset.

5
Point
State
Park
and
Gateway
Center

A twenty-one-year-old major in Virginia's colonial militia, exploring the area in 1753, found the site attractive. "I spent some time in viewing the Rivers, and the Land in the Fork, which I think extremely well situated for a Fort; as it has the absolute Command of both Rivers." The major's name was George Washington.

With a number of fellow Virginians Washington had created a real estate company; land speculation was already an old American tradition. Possession of the Point, as the confluence of the Allegheny and the Monongahela came to be called, would secure their Ohio Company a chance to parcel out that river's valley. The colonies' population was exuberant both in growth and in spirit; this restlessness, our westering urge, promised the investors a good return.

The unrolling of Anglo-American hegemony from east to west later appeared inevitable, a manifest destiny, but it didn't seem inevitable to the Virginians. The stockade they threw together early in 1754 (grandly named Fort Prince George) provoked a country which entertained a different view of America's future. France, long established in Canada and the Caribbean, had linked her possessions with a string of posts along the inland waterways; she intended to dominate America's rich interior. An English-held Ohio would abort this nascent north-south empire. A flotilla carrying about five hundred Frenchmen arrived from Quebec in April 1754 and reminded the Virginians that they had built their palisade on land belonging, by historical right, to the king of France. Fort Prince George's three dozen or so Virginians departed.

The French replaced Fort Prince George with the far more elaborate Fort Duquesne. The Point thus became the conscious projection of power of two very different empires. The conflict between them, and with the Indians, is a principal theme of the Fort Pitt Museum, on your left after the underpass. (We'll return later to the Music Bastion, which you've just passed.)

France's ambition could only be achieved with Native American help, for the French in America were vastly outnumbered. English-speaking colonists had already filtered across the mountains, and Indian raiding parties regularly attacked isolated Anglo-American homesteads. More than once during what was to become known as the French and Indian War, the French and Indians repelled Anglo-American attempts to retake the Forks of the Ohio, and several of Fort Pitt Museum's displays represent the French rout of General Braddock in 1755.

The last French victory occurred toward the end of 1758 when Major James Grant made an ill-conceived assault on Fort Duquesne; 270 of his 800 men, many of them Highlanders from Scotland, were killed or captured.

This war's turning point had come in the summer of 1757. At that time, William Pitt became England's prime minister, with the intention of establishing British supremacy everywhere. To help execute his plan, he appointed General John Forbes, a Scotsman, to command the British forces.

As instrument of so spectacular a will to power, Forbes was an odd choice. Suffering from a bloody flux, he often led his army from a litter slung between two horses. His way of transporting the troops was just as dramatic. To get back to the headwaters of the Ohio, Virginians like George Washington wanted to reopen Braddock's roundabout but easy southern road. Pennsylvanians preferred a shorter but far more difficult line straight over the mountains.

Forbes characteristically chose the direct route. As a participant put it, construction of the road was "a most diabolical work, and whiskey must be had." But a passage over the mountains and through the forest primeval, with its "numberless, damned petryfyd old logs hard as iron," was finally cut.

Fort Pitt Museum

Forbes's grand defiance of nature, which foreshadowed Pittsburghers' historical attitude toward the environment, had its effect. Those in the small French garrison at the Point now knew that Forbes's army—easily supplied and easily reinforced, thanks to the road—could not be turned back. In November 1758, following instructions from Montreal, they set fire to Fort Duquesne and marched to safer land. This was France's final withdrawal.

A monument to the right of the museum commemorates Forbes's victory and his road, still used by the Boy Scouts as a hiking trail and by motorists on U.S. Route 30.

A Presbyterian divine—another Scot—preached a thanksgiving sermon at the smoking ruins of Fort Duquesne. The dying Forbes then sealed his relations both with the place of his conquest and with the statesman who had inspired it. "I have used the freedom of giving your name to Fort Du Quesne," he wrote William Pitt, "as I hope it was in some measure the being actuated by your spirits that now makes us Masters of the place."

British victory had a consequence that Forbes and Pitt neither foresaw nor desired: the American Revolution. Expulsion of France from America meant the end of the threat that made American colonists good Englishmen. So long as they had empire-minded French neighbors, Americans couldn't dream of revolt against England's costly protection. Disappearance of the French, which Forbes's conquest hastened, gave the colonists margin not only for dreams of rebellion, but also, in less than two decades, for the fact of independence.

The Forbes monument refers to the establishment of "Anglo-Saxon supremacy" in America. The phrase grates on a modern ear—but of that supremacy Pittsburgh offers proof aplenty. One stands before you: the Blockhouse.

The emblem over the gate might lead you to consider this structure a monument to the Daughters of the American Revolution. You would not be entirely wrong. In the 1890s that quintessentially Anglo-Saxon organization did save this, Pittsburgh's oldest building, from demolition by the Pennsylvania Railroad.

Sixty years later, in another fierce battle, they fought to keep it out of less destructive yet still, to the D.A.R., suspect hands—those of the Commonwealth of Pennsylvania. The state wanted the building as part of Point State Park. How that battle turned out may be judged from the brass sidewalk plaques around the perimeter stating triumphantly, "Not Dedicated Property of the Fort Pitt Society, Daughters of the American Revolution."

The formidable women did not even bow to the state's desire that only indigenous species be planted in the park. Old ginkgo trees—native to China—still shade their plot. They did agree to demolition of their guardian's cottage—on condition that the state provide a special guard room within the museum, with a window overlooking the redoubt. That's the reason for the solitary opening in the museum's western wall.

The Blockhouse is the only part of Fort Pitt that has remained intact through the centuries. Its date, 1764, and builder's name appear over the door. Colonel Bouquet was a professional Swiss soldier who played an important role in Pittsburgh's early history, first as Forbes's field commander, then in the fight against the Indians.

After the fall of Fort Duquesne no one knew when the French might attack again; and as the Anglo-Americans advanced westward, the Native Americans became still more menacing. This dual threat induced Pitt to order a fortification at the Point that would "maintain His Majesty's subjects in undisputed control of the Ohio." Fort Pitt, the most impressive stronghold on the British frontier, was built in response to this imperative. An even more formidable undertaking than Forbes's road, the massive fort too foreshadowed Pittsburgh's predilection for land-transforming projects.

The pentagonal Blockhouse was built outside Fort Pitt proper so

9

Point
State
Park
and
Gateway
Center

that sharpshooters could repel assailants crossing the moat. But by the time of its construction, 1764, would-be attackers had become far less worrisome than in 1759.

The effectiveness of both Forbes's road and Fort Pitt lay as much in the fear they induced as in any actual exertion of power they permitted. Forbes's road succeeded not because of a real attack, but because the French feared, rightly, that the obstacles it removed meant an attack was now possible. Fort Pitt likewise served more as a sign than as an actual instrument of British power. The Treaty of Paris in 1763 practically ended the French threat in North America.

The Native Americans, thanks in part to Bouquet's abilities, lost their will to fight here the same year. Their last great campaign began in May 1763. Organized on a vast scale by the great Ottawa chief Pontiac, this war almost succeeded in rolling back the white man's presence. The Indians took many of the western forts and lay siege to Fort Pitt.

Bouquet's orders were to restore British power by any means, including that of presenting the Indians gifts of smallpox-infected blankets. He did not resort to that tactic. (His subordinate within the besieged Fort Pitt, where the disease had broken out, did.) Bouquet's experience, which included seven years of bush warfare, not to mention a careful reading of the classics, had prepared him to confront Native Americans on their own terms, without resorting to subterfuges.

To lift Fort Pitt's siege he marched from the east with four hundred men. At Bushy Run, just a day's march from the Point, the Indians ambushed him. It was the kind of attack—ants surrounding a caterpillar—that had destroyed Braddock's army in 1755.

Adopting a complex feinting maneuver Hannibal had used against the Romans at Cannae, Bouquet extricated his men and vanquished the Indians. The mauled but victorious little army soon marched to the Point and ended the ten-week siege.

Bouquet followed up this success with another. In October 1764, he marched out of Fort Pitt with a thousand men to subdue the Delaware and Shawnee, who had been attacking English settlements. This campaign not only brought peace to Pennsylvania and the lake region, but it also awed the tribesmen into returning all the captives—over two hundred—they had taken in raids. Much has been made of Indian ferocity in this period, but many of the captive whites were reluctant to return to their own people. They had grown fond of the Indians and their way of life.

11

Point
State
Park
and
Gateway
Center

With this achievement, Fort Pitt fulfilled its original mandate. Conditions on the frontier were peaceful enough that Bouquet himself suggested in 1765 that the stronghold be converted into "a trading place." That is exactly what young Pittsburgh became, as pioneers streamed through on their way west.

You will find an outline of Fort Pitt's French predecessor, Fort Duquesne, in the grass field toward the fountain. At its center is a bronze rendering, from an original at the Bibliothèque Nationale in Paris, of Fort Duquesne's plan, detailed down to the *aquéduc des latrines.*

As Forts Pitt and Duquesne mark Pittsburgh's birth, so the great fountain before you marks the city's rebirth two centuries later. This rebirth (or Renaissance, as it is called here) had none of the tragic overtones of the birth. But in its way the process was as dramatic, and at least as complex. If Pittsburgh's birth meant mastering a wilderness, the rebirth meant mastering what threatened to become a wasteland.

How bad was it? The rivers brought devastating floods; the air bore so much soot that streetlamps were lit at noon, and downtown businessmen changed shirts thrice daily. The built environment won no prizes either. H. L. Mencken gave a 1927 article about Pittsburgh the title "The Libido for the Ugly." Frank Lloyd Wright, when asked in the thirties what should be done with the city, advised, "Abandon it."

Pittsburgh's birth was a conscious exercise of power. George Washington chose the site to dominate the Ohio Valley. Pitt and Forbes took it from the French to stop their expansion. Bouquet used it to subjugate the Native Americans. The city's rebirth, contrariwise, has been depicted as an exercise in sweetness and light, brought about by the selflessness of those who led Pittsburgh's postwar renewal. Certainly these leaders knew how to subordinate their short-term interests. But that was self-mastery, not selflessness. In fact, they served an ideal of power no less compelling than that which had motivated Pitt and Forbes and Bouquet. Twentieth-century leaders did not want direct dominion over land and people, but over Pittsburgh's economic future. They were not denying their own interests; they were creating a wider field for their fulfillment.

This observation does not detract from their achievement. Communities can die, and the city's elite might easily have let that happen to Pittsburgh, making lives for themselves elsewhere, as Henry Clay Frick and Andrew Carnegie had done. Instead, they sought their own good in that of their town, and that seeking transformed Pittsburgh.

One of the greatest research projects of early twentieth-century sociology, the Pittsburgh Survey, found a striking paradox in the contrast between Pittsburgh's superbly organized, highly advanced economic structure and an underdeveloped and slipshod political structure. But the paradox disappears if you consider that the creation of the economic structure *required* a weak political system. What properly functioning government would permit the rape of the land—not to mention the chilling exploitation of labor—that Pittsburgh's great nineteenth-century industrial expansion entailed?

The stock market crash of 1929 revealed the weakness of unbridled big business. Even Pittsburgh, the most rampantly entrepreneurial and capitalistic American city, got the message: free market forces did not solve all problems. Growth in the manufacturing sector had tapered off by the 1930s, and the physical and mental atmosphere created by industry was stifling and repulsive. People were loath to come to Pittsburgh and delighted to leave.

Enlightened Pittsburghers saw that business as usual was not going to solve the city's problems. They had to reject the wisdom of their forefathers, according to which any increase in a government's activity was an increase in socialism. Nowadays, cooperation between businessmen and city officials is fairly common, but it was a revolutionary idea in the 1940s. Realized on a grand scale, Pittsburgh's private-public partnership became urban America's model for progress.

13

Point
State
Park
and
Gateway
Center

The chief protagonists of this partnership were David Lawrence, consummate politician and Pittsburgh's mayor from 1946 to 1959, and Richard King Mellon, a reserved banker and member of Pittsburgh's richest family. Lawrence aspired to become something greater than a mere Democratic boss; Mellon's place at the nerve center of Pittsburgh's economy afforded him a clear perception of its problems and possibilities.

Some solutions were obvious. Dams were built upstream to control floods. A technique perfected by a St. Louis engineer, Raymond Tucker, made smoke abatement possible. An incident in this campaign reveals Mellon's role, as well as the primitive attitudes some of his peers clung to. The mayor's office and the Allegheny Conference—the group of business leaders behind the Renaissance—had established smoke abatement guidelines. As these were about to be extended to Allegheny County, Pittsburghers discovered that the Pennsylvania Railroad was lobbying against them because the new regulations would curtail sooty locomotives.

The railroad's sabotage of Pittsburgh's progress had been a leitmotif in local history; this time the arrogant company was foiled. Mellon simply telephoned the railroad's president with a protest. The suggestion that the vast Mellon interests might take their business to other, more cooperative rail lines did not need to be spelled out. The railroad dropped its opposition, and the smoke abatement program succeeded.

Smoke and flood control were essential to Pittsburgh's future, but what was that future to be? Whatever prospects heavy industry had, the city needed to create an environment conducive to white collar activity. Long before many others, Pittsburgh leaders foretold the switch from a manufacturing to a service economy.

Visual pollution hindered development almost as much as the atmospheric sort. By the mid twentieth century, the city's birthplace had become a matted and entangled growth of railyards and warehouses, bridgeheads and alleys, sprinkled with a few important old buildings. The desire for a clean slate burned so intensely that the men of the Renaissance decided to save only the Blockhouse and clear all the rest, even the bridges. In a way, this was their most astonishing achievement, for despite its decay, the Point had remained the center of the city's traffic patterns. (You can still see the massive piers of the Point Bridge on the Monongahela shore and the Manchester Bridge on the Allegheny shore, which had intersected where the fountain now spouts.) In a dramatic demonstration of intent, they returned Pittsburgh's heart to something the first settlers might recognize.

The Pittsburgh Renaissance razed better than it built. The consensus that made renewal possible made significant art or architecture improbable at the Point. There seems to have been but one attempt to produce something sublime there, and it met a decisive defeat. Edgar Kaufmann, who had commissioned Frank Lloyd Wright to design Fallingwater in the 1930s, asked Wright to produce a monumental plan. What Wright came up with was less a monument than a social revolution. Earlier, he had suggested abandoning Pittsburgh; now, in 1947, he apparently intended to absorb it.

His thirteen-level "fairyland" would cover the Point with an automobile-friendly shopping-cultural-office complex, topped with a dirigible mooring and a "great overhead insectorium or aviary." The scale was astonishing. The plan specified "total accommodation for persons seated in audience or in cars on ramps: 123,000." When one of Kaufmann's colleagues asked about the price of this architectural entertainment, Wright answered, "Who cares about money? You can tell what God thinks about money by the kind of people he gives it to." Kaufmann quietly placed the plans in his desk; they were never presented to the park committee.

15

Point
State
Park
and
Gateway
Center

What the park got was a big fountain. One tour guide suggests that this fine spectacle "symbolizes" the joining of the two rivers, without explaining the purpose of symbolizing a phenomenon occurring a few yards away. If the fountain must symbolize something, it might represent the achievement of the Renaissance in cleansing the Point of any reminder of the industrial era.

However unadventurous, the fountain does give the Point focus. That's all the more necessary, for the park lacks the visual analogue of its dramatic history. The Monongahela and Allegheny conjoin mildly, and the Ohio River they form does not gratify us with a long westward perspective in keeping with the river's role in American development. In fact, as you see, it turns a corner so quickly that if you didn't know better you might think it was a mill pond. Looking eastward, upstream, the Monongahela is likewise constricted. Only the Allegheny offers something more, as we shall see.

Humans have done even less than nature to provide views here. Mt. Washington is topped by buildings that are flat and insignificant or downright ugly from this vantage; the shore below features a long, gray warehouse. The only things that relieve this southern panorama are the abandoned Lawrence and Company Paints and Varnishes building below, and the Bayer sign above. Originally erected by Alcoa, the aluminum sign subtly spells out "Pittsburgh" during the day and tells the time at night.

The northern shore is burdened by the stadium, whose 1960s-style brutalism is echoed—incredibly, since it was commissioned by the city's premier cultural institution—by the 1991 Carnegie Science Center, a graceless bunker.

The Golden Triangle's skyline, which can make you gasp from a hundred points around Pittsburgh, is uncharacteristically bland at the Point, as disappointing as the other vistas. Paradoxically, the buildings of Gateway Center, in the foreground, form neither a gateway nor a portal to the city, but a wall.

Though aesthetically disappointing, Point State Park is functionally a great success. Heavily and happily used not only by Pittsburghers, but also by visitors, it serves as a model of what riverside parks can do for Pittsburgh. In fact, the success of opening the waterfront here to public access has challenged the city—and Allegheny County, too—to do likewise everywhere within its boundaries. An important step in that direction is the planned creation of two bilevel promenades, one on the Monongahela and a second one on the Allegheny, which will improve relations between Point State Park and the Golden Triangle.

Walk a short distance along the Allegheny—it's the river on your left as you face downtown—and enjoy its lilting sequence of bridges. Before you reach the first of these, walk up the steps to the right. The hummock you cross is planted, like most of the park, with species native to western Pennsylvania. Return toward town, admiring the graceful design of the Fort Duquesne Bridge funneling traffic over the park, a masterpiece of highway engineering as well as aesthetics.

Beyond lie the lower remnants of the original rampart walls of Fort Pitt's Music Bastion. Its size—it is only one of the original five— gives a sense of the sheer physical authority the wilderness outpost must have conveyed. Its juxtaposition with Gateway Center is fitting, for both Pittsburgh's birth and rebirth were marked by mammoth undertakings that startled the world.

Cross Commonwealth Place and walk to the left of the Hilton to see the first portion of Gateway Center—Gateway Plaza, built in the early 1950s. Though not formally identified, its centerpiece is the fountain ahead of you.

Pittsburgh's Renaissance, like its Italian forerunner, had been preceded by a dark age. In Pittsburgh, however, the darkness was literal; its Renaissance would never have taken place if the smoke had not been cleared. David Lawrence tells how Pittsburghers in search of

Gateway Plaza

backing for the rebuilding of the Point approached the president of the Equitable Life Assurance Society: "What are you doing about smoke control?" the businessman asked.

Given that concern, it is not surprising that the original project, financed by Equitable, was inspired by Le Corbusier, the most hygienic of twentieth-century architects. Le Corbusier believed that if cities did not attack their problems head on, they would die. The attack he had in mind was sweeping demolition, which would make space not for people, as you might expect, but for buildings, or rather for "exalted architectural feats," or better yet, for a "magnificent inter-play of shapes assembled in the light." The result would be "to create a destiny for the center of the city, the center that has been razed and so is empty, and therefore free." Planners in other cities often invoked this lofty vision to produce swaths of soulless highrises spaced so far apart that only the hardy dare linger in the surrounding parks. But Pittsburgh's tight site—not for the first or last time—kept the buildings close and the scale human.

Enlivening this green space, as well-used as Point State Park, are the fine 1950s fountain, with its turquoise oxidation, and a limestone sculpture by Henry Chalfant called *Trifoglio,* a conversational group echoing the original Gateway buildings. Note that these structures are not aligned on a single axis; their asymmetry lends them an interest that their architecture alone does not elicit.

Serendipity rather than calculation generated their most affecting trait—the icy light their sheathing emanates. The architects originally specified brick and limestone, then stainless steel, an homage to the city's principal product. But the Korean War made stainless steel unavailable. What you see is a less luminous but subtler chrome alloy steel, faceted to give the buildings that "magnificent interplay of shapes assembled in the light" that Le Corbusier considered essential to modern architecture.

The original project called for at least seven of these cruciform towers. Other designs and more informal siting later prevailed, as

Limestone sculpture, Gateway Plaza

you'll soon see. Before leaving the plaza, notice the historical marker on the left, indicating the studios of KDKA, the world's first commercial radio station.

Exit to the right and cross Penn and Liberty (separated by a median) toward Gateway Center's raised southern portion, Equitable Plaza.

A large but playful abstract sculpture by Mark di Suvero was planned for the Stanwix-Penn-Liberty median, which would have given much needed focus to what is in fact the portal to Pittsburgh, but fear of public outcry discouraged this project. The 1986 Fifth Avenue Place, where tour 3 begins, has created a strong perspective, partly compensating for the absence of the sculpture.

Climb the stairs to Equitable Plaza's checkerboard terrace. Four Gateway Center, the sleek slab on your left, was built in 1960, designed by New York architects Harrison and Abramovitz. It has a handsome stainless steel service core on the other side. Its neighbors, the 1957 State Office Building (on your right) and the oddly surfaced 1958 Bell Atlantic Building (ahead and to the left), lack its sheen and quality. Beyond the bridge on the right is the Pittsburgh Post-Gazette Building. Now the city's only newspaper, the *Post-Gazette* is a direct descendant of the 1786 *Gazette*.

As you walk over the footbridge crossing the Boulevard of the Allies, you'll see an unusual structure on the left. The diamond-patterned steel does not merely sheathe the 1964 building, it is holding it up. Mayor Lawrence had a clear understanding that industry alone was not sufficient to maintain postwar Pittsburgh's economic health; concentrations of corporate administration and research were vital. In fact, most of the buildings of Gateway Center house corporate headquarters and offices, and this building was born IBM. But Pittsburgh's labor history is every whit as important as its entrepreneurial exploits, so it is appropriate that the American labor movement also be represented in the city's prime renewal area. The building now houses the United Steelworkers of America.

Gateway Center

Equitable Plaza

Closing the plaza at the Monongahela River is another Harrison and Abramovitz work, the 1968 Westinghouse Electric Corporation headquarters. Lorado Taft's 1915 bronze tablet inside commemorates George Westinghouse, "Master Workman," who died the year before. A gift of the Westinghouse Veteran Employees Association, it attests to the good relations the genial inventor enjoyed with his workers. (See tour 6 for more on Westinghouse.)

Westinghouse, which acquired CBS at the end of 1995, began and still owns radio station KDKA. The station's early broadcasts, in a studio in a shack atop a nearby building, included local news, live performances, and children's bedtime stories—all punctuated by the sound of passing trains.

23

Point
State
Park
and
Gateway
Center

2

THE OUTER TRIANGLE

This walking tour begins at Stanwix and First Avenue. It may be done as an extension of the previous itinerary, crossing Stanwix from the Westinghouse Building.

Urban Magnetism

A s you come from Stanwix, First Avenue marks an abrupt reduction of scale, a sign of the wall-like Gateway Center's failure to integrate with the rest of downtown. As for the center's name, a reference to the late-eighteenth-, early-nineteenth-century Pittsburgh that outfitted westward pioneers, it would be more appropriate to the area we are about to visit.

From First, turn right on Market and left on Fort Pitt Boulevard. Now dubbed "Firstside," these blocks survive from an era when Pittsburgh was, in fact, gateway to the West. Although the Great Fire of 1845 destroyed earlier buildings, part of the street pattern follows the one surveyor John Campbell established in 1764. The public promenade planned along Firstside will give the area an entirely different ambiance.

The three rivers made possible Pittsburgh's role in opening the continent. The Monongahela wharf, presently hidden under the roadway, had an advantage over its Allegheny counterpart: that river's swifter flow and steeper bank made it difficult to load and unload boats. Even the Mon flooded so frequently that docks were floating rather than fixed.

Through most of the nineteenth century, steamboats lined this

24

stretch of the Monongahela, embarking goods and passengers for the West. The city's geographical position also encouraged boat building. Surprisingly, the industry constructed not only riverboats, but also oceangoing vessels—twenty between 1792 and 1810—the first suggestion of the grand scope of Pittsburgh's economic vocation.

A post–Civil War brick facade at 231, and a cast-iron one at 239 (with sunflowers) enrich this block of Fort Pitt Boulevard. Turn left on Wood Street; the tan brick and terra-cotta building's name, the Conestoga, is another reminder of Pittsburgh's nineteenth-century function. Westward-bound travelers often crossed the mountains in Conestoga wagons, transferring to boats here. Note the 1907 West Penn Building across the street, a rational structure floridly embellished.

Turn left on First to see the fine small facade of 226. Beyond at 200 stands the 1872 Waterfront Building, which enjoys a spirited interior by MacLachlan, Cornelius, and Filoni; Roman architect and ideologue Vitruvius is cited both verbally and visually. The foyer and lobby also feature artwork that helps you imagine Firstside's steamboat era. Backtrack to the right and cross the street to another red brick structure, a 1984 garage that offers a passageway to the Boulevard of the Allies. Its clever design includes a fountain, whose jolly crowd of terra-cotta little people rebuke the recent superrealist bronze works plopped elsewhere in the city, which lack nothing but art to make them alive.

Turning right on the boulevard, sets of twins follow. The 1895 Ballet Building, at 244, sports a handsome blank escutcheon at the corner; for many years, the Pittsburgh Ballet Theatre called this place home. Its not quite identical twin stands next door at 111 Wood Street. Cross Wood for a better view. Farther up the boulevard are 312 and 322, next to a recent YMCA that respects the older structures' materials and proportions, if not their style.

Engine Station No. 1, built in 1900, stands beyond the YMCA. A marker diagonally across the boulevard at the northeast corner of

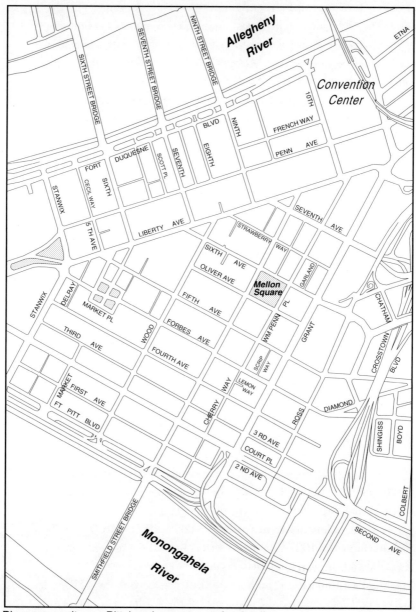

Please consult your Pittsburgh street map for details.

Smithfield and the Boulevard of the Allies commemorates the University of Pittsburgh's founding there in 1787.

Walk toward the river on Smithfield to see yet another architec-• tural twosome, this time not at all in harmony. The Beaux Arts stone facade at 112, a recycled fire station, and its 1881 neighbor at 110 have nothing in common but self-assurance. A final reminder of the Monongahela wharf's oceangoing days stands beyond First on the left, with dolphins adorning the building on the corner of Fort Pitt Boulevard.

Commanding Smithfield, and connecting the wharf to the South Side, is the Smithfield Street Bridge. Built in 1883, it has recently undergone a thorough renovation (see tour 11).

Backtrack on Smithfield and turn right on First, which is lined with a series of well-preserved and restored structures. The interior of Fort Pitt Commons at First and Grant shows nineteenth-century building techniques as they were before the development of structural steel.

Make the immediate left on Grant. Here you have a good view down Grant of both the City-County Building and the Allegheny County Courthouse. From this vantage, the courthouse's central tower still dominates the street, which we will walk the entire length of.

The Golden Triangle, Pittsburgh's unusually healthy downtown, has maintained its magnetic power over the Pittsburgh region thanks to a series of conscious choices. Locating important buildings here, like the two just mentioned, obviously keeps the triangle central. Transportation policy achieves the same purpose. Bus lines so routinely converge in the Triangle that the transit authority specifies exceptions; even in outlying areas, you will see bus windshields with a sign reading "*Not* to Downtown."

Notice the columns flanking the Boulevard of the Allies; they commemorate the 1921 opening of this artery. Conceived by Frederick Law Olmsted, Jr., early in this century, the Boulevard of the Allies gave the East End a direct connection along the Monongahela with downtown, matching the earlier Bigelow Boulevard, which parallels the Allegheny.

The Golden Triangle's predominance continues, thanks to internal improvements as well as land use and transportation policies. The city's renovation of Grant Street, completed in 1990, enhanced this road's already formidable dignity, giving a stroll down it a nearly processional quality. Yet the magnificent sequence doesn't daunt visitors; it invites them to join the parade.

In addition to its status as one of America's noblest thoroughfares, Grant Street constitutes an axis in the city's moral geography. Its public buildings, emblems of collective order, are interspersed with privately built structures, monuments to individual whim. These buildings tell stories of aspiration and meanness, of achievement and folly.

The street's welcoming manner is evident at the outset, where the attractively massed silver octagons of Oxford Centre beckon you inside. The lower floors offer piano music, food, silken banners in open elevator shafts, and shops like Rodier and Ann Taylor. As alluring is the below-street-level terrace, with the first of several pleasant Grant Street fountains.

The Grant Building, across the street, is the work of one of Pittsburgh's finest architects, Henry Hornbostel. The 1927 structure shows his work toward the end of his prolific career, in an art deco mode. At night, the building's rooftop flashing beacon light spells out "Pittsburgh" in Morse code.

Hornbostel's 1915 City-County Building stands next door, his response to H. H. Richardson's Allegheny County Courthouse, just beyond. Designed as Pittsburgh's city hall, with overflow offices from the courthouse, the City-County Building is kin in scale as well as function to Richardson's work across Forbes Avenue.

Though a lesser architect, Hornbostel here had an advantage over Richardson. When Richardson designed the courthouse in the early 1880s, Grant Street had a hump, the remnant of Grant's Hill. In 1912, this hump was leveled to facilitate traffic, befuddling the original Grant Street entrance. In fact, the present entrance is the only part of the courthouse that lacks authority.

The City-County Building's entrance manages to be both impressive and welcoming, proving that mass need not exclude lightness. Like Richardson, Hornbostel used triple arches, but Hornbostel's are extravagantly scaled, creating a high open visage toward the city. The effect of this grand portico, despite a too-weighty bronze of Richard Caliguiri, mayor from 1976 to 1988, is almost airy.

Hornbostel displayed similar flair in the interior, where a high, gold-columned gallery runs from one side of the building to the other. There is much to savor in this courtly promenade, beginning with the elevator doors, which show an infant, a youth, and a man holding city and county buildings from analogous periods in Pittsburgh and Allegheny County history.

Walk through the gallery and exit at the back. The facade of the 1929 County Office Building across Ross Street also offers curious details; a smartly styled bestiary is woven into the column capitals and the frieze. (The plan for this structure originally envisioned nine more stories.) To the right of the County Office Building, and a bit down Fourth, stands the County Mortuary, with an entrance framed by more fantastic animals—mastiff heads biting dragons' tails. This turn-of-the-century project of another fecund Pittsburgh architect, Frederick Osterling, exhibits his Richardsonian vocabulary; Richardson's syntax, however, is missing.

To see the real thing, backtrack on Ross Street and turn right on Forbes; go at least as far as the second side entrance of the County Office Building. Across Forbes is the old Allegheny County Jail, built during 1884–1888 in conjunction with the courthouse.

Here stands power at its rawest; rarely has form so conclusively embodied function. But though the authorities' power to imprison is well expressed, what comes across even more forcefully is Richardson's love for simple shapes and simple materials. The jail might have been merely heavy and forbidding, but Richardson's rock-faced granite, the composition of the chimney shaft, the great arched doorway, all grip us. This willingness to let unadorned materials speak for themselves set Richardson apart from his contemporaries and made him the grandfather of twentieth-century architecture.

In 1995 county prisoners were moved to the new jail along the banks of the Monongahela, and Richardson's jail is being transformed into courtrooms and offices. Its rotunda will be open to the public and feature historical exhibits, such as a collection of homemade weapons seized from prisoners over the years.

Return on Forbes to the Allegheny County Courthouse. This backward approach to what many architects consider the best building in America may seem inappropriate, but, as noted above, the original entrance on Grant Street was altered. It's also instructive to move from the elemental to the elaborate. The jail, a feast of the elemental, is linked to the larger building by a bridge. Here Richardson had Venice in mind, where the Bridge of Sighs served a similar purpose, and the Rialto has a similar form.

Medieval citations abound in the courthouse. But Franklin Toker, in his brilliant analysis, points out that Richardson's basic concept was that of a Renaissance palace. This is especially evident in the courtyard, which is free of carved Romanesque details. Enter from Forbes. Notice how the rhythmically spaced windows punctuate these walls so that they are as open with glass as the jail's are solid with granite; the courts and offices and judicial chambers all have natural light.

Practical considerations played a part in the high towers as well. Richardson here adapted the ventilation system of the houses of Parliament in London. The circular nostrils atop the three-hundred-foot-high front tower were to draw in air which would flow through the building and be discharged through the two towers at the back of the court. Other up-to-date courthouse features included electricity—it was one of the earliest buildings planned for it—and a pneumatic-tube

Allegheny County Jail

system for interoffice memos. The pleasant trees, fountain, and plantings date from the mid 1970s; previously, this space was used for parking.

Enter the building's interior at the courtyard's Grant Street side. Up a flight of steps you see the original entrance, now adorned with murals, and the complex grand staircase. On the third level, carved into the base of one of Richardson's signature arches, a grateful citizenry left a touching tribute to the architect, who died at age forty-seven before the building's completion. Richardson was certain of the structure's importance. When told on his deathbed that a poll of architects named five of his works among the ten best buildings in the country, he commented, "If they honor me for the pigmy things I have already done, what will they say when they see Pittsburgh finished?"

On the way downstairs, notice, to the right of the image of Justice in the center, the mural depicting the Battle of Grant's Hill, the skirmish that cost a number of Major Grant's Scots Highlanders their heads.

After the Civil War, Pittsburgh's industry showed what great things the city was capable of. It also revealed the degradation industrial progress entailed. The courthouse eclipsed the image of degradation with something as strong and progressive as the new factories, but nobler and more rooted. Cross Grant Street to look at the courthouse facade. Notice how the pink mortar enhances the stone blocks. The granite's bulge under the Latin lettering above the entrance shows that men, not machines, built these walls. Consider too the lions, high up because of Grant Street's change in level. These elements help make the courthouse a warm building, despite its massive presence.

Originally it appeared more formidable; Richardson intended the structure to loom over the city like a great castle. But in less than a decade and a half, the Frick Building, a twenty-one-story stone slab in front of the courthouse, interrupted the courthouse's relation with the city, severely diminishing its impact.

The Frick Building casts a harsh light on turn-of-the-century

Pittsburgh. Soon after Richardson's death in 1886, technological advances, not least of them Pittsburgh's production of economical steel beams, made tall buildings commercially possible. The architect of the Frick Building, Daniel Burnham, was a key figure in highrise development. He also helped convince Americans, especially American capitalists, that Greco-Roman models provided the best mode of expressing their power and dignity.

This taste had been dramatically publicized by the 1893 Chicago World's Fair, where, as director of works, Burnham created an idealized (and electrified) Rome-by-the-Lake. His site planning, grand yet rational and harmonious, so enhanced the qualities of the fair's white pavilions, and the experience of the visitors, that it inspired urban America's first great planning movement, the City Beautiful.

Yet Burnham's Frick Building neuters the courthouse, cutting off its original relation with the city. The Frick's height, the style, the machine-finished texture and pallor of the stone, all clash with the public building. What had happened to Burnham's feeling for harmony? He was not insensitive to Richardson's architecture; he himself had produced many Richardsonian buildings.

It wasn't the architect, but the client. Henry Clay Frick wanted his building to be the tallest in the city, and he wanted it in the latest style. Above all, he wanted it right here. The fact that the courthouse uniquely expressed the collective will meant nothing to him. Frick had often demonstrated his disdain for the collective will, most dramatically when he crushed the Homestead strike in 1892. But why didn't his well-developed aesthetic sense move Frick to choose another site? The answer to that question tells much about the splendors and miseries of turn-of-the-century Pittsburgh.

Frick and Andrew Carnegie, who had made big fortunes individually, and an enormous one together, shared a grand vision of the steel industry's future. United by their willingness to invest in technology and their passion for containing other expenses, they were divided by almost everything else—their tastes in art, feelings about public opinion, views of workers. The Homestead tragedy created unspoken resentment in both of them. At the end of the century, a business quarrel over evaluation of the worth of Frick's stock occasioned a total breach.

It proved to be irreparable; years later, the story goes, when both were growing old, Carnegie sent a message to Frick: Might they not meet once again? "Tell Mr. Carnegie," Frick ordered the messenger, "that I'll meet him in Hell."

It was this preference for provocation rather than conciliation that motivated Frick in his choice of sites. Carnegie's headquarters was just next door on Fifth Avenue, where Kaufmann's annex now stands. A Frick building on this particular site would tower over it. Later, Frick commissioned the Allegheny Building around the corner on Forbes, to put Carnegie even more in the shade. Franklin Toker traces this architectural vendetta not only to Oakland and Point Breeze, but even to New York, where Frick's mansion on Fifth and Seventy-first still outshines Carnegie's at Fifth and Ninety-first.

The Frick Building's competently designed exterior does not justify Burnham's assurances to Frick that it was "the most beautiful and practical building in the world, a monument not surpassed in any time or place." But the interior gleams with quality. Grant Street's change of level when the hump was razed induced the creation of the lower lobby.

The snowy marble must have caused even greater pleasure in Pittsburgh's soot-laden days. Now other amenities stand out. The brass telephone booths toward the back look like mahogany; the center gate once protected an operator. There's a cigar-lighting gilt gas-lamp maiden at the newsstand, and a bust of Frick at the center guards a tasteful but hardly inviting marble bench.

Frick's unquestioned business genius did not make him an easy man to work with. One wonders if a half-conscious resentment in those around him inspired the stained-glass window above. It shows the goddess Fortune on her wheel, precariously holding a balance between the good times, represented by the lit side, and the deep gloom of the bad. The artist was John La Farge, who had invented many techniques later adopted by Louis Tiffany. Did La Farge intend the subject as a warning to men like Frick, who rested their whole faith in shrewdness and will? Or was placement of a hot trollop amidst this icy elegance in itself a source of satisfaction to him and Burnham, who had commissioned the window?

As you exit on Grant, note A. P. Proctor's lofty lions, disdaining eye contact with Richardson's across the street. Next door, Frick, wholly out of character, commissioned a lacy Gothic frolic, the 1916 Union Arcade (later the Union Trust Building and now Two Mellon Bank Center). Fashion may have influenced his choice of style, for an even more elaborate late medieval confection, New York's Woolworth Building, had been completed a few years earlier. Visit the interior rotunda; the shopping arcade's playful architecture, both inside and out, may have been intended to induce Pittsburghers to part with their money. Serendipity also had a role. Working with architect Frederick Osterling at the time was Pierre Liesch, who came from Luxembourg, a good place to learn late Gothic.

Frick's will to dominate this area silenced any scruples he might have felt about the inconvenience to others. The Frick Building cost the Carnegie headquarters its light and the courthouse its bond with the city; it also uprooted the congregation of Saint Peter's Church, which moved to Oakland to make room for the building (literally; the stone-by-stone reconstruction stood at Forbes and Craft Avenues until its demolition was decreed at the end of the less reverent 1980s). The Union Arcade stands on the site of Saint Paul's Cathedral, now also in Oakland. Frick booted the Third Presbyterian Church off the next lot to build the William Penn Hotel in 1913. As a visual compensation for these ecclesiastical evictions, the Union Arcade's elevator shafts terminate in churchlike fantasy structures rising from the roof. These, however, are not visible from the sidewalk here.

Far greater delicacy governed the placement of One Mellon Center across Grant Street. It seems to have learned from the Frick Building how not to treat a masterpiece like the courthouse. Where the Frick is pushed up against the sidewalk to maximize its presence and rents, One Mellon Center discreetly pulls away, giving the courthouse air and pedestrians a chance to admire. Even as it doesn't obtrude on street level, so at the top it tapers off, diffidently rather than dramatically. You may find that the 1983 building is not distinguished for much besides its modesty. But the plaza, with its fountain and flora, is mighty cheerful for a bank, and the Scott Burton marble sculpture chairs, a telling counterpoint to Frick's wintry bench, manage to convey both monumentality and a sense of fun. They are comfortable, too.

Moving along, the Civic Arena's silver dome grandly appears—when the trees aren't in leaf—accompanied by an intriguing view down Sixth Avenue. But our itinerary continues on Grant, where the USX Building sits, like the Mellon, on the bias—another very large building trying not to overwhelm its environs. The USX Building's triangular shape also cuts its impact, as does its color, caused by Cor-Ten steel, whose protection lies in a coat of rust. The engineering of this sixty-four-story building—Pittsburgh's tallest—included filling the supporting columns with half a million gallons of antifreeze solution, a method for diffusing heat in case of fire.

U.S. Steel management, who ordered the 1971 Harrison and Abramovitz building as headquarters, earned a reputation in the following decade and a half for callousness and even hostility toward the company's most faithful workers. Employees saw the rusting exterior as an omen of steel's precipitous decline; the corporation's mid-1980s change of name from U.S. Steel to USX inspired bitter witticisms about steelworkers themselves constituting the "ex."

Steel's sharply reduced importance, along with the company's increased energy and real estate interests, meant that USX's specific commitment to Pittsburgh had diminished. When, in 1991, the Pennsylvania legislature was considering eliminating a tax exemption favorable to USX, the chairman suggested that the company might

One Mellon Bank Center

USX Tower

move out of the state. This threat illustrates a noxious side effect of the switch from heavy manufacturing to service industries. Factories bind firms to their localities, encouraging managers' responsible participation in civic affairs. Service industries enjoy far greater mobility and sometimes feel proportionately less compelled to act as stable corporate citizens.

If USX's interesting plaza and fountain fail to afford relief from these considerations, try the 1888 Lutheran Church across the street. The sculpture, *Resurrection,* is appropriate in a town that frequently celebrates its own rebirth. A large Tiffany window representing the Good Shepherd enriches the sanctuary. The church, established in 1837, was the first English-speaking Lutheran congregation west of the Alleghenies.

Buildings like the Frick and the Allegheny County Courthouse set a high architectural standard; the Koppers and Gulf buildings show how successfully the next generation maintained Grant Street's tone. Enter the 1929 Koppers Building and walk through, turning right to the side exit, to Seventh Avenue, noting such rich and witty details as the mailbox, a stylized brass miniature of the building itself. You may enter the 1932 Gulf Building from Seventh, exiting again on Grant; equally fine, the Gulf's detailing is less elaborate than the Koppers'. Both buildings were Mellon projects; in the 1980s, Gulf Oil merged with Chevron and moved out, and the Koppers Company no longer exists.

Egyptian architect and urban planner Hassan Fathy complained in the 1960s that western architects failed in their buildings' summits to marry earth to heaven, as their eastern counterparts had done with domes and minarets. But both the Gulf and Koppers buildings enjoy, if not proper marriages, at least happy relationships with the sky. This will become evident when you look up at the buildings from farther down Grant. Koppers' top is verdigris, copper (what else?) green in the form of a chateau. Gulf's pyramidal point is lit in weather forecasting tones at night: red means fair, blue is precipitation; a solid color means rising temperatures; flashing, falling temperatures.

A couple of federal buildings ennoble this final stretch of Grant Street. Art deco aluminum warriors guard the 1931 Federal Reserve at 717. Offering them a fine limestone flank across the street is the Post Office and Federal Courts Building, the work of Trowbridge and Livingston, who did the Gulf Building the same year, 1932.

Grant Street's high tone hiccups toward the end with the Greyhound Bus Terminal, a building you might be delighted to find in a less exalted quarter. But the nearby Pennsylvania Station makes up for the lapse, providing the street its true spiritual terminus.

Like the Frick and the USX Buildings, this structure's urbanity belies a strife-ridden history. Pittsburghers generally felt antipathy toward the Pennsylvania Railroad—they criticized it first for its slowness in linking the city to the rest of the country; trains began arriving only in 1852. Then they criticized it for its monopoly position, which it exploited energetically. Andrew Carnegie, even though his fortunes began with the railroad, later lived in a perpetual lather at its unfairness to Pittsburgh and to Pittsburgh manufacturers—especially steelmakers.

The company ignited a firestorm in June 1877 when it ordered a 10 percent wage cut, at the same time doubling the size of freight trains at Pittsburgh. The workers, whose wages were already below subsistence level, spontaneously resisted, blocking the tracks. The company asked the mayor to call out the police, which he did not do. Nor were the Pittsburgh regiments of the state militia willing to fight; most of them sided with the strikers.

When the state sent in militia from Philadelphia, their efforts to clear the line were opposed by a large portion of the populace. On July 21, they fired on the crowd, killing twenty people. In the ensuing riot, the mob routed the troops, and well over thirteen hundred railcars were destroyed, as well as 126 locomotives and over a dozen build-

Pennsylvania Station

ings, including Union Depot. It was the most violent civil uprising the country had ever seen.

Against this background, construction of a lavish station looked like a move to soothe Pittsburghers' spirits. The Pennsylvania Railroad's president at the time was Pittsburgher Alexander Cassatt, brother of the painter Mary; his relation to the town and architectural good taste encouraged him to commission Daniel Burnham to design the station.

Altogether a generous structure, the former station wins hearts especially for the rotunda. (The equally grand interior lobby is closed to the public, but you can peek through the windows.) Contemporary exposition architecture perhaps inspired Burnham's 1901 design; the arches and domes multiply the festive effect, echoed faintly in the nearby postmodern busway station, resonantly in the more distant Civic Arena. Penn Station's successful recycling for residential use makes it one of the very few downtown apartment buildings.

This site has always been a traffic nexus. The East Busway, which uses part of the old railroad right of way, terminates here, forming a link with the Amtrak station, the downtown subway, and hence the rest of the light-rail system. Here Penn Avenue, the original route from the east, enters the Golden Triangle; and here the railroad's predecessor, the 395-mile-long Main Line Canal, had its terminus.

The canal, which reached Pittsburgh in 1834, was an extraordinary work—a massive manipulation of nature, as Forbes Road had been three quarters of a century earlier. Immortalized by Charles Dickens in *American Notes,* it included a 1,100-foot-long covered aqueduct over the Allegheny and a final canal tunnel under Grant's Hill. It boosted trade, but the canal never paid its way; the railroad fulfilled its functions after 1852.

The conflicts hidden behind Grant Street's splendors here cease; harmony governs the rest of the tour, beginning with Liberty Center, just north.

Liberty Center includes a Doubletree Hotel, an office tower, and shops. Fruit of the city's public-private partnership, it was built in the mid 1980s during what Mayor Richard Caliguiri liked to call Renaissance II. (It's a sign of how seriously Pittsburgh takes itself that no one ever thought it odd that this city has had more renaissances than Florence.)

Liberty Center's position at a complicated crossroads gave it the possibility of providing focal points for several different perspectives. It succeeds in accomplishing that important urban function while, at the same time, its unified color and fenestration hold it together as a single complex.

You may walk through a currently underused shopping gallery to the convention center, also underused. This building must be considerably expanded, they say, for Pittsburgh to compete successfully as a convention city. One way to make additions more attractive would be to open the center toward the Allegheny. The original building's failure to exploit its riverside site shows how Pittsburghers were unaware of, or hostile to, the appeal of the rivers as late as 1981.

Penn Avenue presents a remarkably intact turn-of-the-century commercial streetscape. Our route, down Penn to Sixth Street, is now the long hinge of Pittsburgh's cultural district. (It is another sign of seriousness that the city should have an *official* cultural district.) Penn Avenue has a different history and layout from the rest of the Triangle. Paralleling the Allegheny, it remained elegantly residential until well after the arrival of the canal and railroad. Retail trade, mostly dry goods and furnishings, took over later in the nineteenth century, producing the present buildings, some of them marred by more recent storefronts. Tourist and convention activities to the east, and musical and theatrical activities to the west, are prompting Penn Avenue's renewal. Loft apartments and small hotels, as well as retail spaces and office uses, are planned. Street improvements, which follow the Grant Street model, complement and encourage this effort.

Penn Avenue innovations are to include a plaza, parking garage, performance space, and multiscreen cinema where the parking lot is at Seventh and Penn, and a riverfront promenade along Fort Duquesne Boulevard, with a riverwalk to Point State Park. Generator of all this activity is the Pittsburgh Cultural Trust, created in 1984 to revitalize the area bounded by Tenth Street and Stanwix, Liberty Avenue and the Allegheny River.

The cultural district's spirited activity not only demonstrates downtown's urban magnetism, it suggests a sea change in attitudes about culture's place in the city. Andrew Carnegie put his institute in pastoral Oakland, even as he built his New York mansion far from the madding crowd. City Beautiful exponents seconded the idea that culture wanted isolation from mundane affairs. The need to decontaminate entertainment facilities geographically held sway beyond the middle of the twentieth century, when the Civic Arena was sited amid an asphalt desert.

H. J. Heinz single-handedly changed all this. He saw an opportunity for a splendid symphony hall in a former movie palace, and seized it. The success of that carefully guided transformation—Heinz Hall—inspired others, most notably the Stanley Theatre's metamorphosis into the Benedum Center for the Performing Arts, which houses the Pittsburgh Opera and Ballet, as well as Broadway shows and other dance events. The Cultural Trust itself was Heinz's vision, turned into a detailed development plan by the now-venerable Allegheny Conference on Community Development, which promoted downtown's first rebirth right after World War II.

The Benedum is on Seventh Street, Heinz Hall is on Sixth, both just south of Penn. The exterior of Heinz Hall, a 1971 rendition of Viennese baroque, is especially handsome. Any opulent old capital would be proud of either theater's interior—here the sumptuously restored Benedum, with its rich dark Wagnerian colors, takes the prize. Its backstage, built new by the same firm responsible for the restoration, MacLachlan, Cornelius, and Filoni, is one of the largest and most efficient in the country.

Michael Graves has designed the Public Theater and Office

Building for the space across Penn Avenue between Heinz Hall and the Benedum, to be built in 1997. It will house the Pittsburgh Public Theater (currently on the North Side) and the Pittsburgh Filmmakers fine art film series. Until this grand scheme is realized, another Trust project commands the Penn-Seventh intersection—Takamasa Kuniyasu's *Season in Spiral.* The enormous vortex of logs and bricks occupies the entire lot vacated by a porn shop. A third and smaller renovated theater, the Byham, is on Sixth Street, north of Penn. Dating from 1907, it now operates under the auspices of the Cultural Trust.

You may end this tour just beyond Heinz Hall at Sixth and Liberty, where the Heinz family created a very agreeable pocket park for downtowners and symphony patrons. Art and nineteenth-century architecture enthusiasts may complete the cultural district loop by following Liberty back toward Grant. River enthusiasts will want to head in the opposite direction to see the Allegheny riverfront park, a bilevel promenade designed by Michael Van Valkenburgh and environmental artist Ann Hamilton, to be completed in stages through 1998.

3

THE INNER TRIANGLE
This walking tour begins at Fifth Avenue Place, whose main entrance is at
Liberty and Fifth.

The Ins and Outs
of Planning

rotagonists of the previous tours were drastic as deities, sweeping clean the sites they wanted to build on—even if it meant
eliminating Indians, or churches, or whole neighborhoods.
More recent planners have preferred to start with context rather than
cataclysm.

A flat space surrounded by hills, the Golden Triangle, like the
Roman Forum, did not so much suggest as command that business be
conducted here. Pittsburghers have continually built on the Triangle's
inherent geographically based strength, lapsing only around the turn
of the century when Oakland lured cultural institutions to its wider
and greener spaces.

Historically, cities and civilization have been nearly synonymous,
but in twentieth-century America, automobiles altered the equation.
In most of the country, flight to the periphery made the central city
lifeless or dangerous.

Pittsburgh avoided this fate because of leaders like David Lawrence and Richard King Mellon, who saw the economic cost of downtown decay: flight, especially corporate flight, meant a loss of tax base
to the mayor and of business to the banker. Their informal partnership

to limit those losses and to increase revenues succeeded. That has been as important as geography in keeping downtown Pittsburgh healthy.

Pittsburgh enjoys a high urban consciousness, which is rare among smaller U.S. cities. At first, after the war, people imagined that what the Golden Triangle needed most was a thorough cleaning. But experience—brutal lessons taught by the Civic Arena and East Liberty's renewal—demonstrated that urban vitality meant respecting complexity, a city's foremost trait. That respect required such a light touch on the part of planners that some of their best work has gone unnoticed.

Watched and nudged by planners and the public, much development in Pittsburgh has a civil quality rare in America. Lawrence and Mellon's vision is now a reality: nine Fortune 500 companies call the city home. They came to Pittsburgh, or remained here, for a multitude of reasons, among them downtown's numerous amenities.

Many refined Pittsburghers would not find Fifth Avenue Place, where this tour begins, a good example of the new urban delicacy. Built in the mid 1980s on the site of the picturesque old Jenkins Arcade, the severely underdetailed skyscraper fails to achieve any grace of profile or proportion. Yet it has its merits. The stubby open point with the pole at its top reminds people of a rocket silo, surely not the worst icon for a factory town trying to go high tech. The portal design of the building's lower portion gives a strong focal point to several important perspectives, a welcome feature in an area newcomers otherwise find disorienting.

Fifth Avenue Place's developers wanted a building taller than PPG Place. Height restrictions north of Liberty—established to maintain good visual relations with the Allegheny, as well as light in the inner Triangle—frustrated this inelegant urge. Other city guidelines required open space softened with plants and pleasant public seating, as well as a strong shopping arcade. Pittsburgh planners normally frown on skywalks, like the one linking Penn Avenue Place (formerly

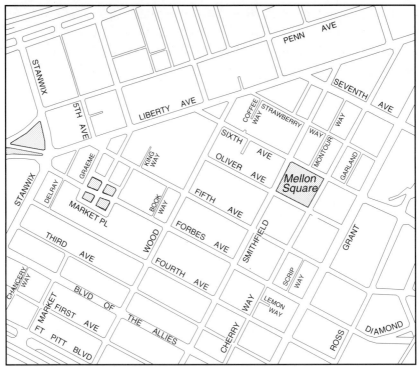

Please consult your Pittsburgh street map for details.

the Lazarus department store) to the arcade and hence to the rest of downtown, as they reduce street activity. In this instance, the department store's health came first, though the effort was not enough to save it. Lazarus has left the city until its new store, aided by city financing, is built at Fifth and Wood, closer to the other large downtown retailers.

Whatever Fifth Avenue Place's shortcomings on the skyline, at sidewalk level its trees and benches make it a good citizen. Architect Hugh Stubbins's creation of an atmosphere of cheerful soft glitz in the retail area also works; outside, the building's warm color, amid so much steely and stony gray, likewise gladdens the eye.

Cross Liberty and admire the lower reaches of Fifth Avenue, where a number of white tile facades—and, in the case of the Buhl Building, white and blue tile in a mannerist mode—outshine older but unkempt cast-iron fronts. Notice the Candyrama owl's baleful gaze at 214–218 Fifth Avenue. He keeps the Market Square pigeons at bay.

Take Market Street by the Buhl Building to Market Square, long the site of a city market. The square's older buildings are modestly scaled, but not without character. Have a look to the left at the corner Oyster House, or the 1902 Landmark Tavern and Nicholas Coffee to the right. These atmospheric structures were restored in 1982 by UDA Architects, when Nicholas's coffee cup Chippendale pediment was added.

Despite its unprepossessing air, Market Square has not only been the object of planners' painstaking attentions, it is, along with Mellon Square, the most-used public space downtown. Its clientele democratically includes the unsavory and the saintly, office drones and committed loungers.

The former city administration squandered some of Market Square's carefully accumulated planning capital. In the early 1980s, the city commissioned New York architects Hardy, Holzman, and Pfeiffer to redesign the space. Their vigorous plan increased the square's usefulness and provided much-needed visual focus; Forbes Avenue's passage through the square was to be marked with grand gatelike pylons. Using budget constraints as an excuse, the administration sloppily cut out the monumental pylons and other important features. It then gave the engineering department—not Pittsburgh's planners, who enjoy a national reputation—the job of realizing what remained of the original concept.

No such negligence affected PPG Place, which illustrates both the merits and limits of Pittsburgh's complex development process. Pittsburghers feared that a large project near Market Square might create an abrupt change of scale there, at the same time blocking the square's midday light. But PPG Industries displayed unusual sensitivity to urban design issues from the outset. They even involved the city planning department in selecting the project's architects. Their choice, Philip Johnson and John Burgee, produced one of the earliest—1979—and most spectacular of America's postmodern corporate headquarters.

The city, in exchange for its help in assembling land for the site, got PPG to develop a whole district, with multiple buildings. For the company this meant a bigger commitment than a simple corporate tower, but it also gave them complete control over their environment. Their headquarters, less than a stone's throw from Pittsburgh Plate Glass' 1883 birthplace, need never fear a neighbor's upstaging or interference.

The city of Pittsburgh establishes criteria for such projects even before the architect is selected. Here one of the guidelines concerned the new buildings' Market Square frontage; both midday shadow and too abrupt a change in scale were avoided by limiting squareside height to sixty feet.

PPG grandly met the city's 20 percent open space requirement with its formal plaza, created in part by closing Market Street. The company also offered, for Pittsburghers' use, the enclosed Wintergarden behind its central tower.

Walk along Market to the plaza, which is just beyond the square. You would expect such intelligent participation in the planners' goals and generosity in the public interest to produce a place, if not wholly warm and friendly, at least beautiful and interesting enough to make you want to linger. That doesn't happen here. It's not just the intentional lack of seating; the plaza affects you like a reverse tanning bed, one that drains you of warmth and color.

Perhaps the main problem is the material. The principal virtue of glass is that you can see through it; above all, you can see out through it while being protected from the elements. Here you're exposed to the elements and can't see in because the glass is the reflective kind, and dark besides. A mirrored surface is only as interesting as what it reflects, and here it mainly reflects itself—although from some angles you get crazy images of Fourth Street. Architectural advertising is an old tradition in Pittsburgh—Alcoa built an aluminum-skinned building, United States Steel a steel one, and Pittsburgh Plate Glass sheathed theirs in glass. But there are risks; metal rusts and corrodes, glass repels.

The main building is literally as well as superficially repellent. To go to the pleasant Wintergarden, you must circumnavigate the lobby. You can't walk through it; it feels impenetrable because it is.

Coming back to the plaza, one wonders if the complex would have turned out better even if glass had not been the principal material. First of all, there is the problem of style. The immediate and not very felicitous precedent was Minoru Yamasaki's World Trade Center in New York. That project, PPG, and real Gothic structures are all characterized by their pointed arches, which were criticized as early as 1624 "both for the natural imbecility of the sharp angle it selfe, and likewise for their very Vncomelinesse." Sir Henry Wotton concluded they "ought to bee exiled from judicious eyes and left to their first inventors, *The Gothes,* or Lumbards, amongst other Reliques of that barbarous age."

Philip Johnson saw Pittsburgh as Gothic, if not barbarous. The city's tight spaces do encourage soaring rather than spreading architecture, like the Cathedral of Learning in Oakland. And there is a

PPG Place

medieval quality in Pittsburghers' devotion to their work. Other harmonies include the main building's derivation from the tower of the houses of Parliament in London, which pays tribute to old Pittsburgh's British heritage, as well as to an image of imperial power, fitting for the world's largest glass manufacturer. Part of the building does work aesthetically, especially from a distance. The top's multiplication of points constitutes an obsessive, even, dare we say, inspired response to Hassan Fathy's dictum that good buildings should marry earth to heaven.

It's hard to know how seriously the architects wanted us to take their work. The street-level treatment, which critic Paul Goldberger found "facile and glib," appears determined to be elegant, even in such graceless details as the lamps hanging from the arcades. The central obelisk cannot convince us of any kinship with its Old World models. If it had to be squat and sturdy, couldn't it at least have been a monolith, rather than an assemblage of blocks? And it should honestly rest on the balls at its feet, rather than on a granite core. No wonder some Pittsburghers call it the "Tomb of the Unknown Bowler."

Both PPG and Fifth Avenue Place (whose top just peeks over this plaza) share the virtue of seeing architecture as a continuing narration, with single buildings as chapters of a longer story, rather than as a chance to make a more or less monumental mark on the face of the city. The one fails on the skyline and succeeds on the street; the other does the opposite. But both share a new moral as well as urban texture: they both make successful efforts to be good Pittsburghers.

The next buildings, a parade of mostly turn-of-the-century structures on Fourth Avenue, also display a common moral as well as aesthetic texture. Here the governing principle was not so much public-private cooperation but happy competition. PPG Place reflects Pittsburgh business' traditional taste for grandeur; Fourth Avenue, which runs through the complex, boldly embodies it.

The parade begins on a restrained note. At 209 stands downtown's oldest commercial building, the 1836 Burke Building, a graceful

PPG Place

Georgian design of Englishman John Chislett. (Chislett later played with Gothic at Allegheny Cemetery, as Johnson did with PPG Place.) Its new owner is, fittingly, the Western Pennsylvania Conservancy. Beyond, at 221, rises the 1905 Benedum-Trees Building, its architectural riches approaching frenzy at the top. The lobby, with its pastel stucco ceiling and various bits of brass, also deserves a look.

At 239, the Investment Building shows how good taste reared its inhibiting head between the time of its neighbors' construction and its own in 1927. The corner obelisks at its upper section gave Johnson his reference for PPG Place. (You have to step away some distance to see them.)

At Fourth and 401 Wood stands Frederick Osterling's 1902 Arrot Building, whose joyously ostentatious exterior finds a match only in its own lobby, small but awesome. Note the brasswork and the fine mosaic details.

Fourth Avenue served as Pittsburgh's financial center; several banks still operate here. The two across Wood Street are dignified, with some nice details like the beehive relief on the 1901 People's Savings Bank. You will discover more captivating details at this same building's 307 Fourth Avenue entrance, the Bank Tower. Here architects Alden and Harlow produced a semicircular staircase that approaches the sublime. Look up the stairwell, then notice the ram's head finial and marble intarsia of the balustrade. Another finely conceived element here, as in Pittsburgh office towers generally, is the mailbox.

At 317 Fourth is one entrance of a much-recycled series of bank buildings, now being prepared as the downtown branch of the Carnegie Library in conjunction with the library of Point Park College. This facade shows the versatile Osterling in an exuberant Beaux Arts mood.

Contextual architecture usually means new buildings are designed to harmonize with their older neighbors. In the Times Building, up and across Fourth at 346, you have an old exterior inspiring its own new interior—context determining text. We owe the successful redo of the 1890 Richardsonian structure—Osterling again—to the Design Alliance.

We're zigzagging. Two former bank buildings stand opposite. Charles M. Bartberger built the Industrial Bank at 333 in 1903; its 1898 neighbor was first of a score of projects Daniel Burnham designed for Pittsburgh. Henry Frick commissioned this one, and bigger works later. Both these architects knew how to design alternately in Richardsonian and in classical revival modes. But, as Franklin Toker points out, Bartberger's building shows a lusty—even subversive—independence of spirit; Burnham's, however honored by time it may be, remains correct but bloodless.

Yet Bartberger is barely known, while Burnham quickly became a historical point of reference, as his Frick Building and Pennsylvania Station show. The Chicagoan's best talent was that of an architectural impresario and general cultural operator—*do-gooder* might better express it, if you could remove the amateurish connotations of that description. As a designer, however, Burnham lacked the dash and vision that made the 1893 World's Fair, where he was director of works, so potent an influence.

Burnham's earlier architectural work drew strength from his partner John W. Root, a man skilled in robust neo-Romanesque design. Upon Root's death, Burnham needed another authoritative point of reference, and he found it not in fellow Chicago architect Frank Lloyd Wright, alas, but in classical antiquity. For him, Greco-Roman architecture provided models to be followed, never subverted. Bartberger had no problem with subversion. He might have smiled at his bank's subsequent conversion for use as a gay disco.

The Fidelity Trust and Standard Life Buildings, at 341 and 345 Fourth, respectively, both have a lively, not to say busy, quality to them, but the star here is the Dollar Bank across the street at 348, built in 1871 to Isaac Hobbs's design, with wings added in 1906. Rarely have magnificence and zest so harmoniously consorted. Some object that the building is all door. But what better way for the banker to do business than to say, "Come in!" You should do so, aware that the lions' original models adorn a papal tomb in Saint Peter's. Inside, on the left, the copper-bronze relief work does not decorate, but rather constitutes, the office walls.

Leave this confidence-inspiring institution by the side door onto Smithfield, noticing the limestone lion head reliefs—one is above you at 309, the other at 303, which we'll pass later. For now, go to Smithfield and Third, guarded by a corner gargoyle; the building is another Osterling work. Down Third you glimpse the rear facade of his Times Building.

Backtrack on Smithfield now, where you soon will be able to distinguish Indians on the facade of Kaufmann's department store, across the street near Forbes. We'll come back to Kaufmann's.

For now, turn left on Forbes, a fairly narrow street whose numerous noteworthy glazed terra-cotta facades need to be freed from later alterations. Another of Osterling's noble bank entrances, rivaling Dollar Bank in grandiosity, will eventually open at 314–318 Forbes into the Carnegie–Point Park library.

Turn left on Wood Street, where, on the other side, the post–Civil War shops adjoining the Arrot Building merit attention, all the more so because they don't clamor for notice the way their contemporary banking brethren did. Backtrack then on Wood, where Roberts Jewelry at 429–431 likewise manifests calm dignity. More lions decorate this facade, both at the cables holding the marquee and above the cornice.

Continue to Fifth Avenue, where you turn right. City planners conceive this avenue as a ceremonial street, in contrast to Forbes. A relocated Lazarus department store, to be built after the 500 Wood Street building and some others are demolished, will anchor this effort. This, the only freestanding downtown department store built in America in the last quarter century, demonstrates Pittsburgh's healthy retail environment.

Here again admire the white tile facades, popular no doubt

Dollar Bank, Fourth Avenue

because they could be cleansed of soot in the bad old days. At Smithfield you arrive at Kaufmann's 1913 creamy terra-cotta corner building. It was designed by St. Louis–born, Beaux Arts–trained Benno Janssen, a German-American like the man who hired him, Edgar Kaufmann.

The Kaufmanns had flourished in the Pittsburgh retail trade since the Civil War era; their enduring fame derives, however, from Falling-water, the house Edgar got Frank Lloyd Wright to design in the mid 1930s seventy miles southeast of Pittsburgh. Wright also built Kaufmann an office in the store, which was dismantled after Kaufmann's death and has become the property of the Victoria and Albert Museum in London. The numerous other Wright-Kaufmann projects included Wright's gargantuan architectural fantasy for the Point.

Across Fifth Avenue rises another Pittsburgh institution, a Mellon Bank so august and profitable it's called the "Cathedral of Earning." The Mellon family has had its headquarters here since soon after the Civil War, when Judge Thomas Mellon left the bench for the bank. Scotch-Irish Presbyterians, the Mellons were canny in business and reserved in private life. Their powerful bank remained the center; the circumference of their operations took in oil and aluminum, real estate and steel. Their descendants, who together constitute one of the richest families in the world, remain active in Pittsburgh business and charity.

Walk through the banking hall, blessedly untouched since its completion in 1924. This, along with the connected 1952 highrise next door, is officially Three Mellon Bank Center; Two is Frick's old Flemish Gothic Union Trust, and One is the Grant Street skyscraper. As you leave the bank on the Oliver Avenue side, note, across Mellon Square, the aluminum spire of Smithfield United Church, which we will visit later.

Most artworks purchased with Mellon money ended up in Washington, where they form the core of the National Gallery, and at Yale University. But the family built a great deal in Pittsburgh, and well;

Richard King Mellon's giant role in the postwar renewal continued an already established Mellon tradition of architectural patronage.

The most successful venture of Pittsburgh's Renaissance was Mellon Square. It got its name not because their property was next to it, but because they created it. In the early 1950s, Alcoa, in which the Mellons had a considerable interest, was considering a move to New York. Cousins Paul and Richard King Mellon came up with a winning alternative: a new Pittsburgh headquarters facing an urban space conceived in the spirit of San Francisco's Union Square.

The plan entailed clearing a whole city block, but the results amply justify it. You can enter the square from Smithfield Street. Aside from the usefulness of the parking garage underneath, the square fills every noon with downtown workers; they could not find a more elegant place for lunch. The original 1955 fountains further animate the square, as does Kenneth Snelson's lively 1977 sculpture, *Forest Devil*. In Mellon Square, Pittsburgh got its most urbane public space—and the Mellons got, in addition to general gratitude, a smart increase in the value of their properties.

The only man who matched the Mellons for building in this area was Henry Frick, responsible for, along with its neighbors south on Grant, the William Penn Hotel, which faces the square. Benno Janssen's design dates from the same year as his new Kaufmann's, 1913; his additions and improvements date from 1929 and include the seventeenth-floor ballroom designed by Joseph Urban. Cross William Penn Place and walk in. In the public rooms, Janssen achieved an air of distinction that is never stiff; as in the square outside, a certain formality doesn't get in the way of easy and happy use.

Leave the hotel and turn right down William Penn Place toward the 1953 Alcoa Building. (Use the William Penn Place entrance, not the one on Sixth Avenue.) It was designed by the New York firm of Harrison and Abramovitz (as were the 1952 part of Mellon Bank Center across the square, and the USX Tower up Sixth). Aluminum siding might seem out of place in so stylish a neighborhood, but in a town where the steel companies have buildings of steel, and the glass companies of glass, for Alcoa not to have used aluminum would have looked like a lack of faith in their product.

The measure of that faith lay in the number of innovations that resulted from the company's determination to use aluminum both structurally and decoratively. Prefabricated aluminum panels, including windows, made it possible to construct the building from inside, without scaffolding. The lobby feels as light as the structure in fact is, thanks to lavish use of the metal. An aluminum Calder mobile graced this entrance for years until it was donated to the Carnegie. Alcoa plans to move from here in 1998 to new headquarters on the North Side, near the Andy Warhol Museum.

Pittsburgh's physical narrowness makes for touching juxtapositions. Nestled next to Alcoa—which still seems futuristic after four decades—is the 1894 red-brick workers' housing transformed in 1930 into what is now the Harvard-Yale-Princeton Club. Fate clearly wanted the cozy institution to be dominated by aluminum, the material of Smithfield United Church's spire as well as of Alcoa's wall.

Turn left on Strawberry Way, where sweetshops and shoe repair shops maintain the scale of the Ivy League club. A left on Smithfield brings you at once to the entrance of the Smithfield United Church. Its spire, the world's first use of structural aluminum, shows how fertile architect Henry Hornbostel's imagination could be. Nothing inside matches it, but the stained glass windows, with historical scenes in the lower sections, are rewarding. The rose window came from the Evangelicals' earlier 1875 structure. The church, whose history as a German-language congregation dating back to the time of William Penn is detailed in a bronze plaque on the side of the Brooks Brothers store, has long demonstrated its faith by its good works, which currently include maintenance of a day care center and a shelter for homeless women.

As we approach Sixth Avenue, one cannot help but be impressed by the clean-lined but lavish terra-cotta–skinned Oliver Building on the corner, completed by Daniel Burnham for the heirs of entrepreneur Henry Oliver in 1910.

Church should dominate our thoughts now, and not merely because of the fine view of the elevator shaft chapels atop Union Trust across Mellon Square. When the Penn family granted land to the German Evangelicals for what is now Smithfield United, they also provided for the Presbyterians and the Episcopalians. The area's sacred quality dates to the time Native Americans chose it as a burial ground; French, British, and Americans until 1854 followed their example. Flanking the graveyard on Sixth, next to the Oliver Building, is Trinity Cathedral, built in 1872, the congregation's fourth church hereabouts.

Presbyterians don't have cathedrals, but if they did, First Presbyterian Church would be it. Stimulated by their neighbors, they outdid not only them, but most baroque basilicas as well. In fact, only Kenneth Clark's historically impossible phrase can do justice to the style: Gothic rococo. First Presbyterian's Philadelphia-based architect, Theophilus Parsons Chandler, Jr., demonstrated his feverish mastery in Shadyside's slightly earlier Third Presbyterian as well. His work here brings to mind a phrase of Blake's: "the road of excess leads to the palace of wisdom." Astonishing woodwork and windows dominate the interior. The woodwork includes thirty-foot-high oak doors separating the rear chapel from the main sanctuary, each weighing two tons; they are hung so perfectly that one person can easily open them.

Louis Comfort Tiffany did a baker's dozen of the stained-glassed windows; the fourteenth, not of his making, is dedicated to the Craigs and Nevilles. Such is the extravagance of this building that the side balconies run right across the middle of these long window openings. Tiffany worked around the interruption by depicting earthly scenes in the lower part, heavenly in the upper. The heads still remain sometimes invisible; that only adds to the building's atmosphere of fertile improvidence. A final instance of wasteful luxury: the church facade contains William Willett's first medallion window—he was a Pittsburgher who pioneered the revival of Gothic stained glass. It has been hidden almost from the beginning behind the organ pipes.

A quasi-sacred institution stands across Sixth Avenue from the church, the luxurious Duquesne Club, over a century old and as powerful a business club as you'll find in America.

Pittsburgh's skyline benefits from the ill-coordinated grids based on the Monongahela and Allegheny banks. Sixth Avenue's terminus, for instance, is on the bias, and all the better for it. Unexpected angles not only thicken and animate the skyline, they excite curiosity on the street level. Irregularity awakens a sense of possibility in us, suggesting that something unusual may be happening. What's around that corner?

The answer to the left on Liberty Avenue is the postmodern CNG tower, where we will soon go; to the right is the 1907 Keenan Building, topped with an exuberant poured-concrete dome. On this side of Liberty, a triangular building has been elegantly recycled as a subway stop, with a Sol LeWitt abstract bas relief on the wall below and classical music piped in all around. Art exhibitions are given on the upper floors (this stretch of Liberty is in the cultural district), and you needn't be shy about going downstairs either: subway trips in the Triangle are free.

Backtrack a little and turn south on Wood, away from the subway. The large Daniel Burnham building on the southeast corner of Wood and Sixth Avenue has been victim of mostly bad alterations since its completion in 1904, but in 1942 the Wood Street facade was brightened by an electrified glass image, *The Puddler*. Puddling was a difficult skill crucial to the nineteenth-century ironmaking process; puddlers had a heroic standing in that paleotechnological era.

Bell Federal Savings at Wood and Oliver shows Burnham in a more graceful light. Unfortunately, it will be one of the buildings demolished for the new Lazarus store. Across the street is Oliver Plaza, where three highrises jostle one another. This late 1960s proj-

CNG Tower

ect cut Oliver Avenue's relation with Liberty and disrupted downtown's retail shopping pattern, hurting office rentals as well as stores.
This awkward plaza has been partly domesticated by tables that
attract picnickers and chess players. A memorial honors victims of a
1994 airplane crash near Pittsburgh. Enter Two PNC Plaza, completed
in 1976 by Skidmore, Owings, and Merrill. (If it's closed, follow the
passage to the left of the building.)

Exit on Liberty where, to the left at 606, you may admire (excepting the inappropriately modernized windows) a 1910 Art Nouveau
store in sculpted white tile. Across Liberty rises the best new skyscraper downtown, the CNG Tower. Kohn Pedersen Fox designed this
mid-1980s tower for specialty steel manufacturers Allegheny International (reborn later as Sunbeam-Oster), who agreed to locate it here if
they could count on the upgrading of the Stanley movie theater nearby.
The Stanley became the splendid Benedum, but another neighbor on
Seventh Street did not fare so well: the Beaux Arts Loyal Order of the
Moose Building was destroyed for a parking lot.

Enter the darkly handsome CNG—named for Consolidated Natural Gas, the building's major tenant—where, toward the back, you may
read of the 1918 Pittsburgh Agreement. Here Slovaks and Czechs, in
the presence of future president Thomas Masaryk, agreed to support a
common destiny in the birth of Czechoslovakia. Marcia Davenport
dramatized the event in her Pittsburgh epic, *Valley of Decision*.

Elegant at street level, intriguing at the top, CNG Tower includes
a handsomely detailed pocket park out its side door. If it weren't for
the unnecessary bronze figures, you might consider the space itself
one of the finer sculptures in the city.

4

THE HILL, OAKLAND, SCHENLEY PARK

This walking and driving tour is divided into two sections, as the entire route may require more than one outing. Part 1 begins at Duquesne University, Forbes Avenue and Shingiss Street, not far from the Allegheny Courthouse. Part 2 starts at the Cathedral of Learning in Oakland.

The Civic Psyche

Part One. Duquesne University to the Cathedral of Learning

Geography makes downtown Pittsburgh's predominance natural. The area immediately to the east, looming over the Oakland business district and both the Monongahela and Allegheny rivers, likewise has significant geographical advantages. Yet the Hill's history has not been what nature intended for it.

For many Pittsburghers, in fact, this mostly black neighborhood practically doesn't exist. Suffering from social amnesia and topographical blindness, they don't see the city as it appears on a map, or as it is. For them, downtown is linked to Oakland solely by Bigelow Boulevard on the north, and on the south by Fifth, Forbes, Boulevard of the Allies, and the magical—because it takes you around all this—Parkway. Their Pittsburgh is a donut. The Hill is the donut's hole.

Downtown's expansion started naturally enough—as does this tour—along Forbes and Fifth. But Pittsburgh's rapid turn-of-the-century development demonstrated a conscious desire for something different from the old town center and, above all, something separate. In the late nineteenth century, institutional Pittsburgh leapfrogged over the Hill into Oakland, forming Pittsburgh's first consciously designed cultural district.

Yet the Hill teemed with life—the lives of immigrants from Europe, Asia, the Middle East, and America's South. From the 1930s through the 1950s, the Hill District boasted one of the liveliest and most prosperous black communities in America. Musicians played great jazz; the Negro League's legendary Pittsburgh Crawfords and Homestead Grays played great baseball. Sadly, that rich history has been forgotten.

If there were such a thing as psychological geography, the Hill would be Pittsburgh's id, the collective unconscious, and Oakland would be the city's superego, all mind and aspiration. This tour explores both realms of the civic psyche.

The itinerary includes the city's three major universities: Duquesne University, the University of Pittsburgh, and Carnegie Mellon University. Architecture enthusiasts will find Duquesne's campus interesting. Situated on the precipitous Bluff, it can't be navigated by car. Park downtown or at the university's garage farther east on Forbes.

At Forbes and Shingiss stands Rockwell Hall, a late 1950s limestone structure with abstract stained-glass windows. This is the campus' new official entrance. Elevators and a bridge take you to the blufftop. The tallest building, ahead of you, is the original red brick Old Main, dating from soon after the school's founding in 1878 by German priests. Centennial Walk, a pleasant brick walkway to the left, connects Old Main with the rest of the campus, greatly expanded in recent years. Note especially Mies van der Rohe's 1968 Mellon Hall and Paul Schweikher's 1967 student union.

Follow the brick road back to Old Main, turning left and then right onto Bluff Street. Here, where once you enjoyed a spectacular vista of the Monongahela, you now have a dramatic, face-to-face encounter with the new 1995 Allegheny County Jail. Old Main, which used to command the bluff, is now overshadowed by this excessively

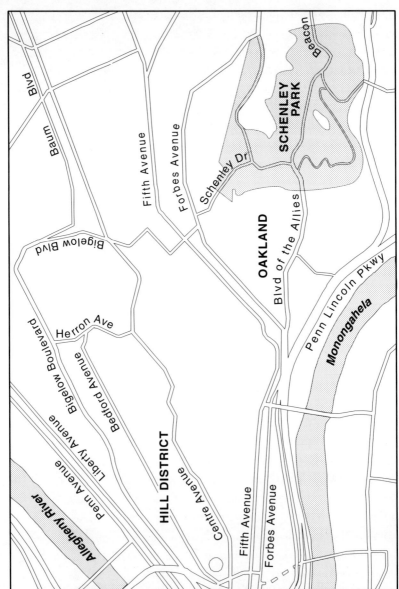

Please consult your Pittsburgh street map for details.

high criminal container. The jail's dominance makes a sad point about the relative appeal of incarceration and education, as solutions to problems in contemporary America. As for the jail's design, Raul A. Barreneche in *Architecture* has called it a "series of truncated cheese graters."

Return to Old Main. Back down McAnulty Drive toward Rockwell Hall at Locust Street stands a fetching piece of work by MacLachlan, Cornelius, and Filoni, the old gym transformed into the Rangos School of Health Sciences. See the picturesque double atrium within.

Drive east on Forbes to Pride; a left takes you to Fifth, where you turn left again. Recycled Victorian buildings show that here was downtown's first growth eastward, before the leapfrogging to Oakland began. A right on Washington Place leads to turn-of-the-century brick and terra-cotta Epiphany Church, the sole survivor of the ill-fated Lower Hill urban renewal ("means Negro removal," the phrase went) of the late 1950s.

Continue on Washington across Centre, driving around the Civic Arena; turn right at Bedford and then right at Auditorium Drive.

America's victory in World War II, as well as Pittsburgh's success with postwar urban projects, lent authority to the notion that big problems wanted big solutions. But big solutions also meant risking big mistakes. On your right is one of them.

The Civic Arena, begot in 1962 of Edgar Kaufmann's desire for an open air opera and other postwar leaders' desire for a Hill more like the newly sanitized Golden Triangle, failed on both counts. Acoustics were wrong for summer opera, and the Lower Hill "cleansing" left an indelible stain on the face of Pittsburgh's Renaissance.

Even if the startling structure had been perfect for opera, it would represent a disaster. The human costs of the Lower Hill project began with the displacement of fifteen hundred families. Their resettlement entailed overcrowding the rest of the Hill and neighborhoods like Homewood, and the harm caused by the disruption of living, shopping, and entertainment patterns is difficult to calculate. This episode

Civic Arena

in Pittsburgh's history has found vivid documentation in WQED's television film, *Wylie Avenue Days*. It is an elegy on Pittsburgh's "Little Harlem," before the one-two punch of 1950s urban renewal and 1960s racial unrest took the heart out of the Hill.

The social engineering implicit in the Civic Arena project spawned an enduring resentment. Many in the African-American community remain alienated from the city's political process, and their estrangement is worsened by an appalling income and employment gap between black and white Pittsburgh. According to a 1995 University of Pittsburgh study, Pittsburgh has the highest percentage of unemployed black males (ages 25–54) and the highest poverty rate for blacks (ages 18–64) among fifty U.S. cities with comparable racial demographics.

Uneasy relations between African Americans and the rest of Pittsburgh cast a shadow over the Lower Hill. But two things lighten the gloom. One is the Civic Arena itself. From afar, it makes an improbable and startling apparition. A visitor arriving from the north on 279 might imagine, given Pittsburgh's metallurgical history, that the earth here had suddenly blistered with steel, and a powerful black girder had been thrust over it to contain it.

From up close, the Arena remains an intriguing exercise in engineering. The cantilevered black structure's real purpose is to accept the dome's sections as they peel back (in two-and-a-half minutes) on fine nights. The building thoroughly responds to Le Corbusier's call for "exalted architectural feats," and the exaltation approaches the sublime—or the corny, if you're not in the right mood—on those occasions when fireworks punctuate the daffy drama of the opening and disappearing dome. The arid tracts of parking lots around this splendor also recall Le Corbusier: he wrote that the way to create a destiny for the city was to free its center—by razing it.

Continue on Auditorium under the giant girder leaping over the arena's dome. Turn left on Centre. I. M. Pei designed the highrise apartment block on the right (1420 Centre) in 1964. On the left at

Centre and Crawford stands Saint Benedict the Moor Roman Catholic Church, long a vital center of activism in Pittsburgh, and now anchor to a development enhancing the Hill's prospects.

Crawford Square, though handsomely designed by UDA Architects, is as far from Le Corbusier as you can get. Developer McCormack Baron and Associates of St. Louis specialize in building not projects, but whole inner-city neighborhoods. Crawford Square is meeting the same success the developer's other efforts have: The first stages, completed in 1996, were quickly filled, and construction of the third stage is well under way. The housing mix—rental apartments, townhouses, detached dwellings—is designed to appeal to a wide range of income groups. The city hopes that those who were forced out by the sweeping demolition of the 1950s will return: "Come Back to the Hill," the advertising billboards read.

Turn right on Miller Street to a sharp right on Foreside Place, which offers a splendid view of the Bluff. Take the next right into the new Protectory Place (unmarked, opposite Vine) to appreciate Crawford Square's urbane style. Notice, for instance, how well furnished the streetscape is, with utility wires underground. Here single rows of trees unify the different blocks; the double row of trees that lines Centre gives the Hill a proper entrance.

Continue across Centre on Protectory. Jog left on Webster, then right on Crawford. After turning right on Bedford, notice the bas reliefs at the entrances of Connelly Trade and Letsche Alternative High Schools, where Willa Cather taught Latin as a young woman (see tour 6). Just before the first stop sign, on your left, at 1727 Bedford, is the childhood home of August Wilson, Pulitzer Prize–winning playwright, bard of the Hill. He grew up in the forties and fifties in a two-room apartment behind the market.

If Pittsburgh has forgotten the Hill, Wilson's ambitious project is to make the world remember it. In plays such as *Joe Turner's Come and Gone, The Piano Lesson, Fences,* and *Two Trains Running,* Wilson uses the Hill of his memory the way Faulkner used Yoknapatawpha

County—to create a tangible landscape for the experience of an entire culture. "The plays' settings," writes Ben Brantley in the *New York Times*, "present this corner of Pittsburgh as a crucible in which the identity of black America has been shaped and tested." Wilson's oeuvre, still in progress, consists of a play about black Americans in every decade of the twentieth century. In August Wilson's work, the Hill is resurrected.

Continue on Bedford to the next stop sign. Go right on Devilliers, then left on Webster. Here, at Erin, rises a religious structure typical of this neighborhood. Zion Hill Baptist Church was born in 1920 as a synagogue; the change is emblematic of the exodus from the Hill of eastern European immigrants, many of them Jewish, and the influx of African-American migrants, many of them Baptist.

Turn right on Erin and left on Wylie, once the Hill's dense central thoroughfare. On the left, at Wylie and Elmore, is the legendary Crawford Grill, which we'll return to. On the right, you'll see Pat's Place, a former cigar store where August Wilson hung out as a teenager, collecting stories from former railroad porters and picking up the rhythms of their speech.

Turn right onto Kirkpatrick, noticing Eddie's restaurant on the corner, another Wilson haunt. *Two Trains Running*, a play about the Hill's experience with urban renewal, takes place in a diner much like this one. Go right on Center and right again on Elmore, which leads directly to the Crawford Grill at 2141 Wylie. The Hill's patchy blocks, a landscape of loss, reiterate the experience of both foreign immigrants and African-American migrants. The first loss was memory. August Wilson describes the Pittsburgh of 1911, where "From the deep and the near South the sons and daughters of newly freed African slaves wander into the city. Isolated, cut off from memory, having forgotten the names of the gods and only guessing at their faces, they arrive dazed and stunned." They sometimes end up feeling like "leftovers" of a stew the white man has eaten. What makes them remember who they really are is music. In *The Piano Lesson*, it's the piano itself which, "carved in the manner of African sculpture," records a family's history. But more often it's a song that pulls people together. In *Joe Turner's Come and Gone,* the magical Bynum (as in "bind 'em") tells lost Loomis, "Now I can look at you, Mr. Loomis, and see you a man who done forgot his song. Forgot how to sing it. A fellow forget that and he forget who he is." In *Ma Rainey's Black Bottom,* Wilson explains, "It is hard to define this music. Suffice it to say that it is music that breathes and touches. That connects." This is the hope for those new Pittsburghers in 1911, whose heart is "kicking in their chest with a song worth singing." It's "to reconnect, to reassemble, to give clear and luminous meaning to the song which is both a wail and a whelp of joy." Lena Horne, Art Blakey, Earl Hines, Billy Eckstine, Kenny Clarke, Erroll Garner, Ahmad Jamal, and George Benson are among the jazz musicians who played here and called the Hill home.

Go left on Wylie. The Carnegie Library on the right beyond Devilliers has been transformed into a mosque. Islam is not new to the Hill; in 1948, three sects were represented here.

Go left at once on Green, right on Linton, and left on Heldman through an odd trace of split-level suburbia. A left on Centre takes you by the Irene Kaufmann Hill House, a settlement house established early in this century to help immigrant Jews. (Another Hill institution reaching out to immigrants was the Kingsley House, which served as the base for the groundbreaking Pittsburgh Survey of 1910, a great experiment in social research.)

Just beyond Devilliers on the left stands the colorful 1927 New Granada Theatre. The Middle Hill, which you're passing through now, is divided from the Upper Hill by Herron Avenue, which is quite a way up Centre. Turn left on Herron. A right on Milwaukee takes you to the 1902 Madison School; notice the simian motif of its entrances. Beyond the school on the right side of Milwaukee is a park with extensive views. Circle the park with a right on Finland, a right on Camp, and a right on Adelaide.

Backtrack left down Milwaukee and turn right in front of the school on Orion Street. Turn right on Webster and left at the end on Blessing, down still wild slopes to Bigelow, where we make a sharp right.

Follow Bigelow for a while, where you may park, if you enjoy walking, in the area of the massive and columned 1916 Schenley High School; otherwise, you may continue the tour by car to the Carnegie, where there is parking at the end of South Craig Street. Be forewarned, however; driving in Oakland is notoriously difficult.

It was not merely an unnatural desire to leapfrog the Hill and its inhabitants that kept downtown Pittsburgh from expanding directly eastward. Industry had made the post–Civil War city so ugly that the national press referred to it as "hell with the lid taken off." Suburban development had begun, in Pittsburgh as elsewhere in the United States, with pre–Civil War railways. But the idea of a new urban order came into clear focus only with the 1893 Chicago World's Fair. Its hygienic grandeur—it was called the "White City"—thrilled millions, engendering a new sense of the possibilities for urban planning. Thus began the City Beautiful movement.

Grandeur required space, and Oakland, unlike the Hill or the North or South Sides, offered that abundantly. Most of it belonged to Mary Schenley, who at fifteen had married a middle-aged British captain and had lived in England ever after. In 1889, she donated three hundred acres to Pittsburgh for a park; at the beginning of the 1890s, Carnegie—always ahead of his contemporaries—got twenty acres of it for what became the Carnegie Institute.

That prepared the way for Franklin Felix Nicola. Nicola bought the heart of Mary Schenley's estate and set about developing, according to City Beautiful canons, Pittsburgh's new "civic center"—the very term shows the Golden Triangle's momentary loss of its hold on Pittsburghers' minds. Nicola rightly feared that the civic center's cluster of monuments and institutions would be lifeless without a residential quarter. He developed a neighborhood north and west of Bigelow Boulevard called Schenley Farms, which has since become a city historic district. Nicola endowed Schenley Farms with amenities lacking even now in most of Pittsburgh. The houses along these sycamore-lined, utility-pole-free streets were built to the most advanced specifications.

Continue down Bigelow and turn left at the T intersection onto Bayard, admiring the Italianate house on the corner at 4405 Bayard. Its Beaux Arts style is more characteristic of Oakland's institutional architecture than of its residences. Just beyond, across Bayard, you see an excellent example of Gothic, which rivals the Greco-Roman Beaux Arts in public architecture hereabouts. Bertram Grosvenor Goodhue vigorously conceived and finely finished First Baptist Church, with its elegant copper flèche, in 1910; connoisseurs observe that Goodhue's Gothic never lapsed into quaintness. Oakland continues to be attractive to religious buildings. Two new ones, First Church of Christ, Scientist, and the Ryan Catholic Newman Center—an oratory—have been erected a block east on Bayard.

Conflicting architectural styles distance Oakland from the City Beautiful model; so do land-use deviations. When Nicola began his development, Mary Schenley had already donated the plot, ideally residential, where the Western Pennsylvania School for Blind Children was built in 1894, at the corner of Bayard and North Bellefield.

Turn right on North Bellefield, where at 135 you see Oakland's third style. The vogue for brutalist architecture has lasted longer in Pittsburgh than anywhere else, a fact both inexplicable and inescapable. Perhaps its proponents take too seriously remarks about Pittsburgh's manufacturing-town roughness. Brutalist architectural aggression, in fact, scars the landscape no less than steel mills did. North Bellefield meets Fifth with another sad comment, the pathetic relic of a church destroyed to make space for the glassy structure you see, Bellefield Towers. Turn left on Fifth.

The City Beautiful movement made Americans want cities to be something more than arenas where greed and whim disported themselves at the expense of grace and the public good. The resultant creation of a civil infrastructure was an incalculable blessing. From an aesthetic point of view, however, the City Beautiful movement had serious defects. Proponents tended to identify order with uniformity, and uniformity is stifling. Oakland avoided that stylistically because no person or group was powerful enough to impose a Beaux Arts or any other single style. But uniformity did govern what kinds of buildings got built, and where: there are nothing but large institutional structures from here to the park. Look, for instance, at the mammoth, stripped-down Beaux Arts building at Fifth and Bellefield, Mellon Institute, one of the best of the institutional buildings. Powerful, perfectly finished, and boring, it looks like the rock-hewn sepulcher of an only partially enlightened monarch.

It's true that sepulchers can be intriguing; but, simply encountered on the streetscape, this one intimidates more than it fascinates. City Beautiful streets don't, in fact, work well for strollers. The buildings tend to be too big, too monotonous, too far apart. Nor can these ponderous structures, the architectural opposites of highway architecture, be enjoyed from an automobile. City Beautiful rhythms were established by men used to the pace of carriages; Oakland, freed of motor vehicles, might be enchanting from a calèche.

These reservations should not discourage you from investigating Mellon Institute. Built in the 1930s by Richard B. and Andrew W. Mellon, the brothers who had founded it in 1911, the institute encouraged industrial research. The Mellons's interest in industrial innovation dated from the early days of their bank, when it backed new processes like that for manufacturing aluminum.

Despite its daunting mass, there are many details to savor in Benno Janssen's creation, especially the materials themselves. Notice the marble paving around the Institute, subdued but very rich. If the columns look solid, it's because they are; these are monoliths, each column weighing sixty tons. The Indiana limestone has a subtly beautiful color and texture.

Inside, touches of aluminum—doors, windows, elevator doors— enliven the determinedly noble atmosphere. Of these, the one that will

Mellon Institute

win your heart is a receptionist's desk in aluminum. Beyond, a handsome wood-paneled library has more the air of an English club than of a place for industrial research. The Institute is now part of what used to be Carnegie Tech. The marriage in 1968 that produced Carnegie-Mellon University seemed destined; Andrew Carnegie believed that research was the soul of universities.

One of the downtown institutions to come to Oakland was Saint Paul's Cathedral, across Fifth beyond Dithridge. Frick's desire to buy the old cathedral's land for his Union Trust Arcade on Grant Avenue prompted the move. Saint Paul's late Gothic Revival style does not stand out among Pittsburgh's many Gothic churches.

More interesting is the building across the street. If Carnegie or the Mellons had been born a couple of generations later, they might have participated in the founding of Carnegie Mellon University's Software Engineering Institute. The mid-1980s structure makes respectful references to its neighbors without mimicking them. Its alignment, height, and limestone base match Mellon Institute, while its entrance reflects Saint Paul's. Walk through. An unexpected delicacy also governs the area beyond the entrance in the back: a metal pergola covered with wisteria offers shade. Turning around, you'll see Saint Paul's framed by the lobby windows. Exit through the back doors.

Go left on Henry to South Craig Street, where you turn right. If you're driving, make the right from Fifth to Craig. City Beautiful designers envisioned their civic centers as monumental courts of honor, set apart and decontaminated, in world's fair fashion, from profane commercial activities, which they confined to concession areas. Oakland's history spares it some of this rigidity. Craig Street's earlier development made its lively heterogeneity possible. Thanks to the recycling of some late Victorian houses, the street has become a fine jumble of housing, offices, and high and low commerce.

At the end of Craig, you have a view to the left of Carnegie Mellon University, where we will proceed toward the end of the tour. Directly across Forbes is the entrance to the garage of Pittsburgh's foremost cultural institution, the Carnegie.

Andrew Carnegie, its founder, puzzled people when alive and remains paradoxical even now, despite Joseph Wall's illuminating biography. One example: He often asserted and demonstrated his love for Pittsburgh, where he spent his youth and made the greatest fortune of his century, but he built his main residence in Manhattan and even then spent as much time as possible off in his native Scotland.

He felt a deep need for community, for the brotherhood that transcends class. But where did he build his great institute? Far from the center of this community, in an area much more accessible to the bourgeoisie than to workers. Workers in any case had little time to enjoy the benefaction, thanks to the twelve-hour day that Carnegie and his peers imposed on them. Most paradoxical of all was the spectacle of this supremely practical man trying to reconcile his immense fortune with his tenacious idealism, the fruits of his Scotch business genius with his heritage of Scotch radicalism. His active but not always accurate conscience told him something was wrong with a society where a single man could accumulate the wealth he had. It told him to build a bridge to the working class. That's the Carnegie.

At first the Carnegie, which celebrated its centennial in 1995, comes across as a cultural flea market, an improbable congestion of dinosaurs and Warhols, of rocks and books, of chamber music and medieval stone clones. It is as if Carnegie had resolved the question of choice simply by having it all. But in truth what he excluded from his philanthropy was as significant as what he included. Early on, he decided he would not give to hospitals or churches, except for donating organs to the latter. Eliminating body and soul as objects of his generous solicitude, he was left with the mind. That suited him entirely, for he aspired to scientific philanthropy, charity to improve not just the lot of individuals, but of the whole race. His peculiar Darwinism encouraged him in this enterprise: Social evolution was inevitable; it came with differentiation, which meant that it was also inevitable (and presumably good) that there would always be rich men like himself.

This reversal of Christ's teaching—that the poor we would have with us always—did not slow him overmuch. He believed that the rich man's amassing of wealth worked for the betterment of all mankind—through philanthropy. Money that might go to booze, left in proletarian hands, served for moral uplift.

Carnegie's certainty that he was spreading sweetness and light alternately infuriated or amused critics. Theodore Roosevelt tired of Carnegie's later efforts for international peace: "if Andrew Carnegie had employed his fortune and time in doing justice to the steelworkers who gave him his fortune, he would have accomplished a thousand times what he has accomplished" in the cause of peace. With regard to his educational efforts, *Blackwood's Edinburgh Magazine* fairly ranted: "Push and screw; buy cheap and sell dear. . . . To get money you must strangle joy and murder peace. . . . In old days, a rich man enjoyed his wealth—and if he did the community 'no good,' at least he did not insult it with patronage."

Paradoxes run through Carnegie's philanthropy, but his institute has been magnificently effective. Through his provision of art and music and science and books, he changed Pittsburgh forever. "It has never been anything but a center of materialism," Carnegie wrote about Pittsburgh. Writer Elizabeth Moorhead confirmed that her native city was "a barren and unlovely place" before the institute, and wonders at another paradox, that it was the materialism of big business that made possible "those immaterial things of greatest worth in our lives today."

Carnegie's belief in progress, or perhaps aesthetic insensitivity, left him with no interest in the old European paintings his partner Frick was collecting. He chose instead to encourage contemporary art through the Carnegie International, a prestigious exposition that has provided the Carnegie's art collection with about a third of its works since the inaugural show in 1896.

Frick's Old Masters ended up on display in New York, and those of the Mellons and other Pittsburgh collectors made their way to Washington, Philadelphia, and New Haven. Later institute patrons like Sarah Mellon Scaife partly made up for those losses; to house the art they gave, Edward Larabee Barnes built the Scaife Gallery in 1974.

This addition, whose entrance is at Forbes and Craig, shows how an architecture of simple materials and unadorned masses can be strong yet not brutal, elemental yet elegant. It maintains good visual and functional relations with the older wing without any recourse to the spiritless architectural "citations"—traditional elements postmodernists tend to use as tools of seduction.

The Richard Serra Cor-Ten steel sculpture, *Carnegie*, installed out front in 1985, displays similar strength and tact. Plain but subtle—see from the Scaife entrance how its angles echo those of the Cathedral of Learning—it manages to command attention without a monument's strutting. More outdoor sculpture graces the other side of the Scaife, in a court that may be approached from the parking lot.

The omnium-gatherum quality of the whole institute reflects in single parts as well. The paintings share galleries, for instance, with contemporary furniture and objects. Moving into the older section, you find turn-of-the-century murals as backdrops for a statue of Amenhotep III, a Calder mobile, and polar bear banners announcing the Wyckoff Hall of Arctic Life.

Museum spaces not to miss include the severely classical sculpture hall and the astonishing Hall of Architecture. The latter looks like a theater where only stars perform, each working to upstage all the others. Here one of the world's largest collections of plaster casts document the history of architecture. This cumbersome 1907 teaching device is in keeping with the City Beautiful preference for models from the past. The hall impresses as much for recording that as for the casts themselves. The 1993 Heinz Architectural Center, a research

Richard Serra's *Carnegie*, Scaife Gallery

and exhibition facility upstairs, handsomely complements the Hall of Architecture.

From the Forbes Avenue entrance to the Museum of Natural History, you may sometimes see the most sumptuous room in the institute—and one of the richest in America—the foyer of the Music Hall. This festival of marble and gold may not have elevated proletarian throngs to contemplation of things of the spirit quite as Carnegie wished, but it certainly elevated the man who paid for it. Here Andrew Carnegie sits on a throne, his evolutionary creed registered below: "All is well since all grows better."

Walk west on Forbes. Across the street on Dithridge is the columned Saint Nicholas Greek Orthodox Cathedral, a 1904 Congregational Church transformed for its present use by means of a shallow gilt dome with Christ the Pantocrator at its center, and a richly adorned metal and mosaic iconostasis.

On the Carnegie side of the street, you may admire the recently restored statues, symbols of the institute's four branches: science, art, music, and literature, incarnate in Galileo, Michelangelo, Bach, and Shakespeare.

Carnegie, the canny idealist, believed that a man who died rich, died disgraced. Before his death in 1919, he gave away $350 million. Of all his gifts, the institute was the one that he most cared for personally, and of its sections, excepting perhaps the dinosaurs, he cared most about the books. Carnegie practically invented the American public library system. You may enter his and Pittsburgh's main library from within the museum through the Hall of Architecture, or by turning left from Forbes around the corner of the institute. Its decor and staff do justice to a fine collection.

The 1908 monument outside the library entrance, by Augustus Saint-Gaudens, commemorates Pittsburgh's political boss at the time of the Carnegie's creation, Christopher Magee. The cornucopia, symbol of abundance, fits a man who lived amid an abundance of gifts, many received and some given. He was one of the people responsible for the creation of Schenley Park.

Cross Schenley Drive at the crosswalk to your left as you face the statue. Helen Clay Frick, who built the Henry Clay Frick Fine Arts Building here, died in 1984 as one of America's richest women. Miss Frick was as paradoxical as Carnegie, but in a different way. Carnegie reflects the dilemma of a capitalist who desires a sense of community, of a man who wants to be both rich and good. Miss Frick was merely eccentric. She had intended this 1965 Italian Renaissance villa to house a museum as well as the University of Pittsburgh's art department, which she funded. The catch was that she didn't want any contemporary art in the museum nor any Germans on the staff.

The university refused to satisfy these wishes. The would-be donor took her millions back to Point Breeze, where she put them to good use, and she left the university this building and some interesting artifacts. Miss Helen, who didn't like moderns, or Germans, didn't mind copies, or fakes. Nicholas Lochoff did the cloister wall reproductions of famous frescoes, twenty-two of which she bought from him in Florence for forty thousand dollars. They form a mural complement to Carnegie's architectural casts. The two apparently medieval statues of the Annunciation were carved by Alceo Dossena in the 1920s.

The Fine Arts building is pleasant enough, but it fails to create any sense of ensemble with its surroundings. Nor does the interesting 1918 Mary Schenley fountain establish a scale for the plaza. The brutalist neighbors to the left (as you face the parking lot), Pitt's Forbes Quadrangle and Hillman Library, are useful to the university, and they have attention-grabbing bulk; however, as architecture, they are execrable. What's even worse, as far as Pittsburghers are concerned, is that old Forbes Field was demolished to make way for Forbes Quadrangle. As cold comfort to baseball fans, home plate was embedded under glass in the ground floor of the building, and the red brick left-field wall remains across the street. A sidewalk plaque marks the spot where Bill Mazeroski's famed home run crossed the wall to win the 1960 World Series.

This area, called Schenley Plaza, was meant to form a noble entrance to Schenley Park. Potentially a very interesting place, it couldn't be more anticlimactic. The parking lot facing Forbes Avenue has recently been landscaped; it now looks like a landscaped parking lot. We turn our backs to it and will approach the park later.

We will also postpone, for a moment, the gratification of visiting the Cathedral of Learning and will look at its immediate neighbors first. Directly across from Schenley Plaza, snuggled up against the Cathedral, is the Stephen Foster Memorial, a theater, museum, and research center dedicated to Pittsburgh's favorite composer. Tour 8 includes the site of his birth.

Follow the stairs and sidewalk behind the Foster Memorial and around the Cathedral to the right. Charles Klauder, architect of the Cathedral and the 1937 Foster Memorial, also designed the 1938 Heinz Chapel with great finesse. Here earth marries heaven with a flair. If its height, pinnacles, and flèche haven't elevated you, the interior may help. The materially and iconographically rich stained glass is by the Pittsburgh-trained contemporary master, Charles Connick. The four transept windows, representing Courage, Tolerance, Temperance, and Truth, are each seventy-three feet high. Notice that cool blue and green dominate the southern sunny side, warm reds and golds the north, giving balance. The chapel's siting has the same grace as everything else about it. It also forms the best approach to the Cathedral of Learning.

Part Two. Cathedral of Learning to Schenley Park

What is most striking about Oakland is not its conscious, calculated City Beautiful urbanity, but an immense folly. For the Cathedral of Learning, from a rational standpoint, is pure extravagance. Yet it is this striking forty-story structure alone which gives Oakland focus.

Without it, the neighborhood would be no more than a ho-hum continuum of Beaux Arts pavilions. Moreover, the Cathedral has become a symbol of the city as a whole. That fact is a triumph of Pittsburgh's desire for the higher things, and a tribute to the will of the chancellor who built it.

There was an analogy between Carnegie's brand of philanthropic social Darwinism and the City Beautiful movement. Each presupposed the separating off of something from the ordinary round of human life. For Carnegie, it was wealth, which rightly, he thought or rather hoped, tended to concentrate in the hands of the few. For the City Beautiful movement, it was the higher civic institutions, which needed to be kept in distinctive quarters of their own, unsullied by everyday activities. Thus money and culture should be set apart from common folk and common purposes. The trouble with this hygiene was that it split the community. Carnegie attempted to mend the fracture by funding culture, but long hours left workers no time or energy to use his library and other amenities.

It fell to John Bowman, chancellor of the University of Pittsburgh from 1921 to 1945, to establish a broader sense of community in Pittsburgh. The school, which became state-related only in 1966, needed money; Bowman found it natural to go to Pitt graduate R. B. Mellon to discuss remedies. Mellon advised him that the way to get Pittsburghers to give was not to talk about money per se, but to get a plan.

The university, which moved to Nicola's Oakland in 1908 from Perry Hilltop, already had a plan. Henry Hornbostel's classically inspired scheme was to cover the patchy slopes of the Oakland end of the Hill with fair renditions of Grecian temples. Bowman, sensing that time had extinguished this City Beautiful concept's allure, got an inspiration. What would appeal to the industrialists and financiers, and at the same time open other minds to what the university represented, would be a tower that, "singing upward . . . would tell the epic story of Pittsburgh."

Bowman conceived a structure of great height—at the original fifty-five stories, it would have been the second tallest building in America—in the most soaring of styles, Gothic. Its medieval garb would link it to the favored church mode, confirming the spirituality of the enterprise; the fact that it was a skyscraper, with art deco details, testified to its kinship with contemporary industrial and commercial America.

The very unconventionality of the idea excited Bowman, for, "If the youth of Pittsburgh grow up with commonplace abilities and commonplace loyalties, what is the future of Pittsburgh?" A landmark grassroots fundraising campaign motivated 97,000 Pittsburgh youngsters to buy a "brick" of the tower for a dime.

The impracticality of thousands of students changing classes at the same time by elevator did not dim Bowman's vision. On the contrary, he was intent on creating an interior as inspiring as the exterior. The great Gothic Commons Room answered his challenge to the architect: "Draw a room that will so grip a boy that he will never enter it with his hat on."

Hats may not always be doffed, but Walkman-plugged freshmen doing their homework on medieval thrones provide one of Pittsburgh's more unusual sights. It is also paradoxical that the main room of a place of enlightenment be so dark. Franklin Toker sees the windowless space as a reminder of Pittsburghers' bituminous and anthracitic origins. In a city so pervaded by darkness—of smoke, of mines, of runs and hollows and mountain valleys—grounding a soaring symbol of light in cavernous gloom was yet another way of bringing together distant poles of the Pittsburgh experience.

The Nationality Rooms, on this and on the third floor, likewise helped fulfill the chancellor's vision. Classrooms inspired by the area's diverse ethnic groups, the Nationality Rooms served to pull Pittsburgh's hitherto ignored ethnic groups into a close relation with the university.

One of the aspects of the Cathedral that appealed to the architect

Klauder was that "the whole structure is unhampered by its surroundings." That freedom jeopardized aesthetic relations with its classically inspired neighbors. Despite their great size, similar materials, and vicinity, the Cathedral and the Carnegie, for example, relate very weakly to one another. But if the Cathedral pays no compliments to the Carnegie, the surrounding lawn and trees do soften and harmonize the prospects around it.

Walk straight through the Commons Room and out across Bigelow to visit the William Pitt Union. Built in 1898 as the elegant Schenley Hotel, it maintains its tradition of hospitality as a center for university student activities, which range from eating and playing on the 1983 postmodern ground floor, to studying and snoozing and schmoozing in the faultlessly restored salons of the main floor. It's all worth a look.

Coming out through the Fifth Avenue entrance, go left to enter another student sanctum, the severe Doric court of the 1923 Schenley Apartments, now dormitories. Leaving the courtyard on the right brings you out on Fifth Avenue. Across Fifth stands the squat symmetrical Romanesque mass of Bellefield Presbyterian Church, also recently restored.

To the right of that—we're heading back east now—rises the picturesque Allegheny County Soldiers and Sailors Memorial Hall. This 1907 product of Hornbostel's vigorous mind contains a military museum and a large auditorium. Before turning left on Bigelow, notice two other institutions farther down Fifth: the Pittsburgh Athletic Association in its convivial 1911 Venetian palazzo, and the forbidding 1914 Masonic Temple, half visible beyond—both works of Benno Janssen.

This area presents City Beautiful's best face, though sorely missed is the colorful Syria Mosque, a Hollywood Islamic auditorium behind the Athletic Association, where the Pittsburgh Symphony long played, and outside a locked door of which Eleanora Duse caught the cold that led to her death in the Schenley Hotel. Demolition of the fraternal

View of Cathedral of Learning from South Oakland

organization's building at the outset of the 1990s prompted Pittsburghers to consider more closely the preservation of the city's urban fabric; this area is now a historic district.

The district includes the 1910 Twentieth Century Club, behind and to the right of the Soldiers and Sailors Memorial on Bigelow, and the 1912 building that housed the Historical Society of Western Pennsylvania until 1991. Its expanding functions prompted a move to larger quarters in the Strip. That's good news for the energetic society, but the move diminished Oakland's role as Pittsburgh's cultural center, as does the loss of the Syria Mosque.

If you left your car near Schenley High School you may return by way of tree-lined Lytton Avenue to Parkman Avenue, which runs into Bigelow a block before Bigelow meets Centre. The tour continues backtracking south downhill, following Bigelow. Turn right at the T intersection at the bottom of the slope that continues as Bigelow. (The same street to the left becomes Bayard.) As you pass Parkman, Bigelow undergoes a name change again, becoming O'Hara Street. We are approaching an immense medical complex, a high-traffic area. At the intersection, turn right onto DeSoto. If possible, pull off to the side and park for a moment. Otherwise, turn left onto Terrace and left again down Lothrop Street to Fifth Avenue, where you turn right.

Hopes that the service industry would be less a violation of the landscape than steel mills are dashed by this conglomeration. For all of the reservations expressed about the premises of City Beautiful planning, one can only lament that the University of Pittsburgh medical center did not follow some recognizable organizing principle. Does mending bodies justify mangling cities? Scientific success underlies this urban failure. Around the time of World War II, discoveries like penicillin marked a great shift in American medicine, from a caretaking to a cure-making profession. The importance of research grew proportionately, and so did the institutions where it took place.

The University Health Center, whose core is this group of buildings at O'Hara and DeSoto, has been the site of research of immense consequence. Benjamin Spock and Erik Erikson's investigation into children's disturbances took place here on the right at Western Psychiatric, 3815 O'Hara. Thomas Starzl pioneered liver transplants at Presbyterian University Hospital, a world leader in all sorts of organ transplants. Jonas Salk's search for a polio vaccine took place on Terrace at what was once Municipal Hospital and now bears Salk's name.

At the bottom of Lothrop you will be forced to turn right on Fifth. To the left on Fifth, and on the cross streets and parallel blocks of Forbes, is Oakland's main commercial center, not on our itinerary. Here's where you'll find student-oriented shops and cafés, as well as a few good restaurants for the grown-ups (especially down Atwood Street).

After making the right on Fifth, you will pass more hospital buildings, with Carlow College on the right. You need to keep toward the left lanes (the lane farthest to the left is a bus lane traveling in the opposite direction). Turn left on Craft Avenue. Here, at the corner with Forbes, once stood the 1852 Saint Peter's Church. The Gothic structure was precious enough for the congregation to move it stone by stone from its original site downtown, where the Frick Building now stands, but not so valuable as to ward off destruction at the hands of developers, who planned an office tower here. Those plans never materialized. Now Carlow owns the site and plans an academic building.

Continuing on Craft you see, on the right, the Pittsburgh Playhouse, a recycled 1906 synagogue. Take a left on Boulevard of the Allies. Stay in the far left lane. At the next light, glance right to see the 1929 art deco former headquarters of Isaly Dairy, birthplace of the Klondike, appropriately clad in creamy tiles.

The Boulevard of the Allies goes gently right at the light; you veer slightly left here onto Zulema, then turn left at the stop sign on narrow Bates. We are now in south Oakland, as far in spirit from monumental Oakland as Naples is from Nebraska. South Oakland was settled by Italians brought in by labor agents to work on the railroad and con-

Oakland Square

South Oakland shrine

struction projects. With waves of new immigrants (especially foreign graduate students) arriving each semester, it's as multicultural a neighborhood as you'll find anywhere. After several short blocks, turn right at the T intersection on South Bouquet Street, where at 379 stands an Italian social hall and mutual benefit society. Notice the canine bas reliefs.

For the tireless, there are steps at the bend where Bouquet and Dawson meet which will take you into the picturesque ravine with its solitary, but not sad, clump of houses immortalized in Michael Chabon's *The Mysteries of Pittsburgh* as the Lost Neighborhood. You will have an easier view of Junction Hollow by turning right on Dawson, then left around Oakland Square.

Continue on Dawson, turn right on Boulevard of the Allies, then take a quick left onto Ward Street. At the end of Ward, turn right and park on Wakefield Street. At Wakefield's dead end is a concrete wall. Just to the right of the wall is a path that leads to a neighborhood shrine. If the Carnegie and the Cathedral of Learning represented conscious efforts at community reconciliation, this homemade shrine pulls things together simply with a brick walk and a little weed control. The Nativity scene on the hillside toward the end is marked "joyful mysteries," but the term might apply to the whole spot. The views—west to downtown, east to Hazelwood industry, and directly below, down the precipitous slopes, beyond the Parkway, where Junction Hollow debouches onto the Monongahela River, to the Pitt- and CMU-sponsored Pittsburgh Technology Center—show that the matter-of-fact old country faith can hold its own with any of the city's glossier attractions.

The Technology Center and the vast tract of land on the other side of the river are the former sites of Jones and Laughlin Steel's Second Avenue and South Side works, once connected by the bridge to your left. Legend has it that the shrine was built on the spot where a steelworker on his lunch break had a vision. The mill blast furnaces would have obscured almost any other sort of view here until the 1980s.

Backtrack on Ward. Turn right on Frazier Street, then left on Dawson, where, at 3252, right side, Andy Warhol grew up.

Make a right on Boulevard of the Allies toward Schenley Park, just over the bridge. This land was an 1889 gift of Mary Schenley, Pittsburgh-born but English by residence; the landscape architect, William Falconer, also came from England. Full of surprises, the park, now 456 acres, merits multiple visits. If you wish another view of downtown, you may want to take an immediate right after the bridge to Overlook Road.

The tour instead continues on to Phipps Conservatory, which means taking the second right, passing a statue of Edward Bigelow, one of the fathers of the park, then driving over Panther Hollow Bridge, adorned with four bronze panthers. The panthers and Bigelow were sculpted by Giuseppe Moretti at the end of the 1890s.

Phipps Conservatory, a gift of Carnegie's partner Henry Phipps, dates from the 1893 Chicago World's Fair, from which some of Horticultural Hall's plants were adopted. Its two-and-a-half acres make Phipps a big greenhouse. But the conservatory's great virtue lies in its exotic and noble architecture; it would be hard to name a more elegant building in Pittsburgh. You can park at the metered parking in front of the conservatory or along Frew Street, which is the first right-hand turn after the conservatory.

For the stroller, there are charming gardens surrounding the conservatory, and plenty of statuary, too: a frightful Christopher Columbus—but the waves are fun; a Robert Burns that Andrew Carnegie wanted here; another Moretti work, *Hygeia,* with Aesculapius's double serpent symbol.

Continue on Frew Street to CMU, which is what Pittsburghers call the school known as Carnegie Institute of Technology until 1968, when it became Carnegie Mellon University. Park your vehicle as soon as you find a place; often that means continuing beyond the campus into the park proper. Enter the campus on foot.

Andrew Carnegie was not so much indifferent to classical liberal

Phipps Conservatory

Christopher Columbus monument, Schenley Park

arts education as he was hostile to it. He noticed an absence of college graduates among successful businessmen, and a prevalence of great men from the ranks of mechanics and common workers: "It is really astonishing how many of the world's foremost men have begun as manual laborers." Consequently, CMU began as a secondary school producing skilled craftsmen. That was in 1900; only in 1912 did Carnegie allow its reorganization as an institution of higher learning—or rather two, the Carnegie Institute of Technology, and the Margaret Morrison Carnegie College for women, named after his mother. Elizabeth Moorhead's characterization was trenchant: "Carnegie Tech was instituted for practical purposes leading to what is called 'success.'"

The tension between learning for learning and learning for doing has been strong in Pittsburgh from the outset; learning for doing has traditionally won. The historian John Funari links this with the particular immigrant values that shaped the city, the Scotch-Irish spurning of Old World culture and their exaltation of hard work. Pragmatic materialism's sway increased with time; it was the sole ideal binding Pittsburgh's multiethnic culture. A Pittsburgh education was primarily a practical education.

Practicality has taken the universities far, however. The University of Pittsburgh recently started graduate business schools in Hungary and in the Czech republic, while CMU has opened a business office in Tokyo. Programs like Pitt's organ transplants and CMU's computer science originated in practical concerns.

Carnegie Mellon University's fathers of artificial intelligence, Herbert Simon and Alan Newell, began exploring the notion that machines might simulate human intelligence in the university's Graduate School of Industrial Administration, where Simon had been investigating how business decisions were made. Their belief that intelligence could be manufactured was revolutionary in the early 1950s; it led CMU to establish a formal computer science department in 1965. Now the School for Computer Science is a leader in robotics as well as in software engineering.

Henry Hornbostel designed CMU's campus after the pattern of the 1893 Chicago World's Fair, a double range of buildings on a midway. But he sought a balance between monumentality and utilitarianism, translating Beaux Arts symmetry and order into something congenial with Carnegie's idea of education. The buildings, in industrial brick, observe functionality as their first principle. Rumors still circulate that Carnegie intended to transform the campus into a factory if the school didn't fulfill its role. In fact, the slope of the long, handsome corridor of Baker Hall—the building on the left as you face west entering the main quadrangle—was not intended to facilitate production-line movements, but simply to accommodate the slope of the hill. Notice within, near Baker Hall's northern entrance, the spiral staircase in beautiful but basic Guastavino construction tile.

The focus of the campus—if you can take your eyes off Pitt's Cathedral of Learning—is the 1912 Hamerschlag Hall, dominated by a classically garbed smokestack. Hornbostel saw the campus as a ship as well as a factory—architects generally mix metaphors—and that inspired the 1899 placement of a bronze prow ornament from the armored cruiser USS *Pittsburgh* on the western brow of Hamerschlag Hall's hill.

Two lapses mar the campus' central scheme: the brutalist concrete building to the right of Hamerschlag Hall, its auditorium jutting out a dozen feet to shatter Hornbostel's symmetry, and the less discordant but equally noncontextual Hunt Library, the green aluminum 1960 structure near the College of Fine Arts. The library interior boasts not only early 1900s cast aluminum doors from the Aluminum Company of America, but also Rachel Hunt's historical botanical book collection.

The upper end of the campus is dominated by Hornbostel's College of Fine Arts (born, typically, as the School of Applied Design), whose interior appointments merit a look. Besides the well-used and elegantly finished Kresge Theater, there are plans of several great buildings inlaid in the floor; the ceiling paintings depict the com-

Westinghouse Memorial fountain

Serpentine Drive, Schenley Park

pleted construction. You enter the dean's office through a replica of the 1656 door of Toulon's Hotel de Ville. Reproductions of classical statues here sometimes cradle Cokes; and practice rooms, rehearsal halls, and gallery exhibitions make this one of Pittsburgh's liveliest spots.

103
The
Hill,
Oakland,
Schenley
Park

As you leave the building, notice the sculpted niches on the facade. Hornbostel designed these five spaces to represent architecture from the Renaissance, Middle Ages, Greece, Rome, and the Orient. When the building was completed in 1917, only the Renaissance niche had been carved. The other four remained blank until 1993, when they were finished over a two-year period by an international team led by master stonecarver Nicholas Fairplay.

Behind the College of Fine Arts is Hornbostel's 1907 Margaret Morrison Carnegie Hall, whose attractive peristyle features an inscription not all women would subscribe to. The futuristic addition atop the roof of Margaret Morrison is just that—Volker Hartkopf's office of the future, called *The Intelligent Workplace*. It's designed as a testing ground for technology that makes buildings more energy efficient and employees more productive and happy. The unique facade, for example, includes devices that let workers control light and heat within.

Other new construction on the ever-expanding campus includes an addition to the Graduate School of Industrial Administration, a well-conceived parking garage delimiting the playing fields, and an enormous student center, all part of a master plan by Michael Dennis and Associates of Boston. A new arts center to house CMU's famous drama department is also on the boards.

Go back to your car by way of Tech Avenue, which intersects Frew. You can reenter Schenley Park by turning right at Tech and Frew. A left after about a hundred yards takes you to the 1930 Westinghouse Memorial fountain. This is another Hornbostel work; Daniel Chester French sculpted the figures and Paul Fjelde was responsible for the six bas reliefs in the hemicycle that represent some of Westinghouse's extraordinary inventions. The beautifully organized monument does justice to a man who did not always receive his due while alive.

Follow this road—it's West then East Circuit—for the Neill Log House of 1790; house, not cabin, because the logs are squared and fitted for durability. Serpentine Drive begins on the right; note its stone wall, but continue on East Circuit to Darlington Road. Go left again on Schenley Drive. Glimpse on the right, beyond the fairway, the white columns of the Pittsburgh Golf Club.

The generation responsible for Schenley and Highland Parks considered parks, ideally, as instruments for "the elevation of people." Edward Bigelow, in fact, proposed civic green spaces for working class areas, but he could not get them approved; the two big parks are in middle- and upper-class neighborhoods. In a way, the beautiful Schenley golf course symbolizes this failure to provide for the working classes. Only in a way, however, because the club does not own the course. The Pittsburgh Golf Club has no course. This one, now open to all, is operated by CMU.

SHADYSIDE, EAST LIBERTY, HIGHLAND PARK
This walking and driving tour begins at Rodef Shalom Temple at Fifth and
Morewood Avenues. You may want to walk the first loop, or even the
whole Shadyside section of the tour.

5

Presbyterians and
Other Primates

B oundaries of neighborhoods, like those of nations, help clarify
personal as well as geographical identity. But neighborhood
boundaries, though often fiercely defended, seldom follow as
clear a line as national ones. Successful neighborhoods like Shadyside
tend to expand; real estate agents see to it, if no one else does.

This tour begins on the border between Shadyside and Oakland.
The two districts call up sharply divergent images: Oakland quintessentially public, institutional, monumental; Shadyside private and
cozily residential.

Yet if you think about it, an assortment of public buildings does in
fact command the quiet streets of Shadyside, by force of social tradition as well as by architectural prominence. The neighborhood's
places of worship, disproportionate in number, also occupy a disproportionate place in Pittsburgh's moral history.

The 1906 Rodef Shalom Temple shares not only Oakland's monumentality, but also an Oakland architect, Henry Hornbostel, who
designed the Soldiers and Sailors Memorial, CMU, and the University
of Pittsburgh's original plan. Much—too much—has been made of
Pittsburgh's masculinity and of its reflection in the built environment.

105

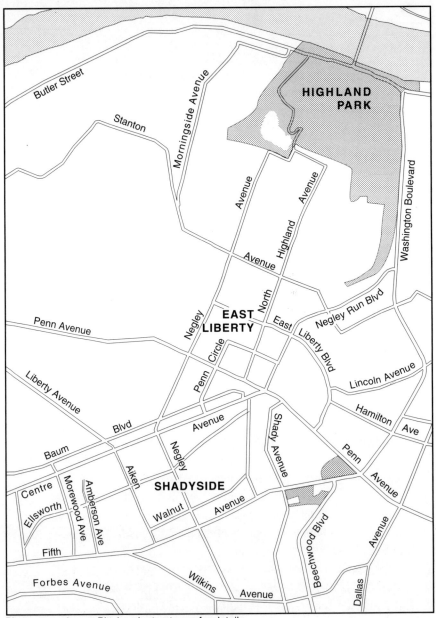

Please consult your Pittsburgh street map for details.

But good local architecture, beginning with the courthouse, does tend to the robust; take Rodef Shalom's massive industrial brick walls, for instance.

107
Shadyside,
East
Liberty,
Highland
Park

Then look at the synagogue's dome. Hornbostel might have given it a seductive roundness; he chose instead to square it, harden it with tile, and cap it almost brutally. Yet with its highly visible green roof and its brightly colored terra-cotta bands of berries and leaves, it is festive, grandly so—the emperor taking his ease.

The vast interior likewise has an original air; it features good quality stained-glass windows that would not be out of place in a church. The congregation, founded in 1854, consisted primarily of Germans from the southwestern provinces; immigrants from the east, of more traditional religious outlook, established the Tree of Life Synagogue, now located in Squirrel Hill. Rodef Shalom was the site of the national meeting of rabbis in 1885, where the Pittsburgh Platform was articulated as the basis of Reform Judaism. It established such innovations as seating by family rather than gender at services.

Walk west to Fifth and Clyde. Rodef Shalom's neighbor, the 1961 Byzantine Catholic Holy Spirit Church, chooses not to sit foursquare on Fifth Avenue, which would put it in competition with the temple, but turns its mosaic-covered facade obliquely toward Oakland and the afternoon sun. The mosaics, as well as the triple stainless steel onion domes at both side entrances, are awkward, suggesting the imperfectly resolved relationship between the church's past and the present.

The street sign at Fifth and Morewood declares that corner part of Shadyside. But nearly everyone would locate WQED's building, across the street from Holy Spirit, in Mister Rogers' Neighborhood. The popular children's show is produced here. WQED was the first public educational station in the country; it remains one of the best. The beautifully scaled and crafted poured concrete walls of Paul Schweikher's 1970 building prove that the brutalist mode in architecture can be more than an exercise in upstaging neighbors.

Just beyond WQED on Fifth Avenue, the 1927 red brick Central

Catholic High School's turrets evoke the medieval sources of the Catholic Church's authority.

One-block-long Clyde Street, which begins at Holy Spirit, finds its focus in the former Christian Science church. Designed by S. S. Beman, the Chicago architect responsible for the denomination's huge neo-Byzantine Mother Church extension in Boston, this dignified but engaging 1904 structure has an interior even more winning in its serene brightness than the Ionic exterior. It's been transformed into a playroom for children at Pitt's Child Care Center.

On Ellsworth Avenue, just beyond the end of Clyde, looms the massive time-blackened tower of the Church of the Ascension, "built in the years 1897 and 1898" a stone over the central door explains. Among Pittsburgh's numerous essays in Gothic, few have the happy siting of this church, whose architect was William Halsey Wood. The style is Tudor Gothic, but the feeling is Richardsonian, both for the massive volumes and for the rock-faced sandstone walls. The sooty patina accentuates the church's grounded quality, a complement to the mystery of the Ascension. The dark stone makes a dramatic backdrop not only for the lipstick red doors, but also for the profusion of flowers that gladden the eye here in the warm season. The interior features an open timberwork roof, a richly carved wood chapel screen, and many representations of the Ascension.

Across Ellsworth Avenue, on the corner of Neville, is Ellsworth Mews—according to its advertising, "elegant townhomes surrounding a European courtyard." The courtyard is as pleasant and functional as the rest of the late 1980s development, which Arthur Lubetz designed, although it's hard to know what is specifically European about it. The project's relatively high density may be thought continental; closely spaced dwellings increasingly characterize all of Shadyside. (Notice down Neville the green apartment building; that would be camouflage tile, were Neville Avenue the jungle.)

Backtrack east on Ellsworth Avenue. Beyond the Church of the

Ascension, two brick pillars mark the entrance to another townhouse development, this one the 1913 Ellsworth Terrace, a dozen rationally laid out dwellings. The phony Victorian duplexes fronting the street date from 1991.

109

Shadyside,
East
Liberty,
Highland
Park

Real Victorian architecture sometimes weds grace to picturesqueness, as it does in Pittsburgh's prettiest house, next door at 4841 Ellsworth, which suggests what Shadyside was like in its earliest years. Situated on a lot the same size as all of Ellsworth Terrace, grace marks its history as well as its appearance. Built before the Civil War and expanded soon after, it is believed to have served as a stop on the underground railroad. George W. Guthrie, the early twentieth-century reform mayor of Pittsburgh, lived here as a child.

Until the 1850s, even the affluent lived in Pittsburgh's crowded urban core; rivers and steep slopes frustrated easy access to the surrounding areas. No one would have called it a classless city, but as a walking city, it inevitably mingled the rich and poor.

Technology changed that. Shadyside opened to development when the Pennsylvania Railroad laid tracks on its northern edge in 1852. Trains made escape from the old city possible, and social confusion made that escape desirable. Innovations like the Bessemer revolutionized the scale and sociology of industry, bringing a huge influx of unskilled immigrant laborers. The arrival of masses of foreigners meant that the old city lost its comforting familiarity.

For all the virtues of houses like the one at 4841, they do represent the fraying of the old walking community. Long before the Civil War, Andrew Jackson Downing gave voice to American antiurban sentiments: "Nature and domestic life are better than society and the manners of towns. Hence all sensible men gladly escape . . . from the turmoil of cities."

Americans' evolving sense of home, the exaltation of family life and of nature, were to accelerate the rail- and then automobile-powered flight from the inner city. Pittsburgh's topography slowed this

4841 Ellsworth Avenue, Shadyside

movement locally. One of the consequences is a higher residential density than you find in other cities; Ellsworth Terrace and Ellsworth Mews offer two examples.

The big 1976 house two doors down at 4875 represents another urban choice. The builder, an Alcoa aluminum heir, could have lived anywhere, and the house is clearly suburban in inspiration. But Alfred Hunt preferred his family's city lot; the Victorian cast-iron fence dates from their earlier dwelling.

The architect, Edward Grenzbach, followed the local tradition: make your buildings from whatever made your fortune. In Pittsburgh, siding capital of the world, aluminum walls usually mean a metal skin posing as clapboard. What you see here are solid cast-aluminum panels. Those garden walls are anorthosite, an aluminum ore. Aluminum pervades the interior too, including a two-story 1937 library added to the original dwelling to house Rachel Hunt's collection of botanical books, now at Carnegie Mellon University.

People moving out of downtown to Shadyside in the nineteenth century were fleeing more than industrial nuisances. One acute observer notes that in migrating from the tight-knit center, with its constant reciprocal surveillance, to the larger lots and detached dwellings of the periphery, Pittsburghers were also escaping their own narrow virtue. Referring to presuburban Pittsburgh, a journalist wrote that "Luxury is a sin to which the ironmaster seldom had to confess." No one would accuse Shadyside's early inhabitants of sybaritic self-indulgence. But their more relaxed style appears in the easy relation the houses have with one another, and their air of unashamed comfort.

Look left to admire the oaks lining Devonshire, a street rich in all its length. We're turning right, where eclectic architecture in a variety of materials—slate and shingle, pebbled stucco and plain stucco, brick and wood, stained glass and leaded glass and diamond glass, sandstone and limestone and cobblestone, along with the verdure, produce an unusually rich texture. Don't miss stony 714, or the copper

111

Shadyside,
East
Liberty,
Highland
Park

box gutters at Devon Hall at 803, or the sooty but successful Queen Anne concoction across the street at 820.

The Biblical Botanical Garden next to Rodef Shalom closes this short walking loop—although the rest of the Shadyside section can be done on foot easily enough for good walkers.

Turn left on Fifth Avenue where, just beyond Morewood on the right, the apartment building at 5000 has what at first glance appears to be a nature mural in the lobby. In fact, it's nature herself, the declivity of Shadyside revealed through floor-to-ceiling glass. On the left a couple of mansions will catch your eye; plane trees, decorative urns, and dilapidated entrance gateposts accentuate the strong eighteenth-century French quality of 5057. 5061, at Amberson Avenue, which dates from 1870, was drastically damaged in a 1987 fire. It has just been meticulously restored.

Turn left at Amberson Avenue where you are greeted by the powerful sandstone mass of Shadyside Presbyterian Church, the historical heart of this neighborhood. From the time a victorious Scot, General Forbes, invited a Presbyterian divine to lead a service of thanksgiving for the conquest of Fort Duquesne, Scots and Scotch-Irish Presbyterians have played the protagonists in Pittsburgh. With Forbes, they led Anglo-Saxons into what is now downtown; with industrialization, a century later, they led them back out.

The church was organized in 1866, helped by East Liberty Presbyterian, as well as by David Aiken, Jr., whose family owned the western end of Shadyside. The Aikens's house gave the neighborhood its name. Sunday school and then evening services were first held in the railroad station—the same station that enabled the Aiken family to develop their land profitably. But the church too played an incalculable role in attracting newcomers.

One of the industry-related problems the Presbyterians were fleeing was the large number of immigrants. The transoceanic saga of these people, brought in as fodder for the mills, has effaced the Anglo-Saxons' own minor migration out to Shadyside and the East End. This

4841 Ellsworth Avenue, Shadyside

Shadyside Presbyterian Church

lesser drama may sound a little like that Mexican soap opera, *The Rich Weep Too.*

One of the church's functions in Pittsburgh was to reassure those who had left their homes that they had not abandoned everything. Industrial transformation suggested an unstable world; earth's elements could become steel, air could become smoke. This flux unsettled even those who were profiting from it. Shadyside Presbyterian served as an anchor against moral drift, proving to newcomers that, however altered their external circumstances were, their heritage remained the same.

Their heritage did. Annie Dillard, writing in *An American Childhood* about the Pittsburgh of old East End families in the 1950s, says it was so thoroughly Scotch-Irish that "it might have been seventeenth-century Donegal." The Romanesque architecture of the 1889 Shepley, Rutan, and Coolidge structure seconded this impression. The vine- and soot-covered church looked as though it had "long since encrusted into its quietly splendid site," looking like "a Scottish rock in the rain."

Since the time of Dillard's observations, Shadyside's outer walls have been scrubbed clean of their antique patina. Have there been similar changes within? If you attend a Sunday service in winter, you will be greeted by ushers in morning coats, an elegant anachronism that will surprise you less if you recall Dillard's description of Shadyside boys as wearing ties "from the moment their mothers could locate their necks."

Young Annie knew men used Shadyside for business connections; the Presbyterian church in general, and this one in particular, have long been criticized as the church of capitalism. Plaques on the left or north transept wall celebrate a variety of technological and patriotic accomplishments, enhancing the establishment tone. Steel plant closures in the 1980s, in fact, provoked attacks on this church.

Just beyond the church at 719 Amberson is the Spencer house, of *The Spencers of Amberson Avenue* fame. This warm and detailed

115

Shadyside,
East
Liberty,
Highland
Park

memoir of Ethel Spencer's childhood from the early 1890s to 1910 paints a remarkable portrait of middle-class life in Shadyside. The burgeoning industrial city required, in addition to waves of immigrant laborers, a growing clerical, sales, and managerial force. Ethel Spencer's father was on Henry Clay Frick's staff. As Michael Weber and Peter Stearns point out in their introduction to the memoir, "The Spencers illustrate the kind of life which, more than the doings of the fabulously wealthy, tempts one to recall the turn of the century as a bourgeois golden age." Like its Queen Anne neighbor at 717, the Spencer house dates from the mid 1880s.

Farther down Amberson, on the left at 5020 in cozy Amberson Place, is the Italianate dwelling of David Aiken, Jr., where Shadyside Presbyterian was founded in 1866. Amberson Place was created, in a manner typical of later Shadyside, when his estate was subdivided.

Backtrack on Amberson Avenue to Westminster Place, where you will proceed left to Saint James Street. If you're driving, park along Westminster for a short detour to the right on one-way Saint James; this affords a look at 918–920, a white board-and-batten double house built about 1860. The house on the corner at 5302 Westminster, also board and batten, with fish-scale shingles, dates from a decade later.

Continue to the end of the block to South Aiken, where a left will take you past an 1893 Frederick Osterling church, to Shadyside's small but dense main commercial area. Notice the old-fashioned Aiken Market. Go right on Walnut Street. Here, despite the extremely unkempt streetscape—the tipsy utility poles might do honor to a frontier town—you may enjoy many of Pittsburgh's best shops, restaurants, and night spots. Walnut Street, in fact, is the most prosperous of the surprisingly numerous examples of the survival of neighborhood commercial centers. These centers testify to the city's complex but focused efforts to keep Pittsburgh's neighborhoods vital.

In Walnut Street's case, the vitality has been excessive. Neighborhood residents have understandably wanted to limit the street's commercial expansion; the more tightly confined retail area, conversely, made these blocks more lively. They long ago reached the critical mass where urban activity in and of itself attracts more urban activity. (In fact, the blocks on Ellsworth Avenue between Summerlea Street on the west and Spahr Street on the east—not on this tour—have benefited from the overflow.)

Some of the architecture amid the jumble has merit. At 5425 stands Frederick Scheibler's 1908 Minnetonka Building, its unadorned quality a surprise, given its date. Lack of decoration meant neither lack of funds nor lack of attention; a closer look at the doorways will convince you of that. Go right on South Negley toward Fifth Avenue and Third Presbyterian Church. Make a left just before you reach the church and park along Kentucky Avenue.

Protestant reformer John Calvin taught that economic activities and the creation of wealth were not of themselves anti-Christian. This view unleashed great energies in his followers. Unfortunately, the acceptance of economic realities went hand in hand with a kind of psychological terrorism, related to his doctrine of predestination. For those of an active disposition, a problem without a solution is not a problem. The impossibility of doing anything humanly to acquire grace meant there was no point in mulling over it—which left more time for business. Success soon became identified as a sign of salvation; men who got on in the world also got smug.

For those of a contemplative disposition, like Shadyside native Elizabeth Moorhead, harsh Presbyterian teachings produced another reaction: "bewilderment and terror . . . darkened my early years." But the Day of Judgment and the fear of the last trump which gave her nightmares left others wholly untouched: "They never took upon them the mystery of things, there was no room for wonder in their settled world. Everything was clear-cut, definite. They were established upon a rock. They *knew*."

Thus a sharp chiaroscuro patterns Shadyside's past, if not its present. The differing effects of the powerful culture Willa Cather called "Presbyteria" could sometimes be seen in the same family. Third

Presbyterian, a turn-of-the-century structure as wild and romantic as downtown's First Church—Theophilus P. Chandler designed them both—had as its prime mover Josiah Thaw.

The Thaws were a very solid old family with great wealth and a great tradition of patronage; the elder Thaw was astronomer John Brashear's principal supporter. Josiah's brother Harry, however, was a crazed libertine. Soon after the completion of this church in 1905, he married the beautiful Evelyn Nesbit. Not long afterward, he killed her former lover, the architect Stanford White. The tale inspired E. L. Doctorow's *Ragtime*.

If scandals and tragedies and writers did not remind us of Presbyterians' participation in the whole human spectrum, buildings like Third Church would. Shadyside Presbyterian was convincing for its earthbound solidity; here we're caught up in an assault on heaven.

The mad bristling quality of the exterior has its counterpart in the interior's rich complexity, which bears comparison not only with its historical antecedents, but also with Bernard Maybeck's contemporary Christian Science church in Berkeley. The elaborate sanctuary is lit by an unsurpassed collection of stained-glass windows. William Willett, who attended church here and had his studio in nearby Point Breeze, next to Lillian Russell's house, did the dim but sublime *City of the Apocalypse* above the balcony on the facade wall. The scandal-struck Thaws may have winced at another work, half-hidden behind the choir loft, *The Wise and Foolish Virgins*. But they may have found consolation in the magnificent Tiffany in the east transept, *Abraham Offering Isaac in Sacrifice*. This window shows how successfully glass artists responded to the nineteenth-century challenge of painting with light.

Continue along Kentucky, at the rear of Third Presbyterian, eastward to South Highland Avenue, where you turn left, soon passing on the right a row of good Second Empire houses. Judge Mellon and others subdivided Shadyside's eastern section into lots smaller, as you

will have noticed, than those of the western end. Continue until you
come to Highland Towers at 340, an apartment building by the Minnetonka's architect, Frederick Scheibler. This 1913 structure,
severely rational in its main lines, decorative and even droll in its
details—note the cement pigeons in the fourth floor cotes—remains
one of the monuments of modernism in Pittsburgh.

119

Shadyside,
East
Liberty,
Highland
Park

Turn right on Alder Street, where 6112 shows what other architects were doing with apartment blocks in 1913. A right again on
unmarked Emerson takes you by the Hunt Armory. To the left on Walnut and Shady is Carleton Strong's Sacred Heart Church, begun in
1924 and finished three decades later. This important church is lovable for a multitude of decorative elements within, as well as for its
robust architecture.

Across the street stands the 1858 Sellers House, which once stood
on a ten-acre lot. It was the rectory of the imposing church commanding the crossroads, Ralph Adams Cram's 1906 Calvary Episcopal
Church. America's most accomplished and certainly most convinced
Gothicist, Cram admired H. H. Richardson's Romanesque work as
"bold, dominating, adventurous, and quite without refinement or sub-
tlety." The words might apply to the forceful central spire of this
church. William Willett did the chancel windows. Calvary is known
for its good works as well as for its architecture.

A third and much smaller church, the Shady Avenue Christian
Assembly, a study in brickwork, stands a short distance to the north at
241 Shady. Go right on Aurelia Street, before the church, where you
will find the entrance to UDA Architects' 1980s complex, the Village
of Shadyside, a successful and dense eastward extension of this neighborhood. A right on Denniston and another on unmarked Marchand
will bring you back to Shady. Continuing right along Shady, you will
cross the East Busway.

Opened at the end of 1982, the busway is nearly seven miles of
exclusive route along the railroad's right-of-way, linking downtown to

Wilkinsburg. Topography has dictated this path since Indian days; East Liberty—the name derives from the free pasture the area once was—began as a stage stop on the Pike to Philadelphia.

Shady Avenue terminates at Penn Avenue, where you turn left, stopping at East Liberty Presbyterian Church, built in the early 1930s. Presbyterian writers like Elizabeth Moorhead and Annie Dillard have chronicled a church whose narrow practicality militated against culture. Pre–World War II commentators, in articles with titles like "Is Pittsburgh Civilized?" or "Pittsburgh: What a City Shouldn't Be," found the city crude and barbaric, thanks to its complacent Scotch-Presbyterian masters.

Yet these same masters were responsible for a remarkable series of churches, as we have seen. The Mellons, whose fortune began in Judge Thomas Mellon's marriage into East Liberty's land-rich Negley family, built not only two of the most splendid buildings in town exactly during the period when magazines were puzzling over Pittsburgh's defects, but they had also begun the collections now at the core of the National Gallery in Washington.

Andrew Mellon, prime mover behind that gallery, once said that "every man wants to connect his life with something he thinks eternal." That may have been his brother Richard Beatty's motive in constructing East Liberty Presbyterian, a spiritual impulse given material form. Depression-era Pittsburghers—many of whom had suffered Mellon mortgage foreclosures—gave a more cynical explanation for the structure, dubbing it the "Mellon Fire Escape."

Whether it was built because of fear of hellfire or a wish for eternity, the church is a triumph as architecture. If Third Presbyterian's pinnacles are an assault on heaven, East Liberty's spire takes heaven by storm. (At least it punctured the pre-Renaissance blanket of smoke.) Its sheer height—only a hundred feet shorter than Mt. Washington—gives it the kind of dominance the Cathedral of Learning has in Oakland.

This was the greatest opportunity of Ralph Adams Cram's life, and he seized it all the more readily because his patrons' cooperation was not only intelligent, but "almost passionate." Cram recounts that his firm occasionally tried to steer Protestant church-building clients toward colonial-style buildings rather than Gothic because of the latter's association with Catholicism. But the best ones all wanted Gothic.

121

Shadyside,
East
Liberty,
Highland
Park

The Mellons went so far as to specify that he was not to feel deterred by "Protestant inhibitions," and as a High Church man he gloried in the fact that this Presbyterian sanctuary could be prepared for a pontifical Mass in half an hour. The stained glass, equally ecumenical in its glory, is by Charles Connick, the Pittsburgh-trained artist who later worked with Cram on the Cathedral of Saint John the Divine in Manhattan. The windows are best seen when no services are being conducted; the church's illumination is Protestant, even if its architecture is not. Don't miss the burial chapel on the left side of the nave. Or the bowling alley on the ground floor.

A true medievalist, Cram declared that the internal combustion machine was even more of a calamity for the human race than gunpowder. What would he have made of East Liberty's car-related "improvements" in the 1960s? The Civic Arena fiasco had convinced Pittsburgh's leaders that total clearance of old neighborhoods was not a good idea, and that, in any case, the inhabitants like to be consulted. In East Liberty they were, and clearance was only partial. But it was enough to do great damage. This had been a thriving commercial center, second only to downtown. The effort to transform it into something like a suburban mall ruined it; the new traffic patterns seemed planned with total avoidance of the area as their goal.

Before rigor mortis set in, wiser planners worked to restore part of the older road system and other neighborhood traits. Some results are evident; from an aesthetic point of view, Penn Avenue is far handsomer with its 1930s deco facades than cluttered Walnut. Across

East Liberty

Penn, the 1915 Regent Theatre, a movie house that closed in the 1970s, was restored to the community as a multiuse performance space in 1995.

Another neighborhood monument enjoying new life is the domed Motor Square Garden, which you reach by driving left on South Beatty, then left onto Baum Boulevard. Also a Mellon project, but built a generation before the great church, it was designed as a market by the refined Bostonian firm of Peabody and Stearns. After an unsuccessful stint as an upscale shopping mall, the vast 1900 brick-and-glass structure now serves the American Automobile Association.

Continue on Baum to South Highland, where you turn left. Henry Frick commissioned Daniel Burnham to design the 1910 Highland Building, slated for conversion to senior housing. As you continue north on Highland, you pass Eastminster Presbyterian Church, with another luxurious collection of stained glass. At 616 North Highland, you pass still another Presbyterian institution, the Pittsburgh Theological Seminary.

Continuing down North Highland you come to Highland Park, a neighborhood whose multitude of big foursquare houses testifies to Pittsburgh's wealth in the first decades of this century. Entrance to the 360-acre park itself is marked by handsome monumental pillars adorned with Giuseppe Moretti's 1896 sculptures. Within are reservoirs and lakes; to the west, left of the entrance, is a big neighborhood-built playground.

Before visiting the Pittsburgh Zoo, you may want to have a look at nearby Baywood, a Victorian mansion reached by continuing westward along the northern edge of the park on Bunkerhill to Mellon Street, where you turn left, followed by a right on Mellon Terrace and a left on North Negley. There you will see the house's extensive grounds. The first right, unmarked Elgin, takes you to it. The 1870s architecture has been altered; more interesting is the site itself, its steep ravine embellished near the crest by artful ruins of turn-of-the-century Gothic battlements.

123

Shadyside,
East
Liberty,
Highland
Park

This estate and its grounds once belonged to Robert B. King, an uncle of Richard King Mellon, and it was the first site considered for the Civic Arena in 1949. Protests from the Highland Park community, and from King himself, were much more influential than the protests from the Lower Hill District, which was razed for the arena. King later gave the property to the city for parkland. The house has since returned to private ownership.

To reach the Pittsburgh Zoo, backtrack and turn north off Bunkerhill onto Hill Road on the park's western edge; follow the signs for zoo parking. (You will be making a left-hand turn onto Washington Boulevard and another left into the parking area.) The escalator from the parking lot is part of the experience here, for one of the recently renovated Pittsburgh Zoo's virtues is the skillful exploitation of its site.

Like Kennywood Park, the zoo originated as a trolley destination. That mundane motive has given way to more exalted ones, of which preservation of species is the most important. From a visitor's point of view, the zoo—including a new primate house and an innovative children's zoo, elevated on rain forest boardwalks—succeeds in the important task of giving us a sense of affinity with nature without sacrificing the animals' dignity. The natural habitats have been enhanced by an abundance of water, and Pittsburgh's green slopes (fully one-third of the city is still undeveloped hillsides) help make the experience both exotic and familiar.

SQUIRREL HILL, POINT BREEZE,
HOMEWOOD, EDGEWOOD
This tour, mostly driven, begins along the edge of Schenley Park at the
intersection of Forbes and Aylesboro Avenues. Visits to Clayton, the Frick
house, must be arranged in advance.

6

The Varieties of
Domestic Experience

The previous chapter led you through residential areas whose
chief interest, besides the zoo, was a series of places of worship. Heading south and east we approach another residential
area; unlike Shadyside, its appeal derives overwhelmingly from the
houses themselves, and from the variety of domestic experiences they
suggest.

Squirrel Hill is in fact a hill; its relatively steep slopes kept it
from developing as early as Shadyside. Electric trolley cars, as well as
the 1922 Boulevard of the Allies link with downtown, encouraged
rapid growth in the second and third decades of this century. That
period accounts for the varied and spirited style of the neighborhood's
substantial houses. Its inhabitants love Squirrel Hill just as it is; the
neighborhood plan, prepared by UDA Architects, has the objective of
"aggressive conservation."

Coming from Carnegie Mellon University (see tour 4), make a left
off Forbes onto Aylesboro Avenue, which you take east. Squirrel Hill's
eclectic manner thickens as you turn left on Wightman Street and left
again on Northumberland Street. The early 1980s house at 5553 is by
the architect Arthur Lubetz. A right on Squirrel Hill Avenue takes you

125

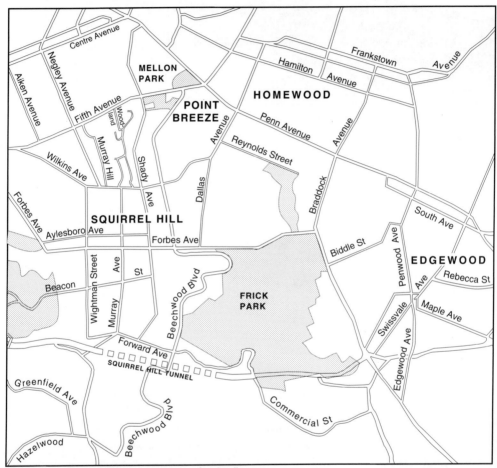

Please consult your Pittsburgh street map for details.

to justly named Fair Oaks Street. Go left to see Robin Road, a short private lane of slate-roofed cottages dating from the twenties, designed by Squirrel Hill resident Benno Janssen and William Cocken. Janssen's work ranged from cozy dwellings such as these to institutions like Kaufmann's department store downtown and the Mellon Institute in Oakland.

Go back eastward on Fair Oaks, crossing Wilkins, to Murray Hill Avenue. At 1180 on the near left corner of Fair Oaks and Murray Hill, is the big square McClung House. Willa Cather lived here for many years, frequently returning even after her 1906 move to New York. Make a right hand turn onto Murray Hill and pull over for a moment.

127

Squirrel
Hill,
Point
Breeze,
Homewood,
Edgewood

The Nebraska-bred author's work—*My Antonia, Death Comes to the Archbishop*—evokes images of windswept prairie and sun-parched desert. It comes as a surprise to find her embosomed in the damp green fastness of Squirrel Hill. Yet this house symbolized care and safety for the author, and she felt no other place could ever be home.

What had brought Cather to Pittsburgh in 1896? A job, first of all, at *The Home Monthly,* then the amenities sponsored by the new Carnegie Institute; above all, perhaps, she was attracted by the "incandescence of human energy" she found here. What brought her to Murray Hill Avenue was a woman. Elizabeth Moorhead called Isabelle McClung "the most beautiful girl I had ever seen"; though younger than Cather, she had a nurturing relationship with the author. Cather had witty and acerbic criticisms of "Presbyteria," as she called Pittsburgh's governing culture, but it does not appear that Presbyteria created much of an obstacle to her relationship with Judge McClung's daughter. Moorhead recounts that the pair often withdrew from family or social gatherings to their bedroom, where they read Russian and French novels, and where Cather worked "in that rich world of imagination which Isabelle always understood and protected."

This was the great romantic attachment of Cather's life. Surviving the younger woman's marriage, the relationship ended only when Isabelle died in 1938. Pittsburgh remained in Cather's work in a handful of short stories, including her most famous, "Paul's Case," a devastating story of an adolescent's attempt to escape industrial, workaday Pittsburgh.

Turn right on roughly paved Murray Hill Avenue, which perhaps unconsciously invented a new mode of maintaining a high tone: exclusion by cobblestone (actually the paving is Belgian blocks). Notice the copper cupola on the carriage house on the left. Go left on Wilkins Avenue, then turn right immediately onto Murray (not Murray Hill; if they connected, and this were easy, it wouldn't be Pittsburgh). Lower Murray Avenue's commercial district, beyond Forbes, is known for its specialty food shops, including kosher butchers serving the neighborhood's large Jewish population. Instead of continuing down Murray, however, we are going left on Forbes and left again on Shady Avenue. After several blocks, a left on Wilkins will take you forthwith to beautiful (and private) Woodland Road, where you turn right.

This elite enclave dates from soon after the Civil War. For the most part, its luxurious houses have friendly relations with one another and with nature; the brick and stone and shingle patterns create a texture as varied as the woods themselves. On the right, however, comes a shock, a house so stark and ascetic that it's hard to think of it fitting in anyplace, least of all on these opulent slopes. But it's here to stay; in 1992 it was declared a Pittsburgh historic landmark. The house's fame and provenance justify the designation, even if its date doesn't—like the house behind it, it was designed in the early 1980s. Its simple geometric forms show architect Richard Meier's International Style allegiance. The abstract composition's sobriety, though poetic, vexes many.

Not that the gaiety of its immediate neighbor—the green-and-white-striped structure—kindles great enthusiasm hereabouts. Yet Robert Venturi, whose seminal work has restored a conscious sense of place to contemporary architecture, intended the house as a response to its site over a creek. Venturi's work implies a desire for fruitful relations with nature, even as Richard Meier's implies an exaltation of reason and technology. The person who more than anyone else alerted America to the dangers of technology and the necessity of respecting nature spent her college years just down the road.

Follow the main road around a bend and to the right, where you will see the Tudor-style Andrew Mellon house on the left; it now serves as the admissions center of Chatham College. The fourth oldest women's college in America, Chatham was founded by Shadyside Presbyterians in 1869 as the Pennsylvania College for Women. Rachel Carson, a Scotch-Irish Presbyterian from Springdale, fifteen miles up the Allegheny River, entered the college in 1925 with the intention of majoring in English; she left in 1929 with a bachelor's degree in science and became a marine biologist.

Like Willa Cather, Rachel Carson found support and inspiration in other women; and for her, as for Cather, nature was an overpowering presence. But Cather felt an absolute horror of grassland; the great outdoors meant solitude. Carson, whose mother would put a spider out of the house rather than kill it, developed a sense of home that expanded to include the universe. The title of one of her biographies is *The House of Life*.

Her teachers at the Pennsylvania College for Women encouraged her interest in natural history and served as role models. Pittsburgh had given her personal experience of the dangers of pollution; her work gave her a shocking insight into its effects elsewhere. Carson documented the damage caused by pesticides in *The Sea Around Us*, published in 1951. In 1952, Chatham gave her an honorary doctorate. But not everyone appreciated her contribution; the chemical industry mounted personal as well as scientific attacks on her. Others felt threatened by an outspoken scientist who demonstrated that a woman's place was in "the house of life" as much as in the home. When *Silent Spring* came out, *Time* magazine accused her of hysteria, called her totally irresponsible, and trivialized the book as an "emotional and inaccurate outburst." But by the time of her death in 1964, antipesticide legislation was well under way, and the ecological revolution had begun.

Continuing down Woodland you will see a sign on the right, just before the road veers left over a bridge, for Fickes Hall. A drive uphill on the right to its parking lot affords a look at another International Style creation, the 1937 Frank House, designed by Walter Gropius and Marcel Breuer. Franklin Toker points out an anomaly: this otherwise relentlessly modern dwelling has social attributes as traditional as its pretentious old neighbors, with entrance foyer, drawing room, and servants' quarters.

Backtrack to Woodland Road and cross the bridge. At the end of Woodland Road, turn right on Fifth Avenue. After a long block, turn right on Shady. On the immediate left is the Pittsburgh Center for the Arts. Organized by artists in 1945, the center offers not only consistently interesting exhibitions, but also art classes and a well-stocked shop; it also houses the Pittsburgh Civic Garden Center. These organizations are lodged in the 1911 Marshall House, facing Fifth Avenue, and in the half-timbered Scaife mansion on Shady.

Mrs. Sarah Mellon Scaife, after whom the Scaife Gallery at the Carnegie is named, was the daughter of Richard Beatty Mellon, of Mellon Institute and East Liberty Presbyterian fame. R. B.'s house, demolished in 1941, stood on the ten-and-a-half acres that now constitute Mellon Park, just next door.

Continue along Shady and make a left on Hastings Street, then left again on Beechwood, down by Mellon Park. Turn right on Reynolds. Leaving behind the Mellons and the Scaifes, we are headed into the heart of the Point Breeze neighborhood, dominated by the Fricks, but also once home to the Carnegies as well. Andrew and his mother lived here until their move to New York in 1867. Tom Carnegie, Andrew's brother and business partner, remained all his life.

Notice Point Breeze's miniature shopping district. The Frick Art Museum appears farther down Reynolds, just after South Homewood;

Mellon Park

park in the parking lot off Reynolds. From here you may enter the grounds of Clayton, the Frick house.

Annie Dillard, who grew up in several houses hereabouts, remembers in *An American Childhood* the impression this neighborhood made on a child in the 1950s. The monumental millionaires' houses, "restful as tombs," still lent Point Breeze "their expansive, hushed moods"; yet it all seemed like Egypt's Valley of the Kings—after the dynasties had ended. There was only one frail link with an age that had passed into history; the "unthinkably old" daughter of Henry Clay Frick was still living, alone in her "proud, sinking mansion." She was at best a flickering presence. No one ever saw Miss Helen.

Elusive though she might have seemed, Helen Frick was not absent to herself; she knew she had a function, knew it in her bones as well as intellectually. She had resolved to cast a warm but clear light on her own experience and on that of her family. She intended to create a bond between them and us. That is Clayton, still proud but no longer sinking.

Connecting the living and the dead was something Helen Frick had practiced from infancy. When she was three years old her sister Martha, a lovable six, died. Henry Clay Frick spent the rest of his life mourning. He surrounded himself with flower-strewn portraits of his "Rosebud." He even had her image engraved on his checks. Helen, in her youth, wore a miniature of Martha around her neck.

It wasn't just a dead Martha she connected to her living father. He seemed as emotionless as marble to contemporaries. Charlie Schwab, like Frick a Carnegie partner and true business genius, as well as the most affable fellow of his age, called Frick a machine, "absolutely cold-blooded." Schwab was certain that "no man on earth could get close to him." But Helen did. The icy genius, who never laughed (although his rages were prodigious) and never told an anecdote, nonetheless regularly discussed business with his little daughter. He even discussed daughters with a man he otherwise shared nothing but business with, Carnegie. He would ask Helen to accompany guests around the house to see the pictures. In later years, Helen convinced her father to finance her charities.

Except where his family was concerned, there was a terrifying grandeur about Frick. Carnegie wanted to be loved; on occasion he even descended into a kind of cuteness to win approval. Frick cared nothing about others' opinions. His perceptions of how the economic process works were so acute and so profound that one wonders if he hadn't read Karl Marx on capital accumulation.

His fortune originated at the end of the 1860s when he learned of coke's importance in the new Bessemer process. He happened to be from the Connellsville region, source of the best metallurgical coke in the world. Frick boldly yet shrewdly—with Mellon backing—set about acquiring a monopoly. He was a millionaire by the time he was thirty-one. But his extraordinary quality came to the fore in partnership with Carnegie. Frick understood that exploitation of labor was a fundamental condition of capitalism. To know such a thing cannot make a man happy, although it might make him rich. But to know such a thing and act consistently with that knowledge makes a man a monster, especially when his chief partner was disarming public opposition by a giant campaign of cultural philanthropy.

The measure of the two men may be seen in how they dealt with cost containment, which they agreed was crucial to financial success in steelmaking. Carnegie focused on the railroads' excessive freight rates to Pittsburgh manufacturers. Despite the fact that rail companies were the mills' best customers, he threatened to lead a popular demonstration against the Pennsylvania Railroad. Frick saw the far greater importance of containing labor costs, and acted coherently. At Homestead in 1892 he so thoroughly broke the steelworkers' labor movement that it remained impotent until 1937.

Frick's conflicts with the world no doubt intensified a need for the intimate harmony of home. In 1881, he married a Pittsburgher of good family and good appearance, Adelaide Childs; in 1882, they bought the house that became Clayton. After the birth of a son and two daughters, they greatly enlarged the 1870 structure according to designs of Frederick Osterling.

This time of expansion coincided with a series of disasters. On 29 July 1891, after a long illness, Martha died. The Homestead strike began the following summer, and on the day of the tragic Homestead riot, 6 July, the distraught Mrs. Frick barely survived the premature birth of a son, Henry Clay Frick, Jr.

On 23 July, an anarchist named Alexander Berkman broke into Frick's office, shot him twice, and stabbed him three times. When the staff and a deputy sheriff were struggling to overcome the would-be assassin, Frick, though bleeding copiously, had the clear-headedness to keep them from shooting him. He pointed to the man's jaw; when the officer managed to get it open they found a capsule with sufficient explosive to destroy them all.

A doctor gave the seriously wounded Frick first aid. Frick then stunned everyone by finishing the work he had come in for—it was Saturday. When he was done, he dictated a statement for the press, declaring that whatever happened to him, the company would continue to pursue his labor policy, and win. On 3 August, as Frick lay recuperating at Clayton, his namesake died, not yet a month old.

A visit to Clayton, designed with a Victorian social call in mind, is not meant to evoke such sad memories. Yet the morbid and even the macabre, occupying a greater place in nineteenth-century daily life than today, do come up. There are the multiple photographs in Mrs. Frick's bedroom, for instance, of her premature baby, in poses that suggest he was still alive when the shots were taken. But he wasn't. There are the constant references to Martha and her death—not just portraits, but also decorative motifs, like falling rose petals in the nursery. A staff member, asked if the ostentatious adoration of Martha hadn't affected her surviving younger sister, replied, "Perhaps Miss Helen had a dent."

But the turbulence did not spoil Helen's childhood, which she recalled as idyllic. It also did not keep her from creating a vivid link between their life and ours. Clayton, far from the grandest or most beautiful of houses, nonetheless enchants visitors.

Life in the house was completely documented; curators were confronted with "the tyranny of abundance" at Miss Frick's death in 1984. Despite the more than nine thousand items left, and despite the Victorian cult of the dead, they have managed to convey not history embalmed, but lives lived. The vitality comes across thanks to unusual decorative elements like wallpaper embossed to look like tooled leather, or aluminum leaf gilt embellishments, or, above all, the large turn-of-the-century painting in the dining room—another reminiscence of Martha, who had appeared to Frick in a vision after the assassination attempt.

There are twists that shed light on the times. The cover of a book in Mrs. Frick's room, called *The Five Talents of Woman*, proclaims it is by the author of *How to Be Happy Though Married*. The staff stairway features a lithograph of a mule draped with the promise, "I'm a non-union helper on Pike's Peak rail." The box he's carrying warns "Dangerous explosives." Some excellent paintings adorn the house, including a Claude Monet landscape intended, the painter himself declared, to please "the discreet bourgeoisie." The library, where this painting is hung, is the work of Frederick Osterling and is the most appealing room in the house.

A final note about Frick's psychology. When he first requested a loan of the Mellons, the lending officer noted that the borrower "may be a little too enthusiastic about pictures but not enough to hurt." Willa Cather associated Presbyteria's suspicion of art with their fear and hatred of human emotions. Only the "undemonstrative" sins like greed or selfishness could be indulged.

Could Frick's suppression of sentiment have been intentional, a device to present himself as the man of business *par excellence?* It is a curious fact that his collection in New York is dominated by portraits expressing great humanity and psychological insight.

If you cannot visit Clayton proper now, you are welcome to have a look at the grounds; the guards get nervous only if you approach the house itself without a ticket. The visitor's center is housed in the Frick children's two-story playhouse. The carriage museum gives another glimpse of Frick vitality; all the vehicles belonged to the family. The star is a 1931 Lincoln, but the 1902 Tuxedo Spider Phaeton also has its merits: Henry Clay Frick raced it. Nearby is a new café for a snack or lunch.

Miss Frick was not in perfect accord with her family's move to New York; she insisted, against her father's wishes, on making her debut in Pittsburgh in 1908. She may have regretted his establishment of the Frick Collection in Manhattan. The official explanation was that smoke from Homestead—that same smoke that gave Frick his fortune—would damage the pictures.

Whatever her father's motive, Helen Frick built her own museum here, opened in 1969. Besides being quiet and luxurious, it has fine small exhibitions, as well as some good paintings. Notice, for instance, the happily juxtaposed Fragonard's *Cook* and Rubens's *Princesse de Conde*. As in their Fifth Avenue mansion, the Frick concerts here are frequent and good.

Leaving the Reynolds lot, turn right, then right again on South Homewood. Go left on Penn, where most of the houses of Millionaires' Row have disappeared. But there is some picturesque architecture: in the third block on the right, just after North Murtland, 6941–6943 Penn shows the hitherto restrained Frederick Scheibler indulging in a number of architectural fantasies, most colorful of which are the ceramic "rugs" thrown over the balconies.

Turn right on North Dallas Avenue, then right on broad Thomas Boulevard. On the left you soon see Westinghouse Park, where once stood Solitude, George Westinghouse's mansion. Westinghouse was of the same generation as Frick, whose house he fitted for electricity; he had a worldly success as striking, though not as lasting, as Frick's. Aside from that, and aside from their living in the same neighborhood, they were worlds apart.

Frick Art Museum

Frick's wealth was intimately bound up with exploitation of workers; Westinghouse's came from a plethora of inventions, most of which he undertook without any profit motive; he regularly failed to seek patents on his inventions. For Frick, home was where he could doff the cold guise of a hard-driving entrepreneur and chat with his family and contemplate his pictures.

Westinghouse's character was so integrated that he could never separate his work from his domestic life. The most astonishing instance of this was when he suspected that natural gas lay beneath this property. His wife liked to have him around, so she encouraged him to drill. In 1883, when they hit the field, more than 1,500 feet below the ground, there was an explosion that blew away not only the flowers but also the derrick and drilling apparatus. The geyser, lit, made a flaming torch that illuminated the neighborhood for weeks.

Pittsburgh's relation to power had always been direct, often leaving terrible scars on men and on the landscape. But George Westinghouse's greatness lay in another relation to power: he domesticated it. Natural gas, for instance, may have momentarily undone Mrs. Westinghouse's flower beds, but her husband's discoveries and his improvements in gas pipe technology made clean-burning gas available to factories and households throughout the city and region. These advances meant Pittsburgh had relatively clear skies until local supplies ran out around 1900. The experience of clean-burning fuel encouraged the antipollution efforts that culminated in the post–World War II cleanup.

Many of Westinghouse's other inventions, including alternating current and air brakes, had the same goal, making power safe for everyday use. Mrs. Westinghouse also had a handy way of putting power in its proper place. She organized indirect lighting in their summer place so cleverly that for years people came to study how she had done it.

Continue driving along Thomas to North Homewood, where turning left you enter Homewood proper. Most people associate the area we have just left with Point Breeze. Homewood's sense of place has been historically so weak to outside eyes that when Ralph Adams Cram was commissioned to design a church for the neighborhood, he couldn't find any "particular associations" to inspire him. He had been studying Catalonian churches and decided to draw on them.

139
Squirrel
Hill,
Point
Breeze,
Homewood,
Edgewood

Homewood began around a Civil War–era nucleus of servants to the nearby wealthy families of Point Breeze. That population increased greatly when Lower Hill urban renewal deprived hundreds of families of their homes. Hard times followed; Homewood native John Edgar Wideman, who was born in 1941, has a character in *Damballah* comparing "rotten" and "raggedy" Homewood Avenue to a gap-toothed mouth a "jive dentist" has worked on. The character wishes that someone would bulldoze the whole thing into a deep ditch and bury it. It bears mentioning that Wideman, who writes as obsessively about Homewood as August Wilson does about the Hill, grew up quite literally on the opposite side of the tracks from Point Breeze's Annie Dillard.

Urban development consciousness fortunately has spread to Pittsburgh's neighborhoods; the new housing and commercial development here got its start with the Homewood-Brushton Revitalization and Development Corporation's use of "layered financing." The neighborhood builds projects that the development group finances through a combination of city, corporate, foundation, and bank support.

Turn left on Hamilton Avenue by an old post office recycled into a farmer's market, and pass the library described by Dillard as her childhood haunt. A right on North Lang takes you to Cram's Catalonian Gothic Holy Rosary Church, more satisfying without than within. Turn right on Bennett Street, where you will see another Homewood anchor, the Homewood A.M.E. Zion Church.

Bennett Place, one of the liveliest works of contemporary Pittsburgh architecture, stands on the left one block beyond. Designed by Arthur Lubetz at the end of the 1980s, it succeeds with its senior tenants as well as on the streetscape.

Make a right at once on Sterrett Street to Hamilton, where another right will return you to North Homewood, which you take left, past more HBRDC housing, back to Penn Avenue.

Turn left on Penn, then right after a few blocks onto South Braddock Avenue. Soon, on the left, you pass the brick and terra-cotta Park Place School, and shortly beyond, Frederick Scheibler's much-praised 1905 Old Heidelberg Apartments. A good distance beyond, you enter Regent Square's commercial district. At the light, turn left on West Hutchinson Avenue.

You are now in Edgewood, an elegantly conceived suburb that owes its origins to the Pennsylvania Railroad, which made commuting possible beginning in 1864. Turn right at the T intersection on unmarked Pennwood Avenue. (The pretty stone borough center—not on this tour—may be reached by a left at the Race Street underpass.) Continue alongside the retaining wall to West Swissvale Avenue, where you turn right.

On the left is the 1916 white stucco California style Edgewood Club; across the street on the right at 124 stands an 1864 Italianate cottage, complete with square cupola. Among the many handsome nineteenth-century homes here, note the board-and-batten dwelling at 235.

At the end of West Swissvale, go right on unmarked New Street, just *before* the Interstate 376 entrance, and right again on Braddock. To the left you see a marker on the site of Swissvale, the home of Jane Grey Swisshelm.

Home is not the first thing that comes to mind in relation to this vital and eccentric woman. You may want to read about her career when you get to Frick Park. Continue on Braddock back to the light at West Hutchinson, where you turn left. After several blocks, turn right onto Lancaster Street, which leads you to Fern Hollow in Frick Park.

Swisshelm's story begins conventionally enough. She was born in 1815 in a cabin across from the cemetery where Trinity Episcopal now stands in downtown Pittsburgh. Her family were rock-ribbed Presby-

Bennett Place, Homewood

terians. In 1836 she married James Swisshelm, a big handsome farmer who had saved her from drowning. Only one thing blemished this romantic picture: James was a Methodist. Worse, he was a Methodist with a mother.

Yet what separated Jane from James, even more than the Methodist mother-in-law, was Jane's own intelligence. She required fields vaster than those of the Swisshelm farm. When the couple moved to Louisville, Kentucky, she saw slavery's ugliest form—men who fathered children of black women, then sold their own offspring as slaves. Jane turned into a fiery abolitionist, and thanks to her pioneering work as a journalist, an effective one.

When she returned to Pittsburgh to look after her dying mother, Jane experienced another sort of bondage, this time firsthand, when she became determined not to return to Louisville. James tried to force her. His signature was necessary on the papers relative to her mother's estate; wives in Pennsylvania were not free to hold property in their own name. He refused to sign. This injustice prodded combative Jane to another campaign, one capped with a grand success. In 1848 she got the Pennsylvania legislature to acknowledge a married woman's right to hold property.

The Swisshelms's living arrangements had been unusual from early in their marriage. James had built Jane a house behind a wagon shop he had bought in nearby Wilkinsburg, while he remained under his mother's roof; Jane in turn kept house for the man hired to run the shop. Later, the couple lived together at the family property here—it was Jane who named it Swissvale. This cohabitation failed when the Swisshelm in-laws came to stay.

Jane moved into Pittsburgh, where her journalism career flourished. She established a number of precedents as the first woman newspaper editor, but she gloried more in her abolitionist and reform successes. Elizabeth Moorhead remembered her as entirely fearless, "a long lean lady . . . who talked more than anybody else, with more emphasis . . . and no one contradicted her." She continued her newspaper career until her death in 1884, in the old homestead on the site where we saw the marker. Pallbearers at her funeral, distinguished Pittsburghers all, included the same Judge Mellon who had defended her husband decades earlier.

Fern Hollow is the heart of Frick Park, once part of Henry Clay Frick's five-hundred-acre estate. You can forget that you're in the city—and that Frick ever did anything wrong.

143

Squirrel
Hill,
Point
Breeze,
Homewood,
Edgewood

7

HAZELWOOD, HOMESTEAD, BRADDOCK
This driving tour follows the banks of the Monongahela River, beginning at
the LTV coke works on Second Avenue in Hazelwood.

Capitalism Triumphs,
for a While

N avigating this first portion of the itinerary is a bit tricky, so
detailed directions are called for. To reach Second Avenue
from the Boulevard of the Allies in Oakland, make a right
turn off the Boulevard (heading east from downtown) at Bates Street
(signs indicate 376 Monroeville here). Second Avenue is reached by
making a left turn at the foot of Bates, just *past* the exit for Route 376.
This approach affords at the light a glimpse of the lively Pittsburgh
Technology Center, a venture of Carnegie-Mellon University, the University of Pittsburgh, and several corporations, built on the site of the
old Jones and Laughlin Second Avenue steel mill.

Now for the tricky part: Follow the signs for Hazelwood and stay
in the right lane. Jog left (still in the right lane) under a train trestle,
then make the right onto Irvine Street. Continue on Irvine—a long
stretch—with LTV's coke works bordering you on the right. Irvine
becomes Second Avenue again after reaching the Hazelwood Avenue
intersection. Upon crossing Hazelwood Avenue, pull over momentarily.

Pittsburgh's topography regularly offers unexpected juxtapositions—the Cathedral of Learning rising, apparently, out of a clutter of

ramshackle asphalt-shingled dwellings in south Oakland, or, vice-versa, out of a green of the Schenley golf course. Sometimes the juxta-positions are less playful. To go from Squirrel Hill, Point Breeze, and Edgewood to this riverbank is a descent in more than altitude. The violence of the change may make you want to shut your eyes. Yet an account of Pittsburgh without reference to this theater of capitalism's triumph, and the proletariat's passion, would be a fairy tale.

The riverbank's ugliness has a meaning. Pittsburgh's very founda-tion, with Forbes Road and Fort Pitt, had required giant disturbances of the face of the earth. In the biblical injunction to "Be fruitful, and multiply, and replenish the earth, and subdue it," few here heard the dictate to replenish; *subdue* sounded sweeter to a town attuned to mas-tery. The visible savagery of the industrial process meant nothing to men dazzled by prospects of almost infinite wealth. Only fools, or visionaries, protested. Wasn't the transformation of raw materials into finished products improving life?

Much-diminished in activity and importance, the brutal industrial areas still denote historical Pittsburgh. Without these grim shores, houses like Clayton and towns like Edgewood would never have been built. What's more, a visitor who neglects the once-thriving flats will have missed the increasingly rare sight of a late-nineteenth- and early-twentieth-century industrial landscape. The destruction of the giant mills—as overwhelming as anything Egypt ever produced—proceeds apace.

Jones and Laughlin Corporation, LTV's predecessor, built the coke works on the last large vacant tract in Pittsburgh; the Hazelwood works complemented the South Side plant across the river and the south Oakland plant where the Pittsburgh Technology Center now stands.

Coke plants like this one owe their historical importance to a technological innovation that over a century ago helped Pittsburgh achieve its industrial primacy. Until the middle of the nineteenth cen-tury, manufacturing steel was so expensive that it served only to pro-

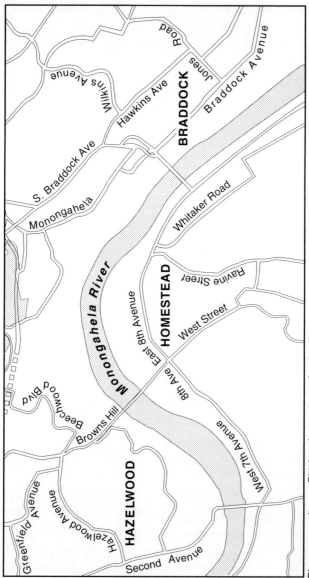

Please consult your Pittsburgh street map for details.

duce small items, like cutlery and hand tools. New industrial needs—
railways needed durable tracks, for instance—spurred research that
culminated in the development of the Bessemer process in England,
which produced steel by blowing cold air through molten pig iron,
removing carbon and silicon. Introduced here by Andrew Carnegie in
1868, the Bessemer process made possible mass production of what
was to become the basic metal of the modern world.

Good coke—the word comes from the soft coal cake produced by a
slow baking—greatly facilitated the Bessemer process; the Pittsburgh
region offered an abundant supply of the finest metallurgical coke in
the world. Henry Clay Frick, who had a quiet but obsessive sense of
coke's value, acquired a near-monopoly over the substance.

Economic destiny thus thrust Frick and Carnegie together as the
great protagonists at the birth of the age of steel. The two men's per-
sonalities differed drastically, but they were both builders rather than
speculators. They shared an imperial vision of steel's future; their
achievement was to bring order out of the chaos of this surging new
business.

Hazelwood's development began as a suburban retreat for the
rich, and it accelerated with the arrival of the railroad in 1861. But its
river frontage across from the South Side iron works made it the ideal
site for coke ovens. The rich left, many for Shadyside.

A church founded in those salad days still stands at the corner of
Second Avenue and Johnston, southeast of the coke works. Organized
in 1870, the Anglo-Catholic congregation commissioned William
Halsey Wood, later architect of Shadyside's Church of the Ascension,
to design this solid 1891 structure with its outlandish bell tower.
Active in charity, the Church of the Good Shepherd brings the evan-
gelical message down to earth in its warm sanctuary as well; excellent
stained-glass windows include an Ascension, at eye level with the
worshippers.

As frisky architecturally, if not doctrinally, is the Hungarian
Reformed Church up Johnston on the left. Titus de Bobula did this Art

Nouveau—influenced building in 1903 for a congregation established over a decade earlier. Notice the curious windows on either side of the entrance.

Continue on Johnston, a long, winding road that becomes Imogene toward the end. Turn right on Brown's Hill Road for the Homestead High Level Bridge. This route, in winter at least, affords views of Homestead and its environs. Once all mill, the vast expanse before you as you cross the bridge is far less picturesque since the 1990s razing of the works that created the town.

Despite this emptiness, we are approaching the single most dramatic site, excepting the Point, in Pittsburgh's historical geography. Homestead was not merely the scene of the strike of 1892, it was the protagonist of that event. Chiodo's, a memorabilia-filled steelworkers' tavern at the end of the bridge on the right, may be a good spot to consider Homestead's history. Pull into the parking area.

When Andrew Carnegie bought the Homestead plant in 1883, he was on his way to creating the world's largest steel company, one whose production equaled more than half that of Great Britain. Homestead's only defect from its owners' viewpoint was that it had a robust, though far from extremist, labor tradition. The contract with the Amalgamated Association of Iron and Steel Workers was coming up for renewal in 1892.

Carnegie, who loved presenting himself as a champion of progressive causes, intended to spend the summer of 1892 in Great Britain. From his partner's point of view, that was fortunate. Vested with full authority over all the Carnegie plants, Frick wanted no interference from Carnegie's occasionally bleeding heart. He knew that Carnegie, as obsessed with cost containment as he was, in fact desired the destruction of union power, however much he might dislike the methods.

The methods shocked everyone. Frick began by encircling the entire plant with a barricade, complete with embrasurelike openings for rifle barrels. Homestead's union men not only had no record of law-lessness, they were homeowners and civic leaders. They felt pride in their work and were protective and proprietary about the plant itself, America's largest open hearth mill. Frick's fortification challenged their personal integrity as well as their sense of justice.

Frick followed this provocation with another; he assembled a private army of three hundred Pinkerton guards. The Pinkertons typically protected strike-breaking scabs. Frick's barricade declared that the men had no right to their workplace; the Pinkertons announced that they had no right to their work.

Frick prudently tried to keep the Pinkertons' arrival a secret. He had them assemble in Ohio, then from near Pittsburgh slip up the river at night in covered barges. But the union had organized a watch; a scout posted on the Smithfield Street Bridge in Pittsburgh spied the strikebreakers and alerted Homestead. It was four o'clock in the morning. The whole town, roused by church bells and factory sirens, was up in arms at once.

They gathered on the shore of the Monongahela. (If plans for an industrial heritage park succeed, visitors may reach the landing site by an extension of Martha Street in Munhall.) Their weapons were clumsy—mostly fence staves and garden hoes—but their massive, though not yet violent, resistance demonstrated their resolve to defend their livelihood.

They succeeded—or so it seemed. The Pinkertons could not disembark. July 6 was steamy; the guards, cooped up in the barges, were suffering from the heat as well as from the assaults of the Home-steaders. At four o'clock in the afternoon, they surrendered their weapons, accepting the strike leaders' assurance of a safe conduct. But now came the horror. Union discipline, solid until then, broke, and the townspeople attacked the defenseless Pinkertons as they staggered forward to what had been promised as safety. Homestead women, armed with umbrellas and blackjacks, proved fiercer than the men. None of the hired guards running this tragic gauntlet escaped injury. Three were killed—compared to only eleven injuries and one death during the battle on the barges.

This is Homestead's double ambiguity. Here, brilliantly creative entrepreneurs engaged in the willful destruction of human capital; here, an entirely respectable workers' movement degenerated into a mob.

Reestablishing order, the strikers held Homestead peacefully until 11 July, when the governor of Pennsylvania sent in eight thousand militia; that enabled the mill to reopen with seven hundred strike breakers. The union held firm. But so did Frick and Carnegie—and they had more resources with which to face the winter. Finally, in late November, the strikers capitulated.

The bosses' success may be measured by the fact that the American steel industry did not unionize again until 1937. Laborers fairly soon gauged the financial aspect of their failure; one skilled worker said, "Before 1892 I made $10 and $12 a day. After the strike wages went down to $7 and by 1903 they were $3. At the same time, the work load increased and my hours of work increased."

Harder to calculate are the human costs of the company's victory. Homestead's expectations had been shattered, its civic heart broken. Two views of progress, of America, clashed in the strike. Until 1892 union men believed that without labor, capital was impotent. Thinking that they were partners in building the enterprise, they brought their faith in democracy to the workplace. The failure of the strike taught them that they were mere commodities, their labor bought and manipulated, or rejected, just as though it were a batch of iron ore or limestone. The sense of participation, America's special strength, was lost in fear and alienation.

Joseph Frazier Wall, in his splendid account of the strike, quotes visitors' impressions of Homestead in the years afterward: The workmen "were cheerless to the point of sullenness," and in the atmosphere "heavy with disappointment and hopelessness, some of the men were afraid to talk, even the Catholic priest." A decade later, with the company spy system well established, the situation had worsened. The Pittsburgh Survey documented this new culture of fear; its authors found no one even willing to admit to the existence of injuries in the mills, where the now-standard twelve-hour day and seven-day week made workers accident-prone: "These men with spirit dead, face a future in which they expect nothing and ask for nothing. They look dull-eyed on a world from which the brightness is gone."

Turn right on Eighth Avenue (Homestead's main street since the mill's World War II expansion devoured First through Seventh) toward West Homestead, and begin to count the stoplights. At the fifth one, veer left; the street sign for West Eighth Avenue is missing. After a short distance, take a sharp left on Basic, followed by a quick sharp right on Doyle. At 540 admire the 1890 house, with ballroom, of George and Perle Mesta. His West Homestead machine works, the largest in the world, were in the enormous recycled buildings just below us; his wife became famous as a hostess and, after her appointment as ambassador to Luxembourg, as the inspiration for Irving Berlin's *Call Me Madam*.

Beyond the Mesta works, former railyards have become a summer water amusement park called Sandcastle. It's a successful venture run by the same people who manage Kennywood, the venerable amusement park upriver, although it's not exactly the kind of business the unemployed of Homestead were hoping would arrive on these vacant shores.

Sandcastle is not on this tour. Backtrack to Eighth Avenue and turn right, driving back through Homestead's commercial district to adjacent Munhall. Beyond the post office on the left is the Bost Building, headquarters for the 1892 strikers, and now slated to open in 1998 as the first structure of the National Steel Museum. Turn right on Library Place, dominated by architect John Comes's Saint Michael's Church. Built by the Slovak community in 1927, the church is topped by Saint Michael on what appears to be a jet ski, riding the bell tower.

Turn left on Ninth Avenue, right on Andrew, then right again on Tenth for Andrew Carnegie's library, a gift to the community in 1898. The architects were the same Alden and Harlow who did the original part of the Carnegie in Oakland. Replete with music hall, bowling alley, swimming pool, and gymnasium, it offered everything necessary for the proletarians' uplift except, the workers objected, the time to enjoy it. "Whatever I engage in I must push inordinately," Carnegie said. He pushed workers inordinately too; tireless himself, he was convinced, despite the protests of his own best managers, that there was nothing wrong with twelve- or thirteen-hour days, with a twenty-four-hour shift every other week. From the steel gazebo on the lawn sloping down from the library, you may enjoy a view generations of steelworkers were also denied—the Monongahela River.

The libraries of the Mon Valley (Homestead, Braddock, and Duquesne) were among the first Carnegie built, and practically the only ones he endowed. Later, Carnegie decided he would only build libraries where there was commitment from the community to maintain them. His attitude proved prescient. Duquesne plowed theirs under for a parking lot; Braddock's sat shuttered for a decade, and the roof caved in. Only Homestead has been in continuous use since 1898. Recently, its sooty exterior has been washed, and the acoustically superb music hall has been restored to its early elegance.

Franklin Toker points out that the number of churches in this section of Homestead makes it a rival to Rome in ecclesiastical density. The strike leaders in 1892 tended to be of the same Scotch-Irish or German background as the mill managers and owners. The strike taught the latter how desirable central and eastern European workers were, "sturdy and submissive." Their lack of English greatly increased the risk of accidents on the shop floor, but at the same time it greatly decreased the risk of protests.

On the principle of divide and conquer, any possibility of labor organization was further reduced by recruiting workers from many different ethnic groups. Black workers, who in any case could not join the all-white unions, were brought up North in railcars to break strikes, then fired or shipped back home afterwards, denied their foothold in the early industrial economy.

By 1907, four out of five unskilled laborers in Carnegie Steel's Pittsburgh works were Eastern European. Loss of their old country, and the imperfect welcome of the new, kept immigrants disoriented. Lacking other organizational outlets, they gathered around their old country churches. Ethnicity and religion were the sole fixed points in a mobile world. But that turning inward separated Slavs even more from the rest of the community; many priests spoke no English, and the churches tended to preserve national distinctions, increasing the Mon communities' civic fragmentation.

Continue on Tenth, whose sacred character climaxes at the corner of Dickson with Titus de Bobula's 1903 Saint John's Greek Catholic Cathedral, built for the Carpatho-Rusyn community. Across Tenth stands the second Hungarian Reformed church on our tour; this one manages to be both classical and Gothic in its architectural forms.

Stay on Tenth, which means a slight jog rightward at McClure Street and then a left back onto Tenth. Glance right and left for more holy monuments. Turn left on Amity Street, on the far edge of the park. Turn left again on Twelfth at the T intersection. A quick right onto Glenn, followed by a left on Fifteenth, brings you to the Russian Orthodox Greek Catholic Saint Gregory the Theologian. Organized in 1913, the congregation built this splendid church in 1950. Be sure to admire it from the back as well; nothing in the Pittsburgh area so wholeheartedly connotes the Slavic east as this silver-domed wonder.

Continue on Fifteenth to Mifflin, where you turn left. Go right on Thirteenth, then left on Margaret and right on Eleventh behind the library. After two blocks, go left on currently unmarked Andrew. At the foot of the slope, go right on Eighth. This road was once a chasm created by the high walls of the mills. Beyond the eye-popping cobalt blue warehouses, after a couple of stoplights, you see across the Monongahela the tall Carrie blast furnaces, which the Steel Industry

St. Gregory the Theologian Church, Homestead

Heritage Corporation hopes to include, along with the Pinkerton landing site on this side of the river, as part of the National Steel Museum.

One proposal for preserving the sense of the giant assembly line that was the Mon is a heritage trail linking specific sites such as these. The trail would also include one of the few amusement parks on the National Register of Historic Places, about a mile and a half upstream, past the Rankin Bridge (be careful not to cross it).

The Mellon name is associated with a number of distinguished Pittsburgh institutions; none of them has been more successful than Kennywood, which A. W. Mellon helped establish in 1899 to attract customers to his Monongahela trolley company. Aficionados travel long distances to enjoy Kennywood's five roller coasters, which, along with other pleasures, afford grand but discombobulating views of the Mon industrial landscape.

Pass Kennywood. The road becomes Duquesne Boulevard, which brings you close—while they last—to the mills that U.S. Steel shut down in the early 1980s. Some statistics: Duquesne households lost purchasing power at the rate of $4,000 a year from 1980–1986. In 1980, Pittsburgh area workers earned $806 more than those in Philadelphia, and $1,433 more than the American average. In 1989, local workers, having lost their mill jobs, earned $2,384 less than their Philadelphia counterparts, and $37 less than U.S. workers. As John Hoerr writes in *And the Wolf Finally Came: The Decline of the American Steel Industry*, "The mill towns, once so alive with the heavy throb of industry, now give off the weak pulse of welfare and retirement communities."

Bear left on the Duquesne Bridge, at the end of which you should follow the sign for East Pittsburgh; it's the second right, but it comes quickly. That puts you on Bowman, which becomes East Pittsburgh-McKeesport Boulevard, and which begins left or north of the bridge. Follow this road, with its alternation of nature and industrial views; do *not* go right at 30.

Heading toward the still partly wooded glen of Turtle Creek, you will glimpse a portion of the largest of all mill complexes, the Westing-house Electric Works, dating from 1894. Shut down in the late 1980s, the complex is being transformed into an innovative industrial mall for small businesses. It has an impressive neighbor eastward in the West-inghouse Air-Brake Works in Wilmerding, not on this tour.

We are going west to Braddock, under the startling span of the George Westinghouse Bridge, a triumph of 1930s art and engineering. Braddock Avenue brings us to United States Steel's Edgar Thomson works. Braddock Avenue affords only glimpses of this working mill; to see Edgar Thomson better, continue beyond to Eleventh Street and turn left. Turn left again at the rough unmarked road just beyond the railroad tracks toward the river; there is a sign for Mon River Lock #2.

This historic plant was begun in the early 1870s on a site already steeped in significance. Here, in 1755, General Braddock's Anglo-American troops suffered an overwhelming defeat at the hands of the French and the Indians—and, saddest to say, at the hands of each other: a large number of the hundreds killed—including a buck-skinned band led by George Washington, mistaken for Frenchmen—were shot by their own confused compatriots.

The Edgar Thomson works marked Andrew Carnegie's decision to concentrate on manufacturing steel. Joseph Wall suggests that Car-negie's experience in bridge building may have convinced him that the age of iron was over. A brilliant engineer, James Eads, had spec-ified steel for key portions of the bridge he was building over the Mis-sissippi at St. Louis. The choice chagrined Carnegie, whose Keystone Bridge Company built with iron. Engineers and scientists concurred that Eads was right in his insistence.

The importance of bridges in America had multiplied with the rapid expansion of railways which, in turn, meant nothing less than mastery of the continent. Carnegie named his works—in 1875 the most advanced Bessemer plant in the world—for an old colleague who happened to control the Pennsylvania Railroad. The Bessemer pro-

Edgar Thomson Works, Braddock

Carnegie Library and Carnegie Hall, Braddock

cess made possible the economic production of durable rails, and therefore Carnegie expected railroads to be his best customers.

It would be hard to exaggerate the splendor of the financial and industrial structure Carnegie and his partners created. True, dazzling economic prospects clarified their vision; still, it was their work as individuals that made those prospects realities. Carnegie's pride in what he was building in Braddock was justified. His empire failed to impress at least one of his contemporaries, however, his idol the English social philosopher Herbert Spencer. Carnegie, with great difficulty, got that ideologue of progress to visit Pittsburgh and Braddock. Spencer's response to the tour was, "Six months residence here would justify suicide."

The Pittsburgh Survey, the great sociological investigation conducted in the early years of the century, repeatedly showed surprise at the disparity between Pittsburgh's astonishing economic-technological evolution and its weak civic and social structure. The paradox is only apparent, however. Such devastations of the land, not to mention of the populace, as the steel industry perpetrated, were possible only because the civic structure was weak. It was because society did not protest that industry could develop in the first place.

Mon Valley towns show the consequences of this political neglect today, and none more clearly than Braddock. Here is a real paradox: the only town left with a still functioning mill is the one most degraded. To see its downtown, backtrack to Braddock Avenue and turn left. Before turning, notice at the intersection the historical marker honoring Father Kazincy, Braddock's famous labor priest, who supported the workers in the Great Steel Strike of 1919. This massive strike, which idled 350,000 men, was called the "Hunky Strike" because Eastern European workers were by then in the vanguard of the labor movement.

The overwhelming air of abandonment makes a mockery of the long industrial primacy of this area. Yet there are glimmerings of life. Turn right on Library Street, where you find Carnegie's first American

Braddock bar

library, built in 1888 and currently under renovation by the Braddock's Field Historical Society. After years of neglect, the building is
being brought back to the community piece by piece. The gymnasium
recently reopened.

In 1889 Frederick Osterling built at 541 Jones—Library becomes
Jones going uphill—a house for Charles Schwab, also restored.
Schwab, at twenty-seven Edgar Thomson's chief superintendent, had
shrewdness comparable to Carnegie's and Frick's; he also had the
vivacity of the former and the coherence of the latter. None of Carnegie's conscience-salving benefactions for Schwab, who was to
create—and dissipate—his own great fortune: "I disagreed with Carnegie's ideas on how best to distribute his wealth. I spent mine!"

Braddock's history, recently documented in Tony Buba's much-
acclaimed films, had its most compelling narrator in Thomas Bell,
author of *Out of This Furnace*. Backtracking to Braddock Avenue,
then right toward Rankin, his words seem appropriate: "The flatter
expanse of Braddock lower down was a uniform, soiled colorlessness."
At the foot of "this dingy plain" ran "the glintless river." The Mon at
night had more drama; his character Kracha, out on the river, looks
around: "The blast furnaces at Rankin flared intermittently through
the rain, like half-smothered fires; on the Homestead side a Bessemer
convertor vomited yellow flames toward the low-hanging clouds and
cast a sheen on the river. There were similar, if fainter, pulsations in
the sky to the north and south as far as the eye could see . . . Kracha
huddled in the stern of the rowboat and contemplated the dark waters,
the restless fires, the unnatural sky; and for the first time since he'd set
foot in America, felt himself in a strange land."

Continue along Braddock Avenue through what remains of Braddock's commercial district. Signs for Pittsburgh begin farther on. If
you wish to continue to tour eight, Braddock Avenue leads to Penn
Avenue, where you will turn left.

8

THE STRIP, LAWRENCEVILLE, BLOOMFIELD
This walking and driving tour begins in the 1100 block of Penn Avenue.
Start by driving east from downtown on Penn. This area is called the Strip
District.

From Cradle to Grave

The twin agents of innovation and immigration made possible
the Monongahela Valley's massive industrial development (discussed in tour 7). Like the Mon, the Allegheny's banks also
incubated new industries in the nineteenth century. Unlike the Mon,
however, the Allegheny—at least in the Strip—still specializes in
cradling start-up enterprises. And where immigration degenerated
into exploitation and ruin in Mon Valley communities, here we will see
immigrant-built neighborhoods that are strong and still desirable.

The railroad, that great impulse to industrialization, marks the
beginning of this tour. A metallic strain, a faint, drawn-out screech,
often sounds through the area around Eleventh and Penn. It comes
from trains moving slowly along the old Pennsy tracks above.

That assonance makes a melancholy backdrop to these blocks,
which suggest what possibilities lie in recycling warehouse and loft
buildings. At 1133 Penn Avenue stands an 1892 Frederick Osterling
sandstone-faced structure, now offices renovated by UDA Architects.
Turn left at Thirteenth Street. At Smallman broods the former Chautauqua Ice Company building, which acquired its massive look by
storing ice, as well as the horses and wagons that delivered it.

Its less weighty but more important new vocation is as home for the Senator John Heinz Pittsburgh Regional History Center. These far bigger quarters suit the old Historical Society of Western Pennsylvania's desire to put a human face on social history. Here, academic concerns intersect with average Pittsburghers' curiosity about their past. Visitors can board a 1949 trolley and enter reconstructed homes from the city's pioneer, industrial, and baby boom eras. (In keeping with the building's original mission, a refrigerator in the cloakroom will store the fresh fish and produce you've purchased in the Strip.)

Not all the Strip's new leisure-time activities aspire to the Historical Society's cultural tone. From the 1500 block of Smallman you may enter Boardwalk, a riverside entertainment complex with a glitzy disco, restaurants, and docking for cabin cruisers. The presence of pleasure craft where timber rafts and oil barges once moored is another innovation, possible thanks to a cleaner river.

Turn right onto Smallman. The Sixteenth Street Bridge, the second bridge you pass under, was designed in 1923 by Warren and Wetmore, architects of New York's Grand Central Station. Look up and left to see its sculptures bearing armillary globes by Leo Lentelli.

Just beyond, on the right at 1600 Smallman, another entertainment complex occupies another recycled warehouse. Metropol features "industrial dancing"—a sign of how Pittsburgh, and the world's, economy have lightened up. Its impressive big-city high-tech style will make futuristic music fans feel right at home. Enjoying an equally large but not so challenging space is Rosebud, a café next door.

Across Smallman, between Sixteenth and Twenty-first Streets, stretches the 1926 produce terminal, once a link between the Pennsylvania Railroad, which had its switching yards here, and produce trucks. The city of Pittsburgh showed good sense in keeping this quintessentially vital trade in town, even after the railroad left.

The Strip's success derives from its multiple purposes, which keep the streets and restaurants active at all hours. Action sometimes

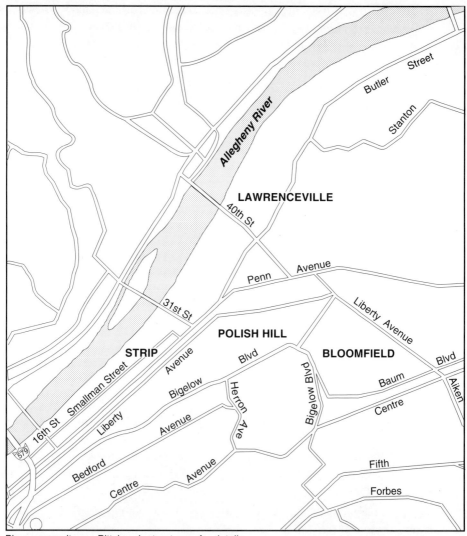

Please consult your Pittsburgh street map for details.

entails friction; dancers, industrial though they may be, occasionally make traffic problems for the fruit and vegetable truck drivers, who also come out late at night.

Park near Saint Stanislaus Kostka Church, which dominates the eastern end of this busy space with a "Here I am and here I'll stay" air. That assertive look may come from the 1892 church's survival of the 1936 flood and an explosion the same year at the nearby City Banana Company. Or it may have come from its Polish builders, experts at putting down roots hereabouts. The handsome interior features extensive murals.

Pittsburgh's confined site has even now kept its scale more human than that of most American towns. But the old city was a walking city, and nowhere can you experience what that was like better than in the Strip. The district is especially lively on Saturday mornings, but it offers its pleasures weekdays as well.

Many of these pleasures are haphazard—the odd encounter, the new shop, the exotic herb. It would be wrong as well as tedious to do a complete inventory of the Strip's attractions; they change often enough to keep the area in the urban vanguard. Let the following suffice to encourage individual exploring.

Catty-corner from Saint Stanislaus, at the head of the produce terminal building, is the Society for Contemporary Crafts, located here since 1986. Excellent craft exhibitions, an attractive shop, classes, and a resource center for craft artists are among its offerings. The society's permanent collection dates from 1972.

Such cultural amenities, along with the shopping and entertainment facilities here, may accelerate redevelopment of one of the Strip's many historically significant industrial complexes. Beyond the church to the left on Twenty-third and Railroad Streets looms the old brick Armstrong Cork Factory, built at the beginning of this century according to Frederick Osterling's plans. Thomas Armstrong transformed the cork business—and thus the old Pittsburgh bottling business too—by adopting new machines in cork cutting. The riverside

165

The
Strip,
Lawrence-
ville,
Bloomfield

complex has been targeted for development, including housing, which might one day give the Strip the residential element it richly deserves.

Back on Smallman at Twenty-third Street, Benkovitz offers elegant seafood, or you can get pig snouts and ears at Farmer's Choice, a block south off Twenty-second at 2123 Penn. Continuing west on Penn you pass purveyors of coffee and garden produce; turning left on Twenty-first you find an Italian hangout called La Prima Espresso, which has delicious pastries as well as excellent espresso.

At 2010 Penn stands the oldest Strip business, Pennsylvania Macaroni, one of many Italian establishments here. Oriental, Mexican, Middle Eastern, and Greek foodstuffs also await you hereabouts, as do bakeries whose styles range from dainty to hearty.

The Strip's restaurant style never budges from the hearty. Old Pittsburgh cookery can be had in Deluca's, 2015 Penn, at breakfast, and at Primanti's, two and a half blocks down on Eighteenth toward Smallman, twenty-four hours a day. Primanti's combines an entirely Pittsburgh sense of efficiency with a strong local idea of nutrition; they put your french fries *inside* the sandwiches. If you didn't go to Benkovitz, or even if you did, Wholey's at Penn and Seventeenth also has an impressive array of seafood in a different and even livelier atmosphere.

The tour continues—more easily in a car now—eastward. Go south to Liberty Avenue, which parallels Penn, and turn left. At 2425 Liberty, at the corner of Twenty-fourth, stands the 1870 headquarters George Westinghouse built for his booming air-brake business. Typifying his lifelong interest in taming power, Westinghouse's invention of a brake using compressed air to bring trains to a rapid halt enhanced both the speed and safety of rail travel. He came to Pittsburgh to get financing for production and succeeded magnificently; his later plants run for miles along Turtle Creek.

This handsomely recycled building now houses a robotics firm, showing the persistence of the Strip's innovative tradition. Go left at the light just beyond it on Twenty-fifth Street, then right at Smallman, noticing the interesting recycling of 2837. At 3220, on the right just before the railroad trestle, a plaque marks the birthplace of the aluminum industry. Here in 1888 the Pittsburgh Reduction Company produced the first commercial aluminum ingot. The inventor of the electrolytic process, Charles Martin Hall, came to Pittsburgh as Westinghouse had, to find financing for his invention. He succeeded too; his company is now called Alcoa.

167

The
Strip,
Lawrence-
ville,
Bloomfield

Rather than heading into the industrial warren toward the river, with its numerous post–Civil War metalworking plants, turn right on Thirty-third, left on Penn, and right on Thirty-fourth. In front of you on Liberty stands the Pittsburgh Brewing Company, home of Iron City Beer. This Victorian complex boasts another innovation, produced in 1962 in conjunction with Alcoa: America's first flip-top can. Notice the terra-cotta bas relief of Ceres, her hair gilt wheat, at the entrance. The brewery is open for visits.

Make a right turn onto Liberty, then a left on Herron Avenue, which is to the right of the brewery. Now you're climbing Polish Hill, a neighborhood built by the Strip's factory workers. You will be turning right on Brereton, a block before the stoplight at the top.

Though not a melting pot, Pittsburgh is a rich stew; the pronounced flavors of its many ethnic groups all but overwhelm the Scotch-Irish Presbyterian stock of its first settlers. Their powerful legacies make us forget that most immigrants' reaction to Pittsburgh was to leave it. Newcomers had a difficult time here even before the horrors of industrialization. "An excellent place to do pennance in," one early traveler called it. "Pittsburgh is by no means a pleasant town to a stranger," another wrote.

Obviously many strangers stayed and made good. Yet leaving the old country, and coping with innovation in the new, were wrenching experiences. Pittsburgh Poles' way of dealing with the upheaval in their lives was to seek stability at all costs. That meant they focused on home and family rather than individual advancement. Low in school attendance, Pittsburgh's first Poles were highest in home ownership. Paradoxically, this neighborhood, the most precarious from a topographical point of view, has an immediately perceptible solidity. Polish Hill's look of ease with itself and its position was attained only by dint of generations single-mindedly pursuing the goal of home and hearth.

Poles built churches almost as rapidly as they did houses—grand and noble churches. Saint Stanislaus in the Strip was the Polish parent congregation; the Immaculate Heart of Mary Church on Brereton Street was built in 1904, within ten years of Polish settlement here. Its architect, William Ginther of Akron, handled the tough site brilliantly, establishing an authoritative Roman presence on the Pittsburgh skyline. Satisfying from any number of viewpoints, the green-domed church displays its truest character in juxtaposition with the asphalt-shingled dwellings along Paulowna Street, which you will see shortly.

A domestic touch greets you as you enter: in the holy water font sits a coffee percolator, which a strip of masking tape declares "Holy Water." Aside from that, Immaculate Heart's interior is impressive; the best view is from the corner to the right of the altar. Renaissance-style oak and gilt altars and confessionals, expertly conceived and executed, enhance the interior's accomplished design. The stations of the cross and window inscriptions are in Polish, but the Roman Catholic church's universality tempers this ethnic spirit. A photograph of the Polish pope, for instance, is inscribed in Italian, "Papa Giovanni Paolo II."

Turn left on Thirtieth Street, then left again on Paulowna. At the light turn left on Bigelow, a magnificent boulevard built in 1900 to connect the Allegheny area of the East End with downtown. Follow the signs for Bloomfield; that means crossing Bloomfield Bridge, which affords a fleeting view of what looks like a Cubist painting of an Italian hill town.

The look is no accident; Bloomfield is Italian, largely settled by immigrants from mountain towns in Italy's Abruzzi region. Abruzzesi, in fact, constitute a big portion of Pittsburgh's Italian population,

Polish Hill

which in turn outnumbers other recent immigrant groups. The harshness of their native region—the mountains make it cold and barren—prepared the Abruzzesi for tough conditions in western Pennsylvania.

Unlike the Poles, nearly all of whom worked in metal production, the Italians practiced a variety of trades. Iron crafts, common in many of their hometowns, gave them a start here; but their skills in construction, cobbling, tailoring, and cooking have also profited them.

At the end of the bridge, turn right on Liberty. Bloomfield, like the Strip, can be appreciated best on foot. Liberty shares the Strip's vocation for feeding people; it smells good. By strolling a block or two west of Liberty you can see what those Cubist slopes look like up close—tight, neat, spare, just like the compact mountain villages that sheltered Abruzzesi in their homeland.

Leaving Bloomfield by car, continue down Liberty a good distance to Baum Boulevard; turn left at the light. Here you may admire the First United Methodist Church of Pittsburgh, a strong 1893 sandstone sanctuary inspired by Richardson's Trinity Church in Boston, and by Shadyside Presbyterian here. The interior feels more spacious than Shadyside, thanks to big windows adorned by gold-winged angels above, with rich Tiffanyesque inserts below. On the west side of the church stands a World War II memorial representing the three branches of the military.

Continue a short distance east on Baum, then turn left on South Graham. This is Friendship, a very solid-looking but lively neighborhood dating from the late nineteenth century, settled mainly by middle-class Germans. There's a lot of renovation in this area, with new owners attracted by the concentration of big, handsome homes. Continue to Friendship Avenue, where a right takes you by Charles M. Bartberger's 1899 Friendship School, with its cream glazed terra-cotta details. Notice the Richardsonian church on the right, but turn left on Roup.

A left on Penn takes you quickly by, on the left, a smaller but richer terra-cotta facade, that of Lackzoom Acidophilus at 5438. Lest

Bloomfield

the name suggest a quackish nostrum, you should know that Lack-zoom became the General Nutrition Corporation.

As we head west we pass on the right—farther down Penn and through a neighborhood called Garfield—the elaborate 1888 Richardsonian Romanesque entrance of Allegheny Cemetery, with a curvilinear wrought-iron gate at the center. Our itinerary will take us to the other entrance of this romantic place after Lawrenceville, which begins here with Saint Francis Hospital.

On the right, at the corner of Penn and Fortieth Street, stands Canterbury Place, thoughtfully expanded housing for senior citizens. Continue on Penn. On the opposite side of Fortieth stand buildings remaining from Lawrenceville's first industrial function, an arsenal.

The neighborhood—until 1867 an independent borough—was founded in 1814 by William Foster, father of the composer Stephen. The name honored the War of 1812's Captain James Lawrence, who commanded "Don't give up the ship" just before dying. His crew did, but he became a hero all the same. Foster had the area's military vocation in mind; a few days after purchasing this large tract, he sold thirty acres of it to the government for an arsenal. It remained active until shortly after the Civil War.

Farther on Penn at 3600 stood the house where Stephen was born on the day both John Adams and Thomas Jefferson died, the Fourth of July 1826. The Fosters were pioneer aristocrats; their White Cottage here apparently was designed by Benjamin Latrobe, architect of the Capitol and the White House in Washington. Stephen's sister married President Buchanan's brother, and their father William was twice mayor of Allegheny City, where Stephen spent most of his life.

If there was such a thing as an Establishment in nineteenth-century America, Stephen belonged to it. Yet his songs—"Beautiful Dreamer," "My Old Kentucky Home," "Old Folks at Home"—nearly always express nostalgia, loss, and homesickness. What does it say about pre–Civil War–era America and Pittsburgh that so bright and well-born a son suffer the kind of alienation you might expect from immigrants? The paradox is that here the immigrants give lessons in putting down roots, while the longtime American sings of rootlessness. Stephen's life accorded with his songs of privation and grief. He died at age thirty-seven with thirty-eight cents in his pocket.

173

The
Strip,
Lawrence-
ville,
Bloomfield

The house you now see at 3600 was built by an early Carnegie partner, Andrew Kloman; their iron works stood along the Allegheny shore. A philanthropist bought the house in 1914 for Stephen's impoverished daughter; it now serves as offices for the American Wind Symphony, and the house can be visited by special arrangement.

Since the closing of its steel mills in the 1970s and early 1980s, Lawrenceville has been holding its own. But not until the beginning of the 1990s has there been any new construction. You now see new townhouses as you approach Doughboy Square. Named for the World War I soldier on the monument, Doughboy Square is not so much a square as a triangle.

Turn a sharp right around the statue; we're heading east on Butler now. Many Germans settled in Lawrenceville; at the turn of the century they commissioned John Comes to design them a high and distinctive church, Saint Augustine's. It rises over Thirty-seventh Street, above Butler, and may be approached by car on Thirty-sixth or Thirty-eighth. The striking interior features ambitious murals; the high-quality stained glass sheds light on the ethnic and linguistic mélange immigrant churches must have been around 1900. One window was given by Frau Josephine O'Reilly, another by Familie Schultis.

Butler Street, Lawrenceville's chief commercial street, is intact enough for people to find a rough charm in it. Not at all intact, unfortunately, are the buildings Benjamin Latrobe planned for the U.S. Arsenal on either side of it at Fortieth. Charles Dickens called it "pretty" after his 1842 visit. Latrobe had come in 1813 to supervise steamboat construction for Robert Fulton. That entrepreneur eased Latrobe out of the venture as soon as it was underway, leaving Latrobe and his family stranded. After the work at the arsenal, they left in 1814.

A piece of the arsenal—which was a large industrial complex

Allegheny Cemetery

employing over a thousand workers—may be seen in the park behind Arsenal Middle School at the corner of Butler and Fortieth Streets. There a stone powder magazine remains buried under the slope of the hill.

175

The
Strip,
Lawrence-
ville,
Bloomfield

The bridge commemorates George Washington's fateful crossing here on a wintry night at the end of December 1753. The icy Allegheny tipped him off his raft. As at Braddock's rout a year and a half later, Providence was watching over the young Virginian; he arrived at the Indian village that stood here with nothing worse than frozen fingers.

Lawrenceville continues to attract large-scale projects and innovators. The Carnegie Mellon University Robotics Institute and NASA have renovated, with city financing, an old foundry building along the river between Fortieth and Forty-third Streets (not visible from Butler Street). The enormous complex develops robots to harvest wheat (planted on the site), dig mines, and explore the heavens.

Which brings us to Allegheny Cemetery. Continuing east on Butler, you see English architect John Chislett's Tudor Gothic entrance. His Burke's Building still stands on Fourth Avenue downtown. Hired as superintendent, Chislett surveyed and laid out the grounds, the first hundred acres of which were bought in 1844. At the office just beyond the entrance they welcome you with a map and brochure.

A visit to the Frick house, Clayton (see tour 6), testifies to our ancestors' different attitude toward death. The rapid multiplication of elaborate rural cemeteries after the model of Boston's Mount Auburn before the Civil War may seem to be an aspect of Victorian morbidity. But, in fact, the origin of such cemeteries has much in common with that of suburbs—as do their ground plans, for that matter. Both suburbs and cemeteries became popular as a means of escaping the industrializing city.

Andrew Jackson Downing saw the attraction clearly. The great merit of these places—in the absence of public gardens they were

Monument in Allegheny Cemetery

popular as picnic destinations—lay not in the fact that they were burial grounds, but "in the natural beauty of the sites, and in the tasteful and harmonious embellishment of these sites by art." Visitors enjoy the "double wealth of rural and moral associations. It awakens at the same moment, the feeling of human sympathy and the love of natural beauty. . . . His must be a dull or trifling soul that neither swells with emotion, or rises with admiration, at the varied beauty of these lovely and hallowed spots."

177

The
Strip,
Lawrence-
ville,
Bloomfield

Another perplexity moderns feel in monumental or romantic cemeteries has to do with what Walter Kidney calls the "boldness of entombment." In cemeteries, eternity, or at least durability, has hitherto been the ideal; stone and marble records of a life were a demonstration that life was taken seriously. And funerary monuments were the one opportunity ordinary people had to commission works of art. Allegheny Cemetery's angels and obelisks may rarely thrill as works of genius, yet they do suggest that the quest for permanence, so evident in Pittsburgh's immigrant neighborhoods, found its most beautiful expression right here.

Like other segments of this tour, Allegheny Cemetery invites exploration. The Butler Street office is generous with maps, and the Allegheny Cemetery Historical Association has traced a route, with special markers leading to Stephen Foster's burial place. Other luminaries resting here include Lillian Russell, Harry Thaw (see tour 5), Josh Gibson (great slugger of the Negro Leagues), and many of Pittsburgh's barons of industry. By all means follow the ACHA route, and remember to look through the door of the Winter tomb, not far from the Penn Avenue gate, to see Egyptian scenes in stained glass. But here, as most places in Pittsburgh, it pays to strike out on your own.

9

NORTH SIDE

This driving and walking tour begins at the North Shore's Allegheny
Landing, a sculpture park near the intersection of Isabella and Federal
Streets. It's a long tour and may take more than one outing to complete.

Solos

Polish Hill, Bloomfield, and Lawrenceville form immigrant cho-
ruses, singing of home; they give deep tones to the symphony of
Pittsburgh life. Such social harmonies are not the North Side's
forte. But this section of Pittsburgh does, in brilliant contrapunto, offer
splendid solos.

Plotted in 1787, Allegheny City, as the area was known historically, began to attract settlers only around 1810. Intended as the seat
of Allegheny County, the nascent town saw Pittsburgh usurp the honor.
That was not to be the last aggression from across the river. Allegheny
City nonetheless prospered, rivaling its larger neighbor in industrial
variety, in social prestige, and, above all, in public amenities.

The tour begins with one of the more recent of such amenities,
Allegheny Landing. The park is located next to North Shore Center at
Isabella and Federal Streets, between the Sixth and Seventh Street
Bridges. Park in this area and explore. The greensward is dominated
by two postmodern mosaic and pebble-textured cement sculptures by
Ned Smyth. The upper one, *Piazza Lavoro*, represents an exaltation of
labor, the other, *Mythic Source*, with its sea monsters, is an evocation
of water's mythical function.

Getting visitors down to the water itself constitutes the park's principal merit. Here coal barges and jet skis, the *Good Ship Lollipop* and floaters on inner tubes provide an aquatic vaudeville. Old water-fronts present a big challenge and a big opportunity to cities like Pittsburgh. How do they mediate water and land, the fluid and the fixed, nature's work and man's work?

Here the transition succeeds. This landscaped and art-spattered slope is inviting; the steps put Franklin Toker in mind of the seventeenth-century Porto di Ripetta on the Tiber in Rome; the board-walk itself, and cunning details like the fishy drain spouts along the river wall, combine to make a pleasant stroll. For special events, you may also catch a water taxi here; it will take you to Pirates and Steelers games and concerts at Three Rivers Stadium.

These foreground details set off a spectacular picture, a grand view of downtown Pittsburgh. Triple suspension bridges transect the Allegheny in the middle ground. Built in the late twenties, they are endearing for their pretty self-anchoring suspension form, dictated by aesthetic rather than engineering considerations. Only the color, sick canary, leaves something to be desired. Their elegant lines call for better treatment—perhaps black, with gilt details. That would make the sports fans happy.

Then there is the skyline itself. Here again you can see how Pittsburgh's topography, demanding density, excludes banality. The effect is augmented by the odd angles the buildings present, thanks to the uncoordinated grids of the eighteenth-century street patterns, and thanks also, in the case of buildings like the Mellon Bank and USX, to architects' preference for siting their buildings on the bias. To the right appear the steel Gateway Center buildings, seen here without their grove of trees; in a certain light they look like blocks of ice.

A son of Allegheny City who greatly contributed to Pittsburgh's livability was Henry Phipps, Andrew Carnegie's childhood friend and lifetime business colleague. Phipps was (as Joseph Wall puts it) "quiet, timid, self-effacing," and devious to the point of perfidy. Trembling, he stabbed more than one colleague in the back. Usually anx-

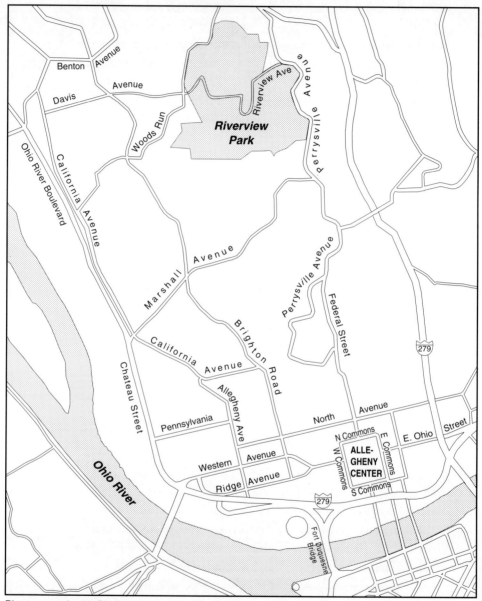

Please consult your Pittsburgh street map for details.

ious as a hen, in his balancing of books and floating of checks he was splendidly cavalier. Like Carnegie, who said, "Allegheny was my first love," he never forgot the place of his childhood, making it the object of several charitable efforts.

He also embellished its view by building up his downtown real estate in full sight of the north shore. The significant vestige of this effort is the Fulton, the arched highrise just beyond the Sixth Street Bridge. With its now-demolished companion across Sixth Street, the Fulton made a fine portal for the Golden Triangle; it still resonates with the arches and parabolas of the sister bridges.

Back now on our own side of the river, UDA Architects designed the 1984 North Shore Center as the first phase of a lowrise development, including housing, intended to follow Isabella Street up to the Ninth Street Bridge. Despite such important projects, the North Side is richer in good recycled old buildings than in new architecture. Walk back up to Isabella and Sandusky, heading toward the Ninth Street Bridge. Number Four North Shore, a turn-of-the-century warehouse renovated in 1984 by Williams Trebilcock Whitehead, serves as a handsome example. Farther down Isabella stands the presently isolated 1917 studio of Frederick Osterling; notable for its great glass facade, unusual for the period, and for its fine Gothic tracery, it is an elaborate echo of the architect's Union Trust Building on Grant Street.

Return to Sandusky and UDA Architects' 1994 SMS Building, whose main entrance is around the corner on Sandusky. This building continues the fine Pittsburgh tradition of eye-catching architectural advertising. The American headquarters of a German steel engineering firm, its extensive use of steel within includes the countertop at the receptionist's desk. Between this building and the river will rise, in 1998, the new Alcoa headquarters. The glass and masonry structure by Design Alliance will have only touches of aluminum, the downtown landmark building having proved aluminum's worth long ago.

Across the street on Sandusky stands the 1910 white tile building—formerly Volkwein's music store and originally a warehouse for oil, steel, and mining supplies—that's been renovated as the Andy Warhol Museum. Architect of the early 1990s project was Richard Gluckman with UDA Architects, master planners of the North Shore Center.

Pittsburgh-bred Andy Warhol rarely gave a straight answer to personal questions. Was it something about the city—perhaps its historical roughness—that drove him to falsity? Andy may have been like Auntie Mame's friend Vera Childs. In the film, Patrick, Mame's nephew, is watching her being carried upstairs, senselessly drunk.

> Patrick: Is the English lady sick, Auntie Mame?
> Mame: Oh she's not English, darling, she's from Pittsburgh.
> Patrick: She sounded English.
> Mame: Well when you're from Pittsburgh you have to do something.

Andy clearly felt he had to do something. After studying at Schenley High School, where he was graduated in 1945, he continued his education at what is now Carnegie Mellon and, one summer, dressed windows for the downtown Joseph Horne Department Store. But to pursue his career he fled. He rejected Pittsburgh's provincialism, and Pittsburgh returned the favor, showing little interest in him even at the time of his greatest success. These circumstances have called into question the appropriateness of establishing a Warhol Museum here.

Yet Warhol had much in common with Pittsburghers. He chose to work in a Factory—his name for his studio. The Carnegie's selection of this building, a former industrial warehouse, and Gluckman's architectural treatment make a visit to the Warhol a little like a visit to Andy's Manhattan Factory.

There he produced things in series—multiple images inspired by the consumer society. Multiples meant art could share with consumer products the characteristic of uniformity but, being art, would be eternal. His taste for replication, the premise for modern manufacturing, went so far that he tried replicating himself, sending out a look-alike to give talks in his name. He even dreamed of an Andy Warhol robot that would represent him in eternity.

He didn't get the robot, but he has a museum. One-artist museums, unusual in the United States, are less so in Europe and especially in France, where the most successful example is the Picasso Museum in Paris. That is a flattering analogy. Curator Mark Francis makes another that might please Andy even more: Graceland. Elvis's macabre memorial must surely have appealed to an artist who, behind the smoke screen of self-promotion and trickster tactics, was seeking eternity. This point was made abundantly clear by Andy's obsessive collecting. A large repository of his famous "stuff" is part of the museum's holdings, displayed along with his art.

Critics who doubt the appropriateness of Pittsburgh as site of the Warhol Museum might also smile at the idea that the puritanical Andrew Carnegie is supporting, so to speak, a pop artist, for the Carnegie (with the Dia Foundation) is running the museum. Yet the two Andys share much more than their now-intertwined legacies. Andy Warhol, as a boy, took art classes at the Carnegie in Oakland. Andrew Carnegie was a North Sider, living his teenage years on Rebecca Street. Warhol, willy-nilly, has become a North Sider too.

Both men were masters of self-promotion, and both manipulated the media in much the same manner, presenting a mediagenic personality as the real one. Yet, in fact, both Andys were highly elusive, especially when it was in their best interest. Carnegie, an inveterate self-publicist since his teens, managed to lay low to the point of invisibility throughout the Homestead tragedy. As for the artist, no researcher yet has a hold on the real Warhol; a museum to the man would be less interesting if his character had already yielded up all its secrets.

A final similarity. It wasn't just that both men got their money from factories that produced multiples. Both Carnegie and Warhol had an emphatically modernist and earthbound sensibility. Carnegie rejected old paintings for his museum; he wanted a collection of con-

temporary works. He, like Warhol, feigned an anti-imagination posture, entirely in contrast with his creative deeds. "Pioneering don't
pay," he would say. "People's fantasies are what give them problems,"
Warhol would reply.

Backtrack to Federal Street and, by car now, turn right, passing
under a colorfully embellished railroad bridge, to Allegheny Center
Mall, the most useful feature of which is its garage. You will be going
right and then quickly left on East Commons. Park here; mall mer-
chants will validate your garage ticket for a free hour.

At the beginning of this tour, we suggested that Pittsburgh had
victimized old Allegheny City. History provides many examples,
including the smaller city's annexation by the larger, which occurred
in 1907. Allegheny fought the takeover all the way to the Supreme
Court. No more dramatic proof of the rightness of that battle could
exist than this garage—for here was the heart of Allegheny City. Allegheny held onto its social primacy a while longer, but by the 1930s the
powerful families had all moved out, many of them to Sewickley and
Sewickley Heights, where they had long owned summer homes.

Given its proximity to downtown, the postwar Renaissance was
bound to affect this area. Alcoa, in fact, sponsored a drastic cleansing
in the 1960s. The core of old Allegheny, 518 buildings, was destroyed
for a housing, office, and shopping complex—the mall above us.

It would be easy to poke fun at this enterprise, especially since it
has not been a great commercial success—as you see when you take
the escalator upstairs. More interesting is to consider the attitudes
toward the old city, and therefore toward history, that lay behind Allegheny Center. Nowhere is the fundamental disdain for the past more
clearly revealed than in the treatment of street patterns here—or
rather in the obliteration of them.

Federal Street, one of the few thoroughfares in Pittsburgh with
sweep and perspective, got corked and canceled by this mall. Going
out the north side of the shopping mall, you see that not even the
memory of the street has been preserved, as it might have been in the

Former Buhl Planetarium

Allegheny Square, Pittsburgh Children's Museum in background

mall entrance, for example; the central portal on the north side couldn't be more forbidding, despite its flags and flower boxes. The mall works as a fortress, protecting shoppers from the city that used to belong to them. Even the elevated stone-walled planters have the quality of bastions. Pedestrians from the surrounding area who don't get shunted aside by the garage's walls have only controlled access to the center above.

They wanted it sanitized, but it's mostly sad. Yet while renewal destroyed Allegheny City's commercial heart, a series of monumental public buildings remain, thanks in part to preservationists' protests. Coming out of the center northward, you find on the left a big below-level fountain, which, when it's turned on, creates a water dome in harmony with the copper ones on the buildings beyond it. To the right is the Carnegie Library, which we shall return to.

On the left, the sleek limestone structure with handsome bas reliefs—there are two on the sides as well as the pair on the facade—was built in 1939 for Buhl Planetarium, which since has moved to the Carnegie Science Center (see below). This unusual windowless building, now shuttered, belongs to the city; its future is uncertain. The 1897 post office next to it has been the Pittsburgh Children's Museum since 1983. Its hands-on exhibits, puppet collections, Lucky's Climber, and Warhol Gallery make it the liveliest place in town.

The post office was saved from demolition by the History and Landmarks Foundation, whose headquarters were here until they moved on to bigger things at Station Square on the South Side. A number of architectural fragments remain hereabouts, including the Belgian blocks and streetcar tracks of old Ohio Street, another truncated thoroughfare. Some are unidentified, giving off a poignant whiff of Easter Island. Left of the museum, on the same side of the walk, you see a giant ivy-enshrouded bronze remnant, with a magical patina. A shield with symbolic figures on either side, it formed part of the Manchester Bridge. Flora-bound and grounded, it may be more impressive now than when it rode high above the Allegheny. The sculptor was

Charles Keck, a student of Augustus Saint-Gaudens and Daniel Chester French.

Something of the passion that preserved these relics comes through on a plaque at the east entrance to the walk. In unusually frank tones, it commemorates the Allegheny Market that stood here, "one of the most beloved buildings in Pittsburgh . . . demolished in 1966 by the Urban Redevelopment Authority of Pittsburgh to make way for a high-rise apartment house." Willa Cather, among others, commemorated the lost market as "one of the best in the world."

Backtrack to the Carnegie Library, Carnegie's first after the one in Braddock. Built in 1889 by the architects of the Library of Congress in Washington, Smithmeyer and Pelz, it included a music hall that now houses the Pittsburgh Public Theater, a deservedly well-funded and well-attended institution. The Public, however, is slated to move downtown in 1997 when the Michael Graves building in the cultural district is built. This departure, along with the Buhl closing, has many North Siders worried about the cultural vitality of this area. Beyond the library stands the IBM building, a 1966 Mies van der Rohe cube.

Andrew Carnegie's double-mindedness about workers, his honeyed words and relentless exploitation, should not blind us to the magnanimity that marked many of his actions. As a boy, along with other Allegheny lads, he had been allowed to use the private library of Colonel James Anderson. As an adult engaged in a vast philanthropic effort to make books available all over America and Britain, he erected a monument crediting Anderson as the "founder of free libraries in Western Pennsylvania." Daniel Chester French beautifully translated Carnegie's generous recognition into stone and bronze. The monument was dismantled in the renewal effort of the 1960s; in 1988 was it reassembled across from the library's main entrance.

You may want to return to your car now, unless you are a fanatical walker. Exit on East Commons, where you are forced left. As you turn right on East Ohio Street, you will go by Allegheny Commons East, a

Manchester Bridge remnant, Allegheny Square

Colonel Anderson tribute, Allegheny Library

tightly organized 1966 rental project inspired by Italian villages. It's not rich, but it works; Tasso Katselas designed it with unusual tact.

Go right on Cedar, then left on Pressley, toward the end of which stands the Priory, a successful inn in a building of considerable character. You turn left on Nash Street and immediately left again on Lockhart Street, on which fronts the Priory's Grand Hall, formerly St. Mary's Church, an interesting 1854 structure. Lockhart returns you west by Deutschtown Square—the dictionary-correct spelling is a clue to the gentrification of what historically was Dutchtown, or, alternately, Swiss Hole. The neighborhood was Pittsburgh's first ethnic enclave.

Go right on Cedar and again right on East Ohio; the old commercial row's restored facades are a response to the city's encouragement of historic streetscapes. A left on Middle Street takes you by the venerable Max's Allegheny Tavern; a left on Tripoli takes you by another successful recycling enterprise, the School House Apartments.

A right on Cedar and a quick left onto East North Avenue takes you by Allegheny General Hospital. (You will be continuing west down North Avenue.) This distinguished institution, long a favorite charity of Pittsburgh patricians, anchors the North Side's economy. It has avoided the sprawl that makes Oakland's medical center a visual nuisance, yet it has expanded and modernized mightily. Within, the decorator of the 1930s lobby displayed Hollywood taste through an Assyro-Babylonian filter, giving medical history the treatment usually reserved for movie palaces.

Proceed west on North Avenue. The degraded commercial area around Federal Street has been targeted by the city for redevelopment. Plans include a new building for Allegheny General and rehabilitation of the Garden Theater. Notice the lively Victorian architecture of the houses, especially beyond Arch Street. We are approaching the Mexican War Streets, a neighborhood laid out in 1848 by William Robinson, who commemorated heros and battles of the war in street names. Its borders, like Shadyside's, tend to expand. The neighborhood's vitality got a potent stimulus in the mid 1960s from threats of urban renewal of the sort that produced Allegheny Center. The Pittsburgh History and Landmarks Foundation led the fight to preserve not only the buildings, but also the racial makeup of the area.

Turn right on Resaca Place, where the intimate and harmonious scale of the neighborhood is at once apparent. The Queen Anne house at 1201, on the left by the alley, shows in its towerlet and other details what extensive aspirations can find expression in a compact space.

Go right on North Taylor Avenue toward Sherman to the Greek Revival Allegheny Widows' Home, a complex around a courtyard that originated as an orphanage. The large central building was designed in 1838 by John Chislett; his later work included the Butler Street entrance of Allegheny Cemetery. After the Civil War, row houses were added for widows; since its 1984 renovation, the buildings have served as housing for the elderly.

Turn left on Sherman and left again on Jacksonia, where you may park at 505 to visit the Mattress Factory. Artists consider this too-little-known alternative museum, which specializes in installation art, the finest facility of its sort in America. The Factory's ephemeral installations generate excitement and controversy; some of the eleven permanent ones induce meditation. The latter include James Turrell's light works at the Sampsonia Way building (the one we're in), and Bill Woodrow's *Ship of Fools* at the 1414 Monterey house, a block to the west at the corner of Jacksonia and Monterey. The city has shown both vision and good sense in selecting the Mattress Factory as developer of the North Avenue–Federal Street project.

Continue west on Jacksonia where, catty-corner from the little park, you see at 613 a beat-up tin rendering of H. H. Richardson's stonework style. Turn left on Buena Vista where, toward the end, 1201 shows the same striving for completeness as 1201 Resaca; this one's tower is sandstone.

Turning right on West North you have a good view across the park of PPG Place's Gothic glass skyscraper. Go left on Brighton Road, then left again on West Ohio Street into West Park. In 1819 Allegheny

1234 Resaca Place

set aside a hundred acres as common pasture, part of which was laid out in 1867 as this park, which attracted Pittsburgh's elite; the city across the Allegheny River had no parks until a generation later.

If you want to stop now, the park is a lovely place to stroll. A couple of war memorials—the column on your left for Civil War soldiers, a less obvious commemoration of the Spanish-American War by Charles Keck across the lake—and the National Aviary enhance the grounds. The latter, a post–World War II reevocation of Henry Phipps's 1887 conservatory on the North Side, had been threatened with closing because of city budgetary problems until 1993 when it received national status.

In May, this sleepy pasture comes alive as site of the annual Pittsburgh Children's Festival, one of the very few outdoor events of its kind. Also in summer, be on the lookout for Gus and Yiayia's bright orange, old-fashioned ice-ball stand, a North Side tradition since 1934.

Back in your car, turn right, after the bridge, on unmarked Merchant Street, which takes you under a rail overpass to the red brick Clark Building, home of the Clark candy bar. Turn right on Martindale; you'll be forced left at Scotland Street. Follow the blue signs for the Carnegie Science Center. You'll be making a right-hand turn onto Route 28 South, then veering to the left, which will bring you, with a left on Allegheny Avenue, to the Carnegie Science Center entrance.

With the Strip's Society for Contemporary Crafts and the Regional History Center, the Golden Triangle's cultural district and the North Side's Warhol and Children's Museums, and, finally, the Carnegie Science Center, the Allegheny-Ohio River corridor has magnetized a significant portion of the city's cultural life.

The grandest addition to this cultural scene is also by far the most disappointing. The 1991 Science Center's exterior has been compared to a sewage treatment facility, the interior to a Toys-R-Us in a parking garage. Its boosters, and they are legion, call it an amusement park for the mind. But no one can explain why they commissioned a humorless brutalist to design an amusement park. The enterprise's heavy-handedness appears so not only in comparison to Kennywood, but also in relation to other such institutions in the United States. One of the oldest, San Francisco's Exploratorium, recycled a World War I storage facility for its quarters—yet it sparkles with a degree of wit and intelligence that no amount of boosterism can replace.

It may turn out that the center's interactive exhibits and frequent crowd-pleasing shows will make visitors forget—since they will never be able to forgive—the Carnegie's failure to provide the city with a building worthy of this magnificent site.

Leaving the center you go right toward the river, then left along the riverside Roberto Clemente Park, a model for the linear park that one day may link all Pittsburgh's river neighborhoods. A bronze Vietnam War memorial stands partway down in the park.

Turn left again around the 1971 Three Rivers Stadium, where Pittsburgh's often victorious Pirates and Steelers play. Here, too, the city missed an opportunity to capitalize on a remarkable site; only the name relates it to the rivers. A proposal for a horseshoe stadium, dramatically open to downtown's skyline, was rejected. A historical relation, on the other hand, was reestablished here. Pittsburghers always associate baseball tradition with Forbes Field in Oakland, destroyed at the beginning of the 1970s. But the sport's original home was right here; on this ground stood Exposition Park, where in 1903 the Pirates played Boston in the first World Series.

Turn left on Reedsdale Street (28 South) and immediately right to the Clark Building, retracing your way on Scotland, Martindale, and Merchant back to West Park. Go left on West Ohio to Brighton, where you turn left, admiring the mansions. The old elite, showing yet again Pittsburgh's truly urban soul, preferred Allegheny even after the East End became fashionable. The East End, although annexed by the city in 1867, remained suburban in its distance from the center and in its class composition. Allegheny was not classless, but as a walking city, where face-to-face relationships characterized daily life, it had urban rather than suburban quality.

A number of commanding dwellings were razed to build the 1973 Community College of Allegheny County, a Tasso Katselas project that exhibits more life than his Science Center. As you turn right on Ridge Avenue, you will see several surviving mansions, including the splendidly gated Byers-Lyon house at 901, now the college's student union, just beyond Galveston Avenue. Make a right-hand turn at Galveston. At the intersection of Galveston and Lincoln Avenue, you see the school's Visual Arts Center, a recycled late Victorian structure.

Continue a few blocks to Beech Avenue and park. The neighborhood we are about to visit is formally called Allegheny West. At 850 Beech, to the right of Galveston, stands the place Gertrude Stein was born on 3 February 1874. A plaque quotes her: "In the United States there is more space where nobody is than where anybody is. This is what makes America what it is." She might have had a different view had she remained longer in densely populated Pittsburgh. But she left for Vienna in 1875, returning to America in 1879—to Oakland, California, where there was "no there there." She spent her long adult life in Paris, writing and receiving visits and collecting art. But toward the end, she conceded, "There is something in this native land business."

A proverb of the era said that when good Americans died, they went to Paris. Stein wasn't the only good American from hereabouts who made the choice. In fact, she had been preceded by Mary Cassatt, the Impressionist painter, whose brother commissioned Daniel Burnham to do the Pennsylvania Station. The Cassatts lived for a while on Rebecca Street, where both Carnegie and Phipps spent their youthful years; it is now called Reedsdale Street and faces the stadium's parking lot. The aristocratic Miss Cassatt would not have liked that; but then her Pittsburgh roots perhaps did not interest her. In 1908 she went to see the already well-known Miss Stein in her Paris apartment. She found the paintings and the people dreadful.

Another Allegheny native who left to make her artistic fortune elsewhere was Martha Graham, born into a strict Scotch-Irish Presbyterian family. She remembered the town as "completely bleak, and lacking in life, brightness, and any discernible beauty. . . . Pittsburgh was dark, as if the city was spun entirely out of evening and dark thread."

A stroll on Beech may dispel this view. To the right of the Stein house, notice the Richardsonian house with pink mortar. Then head west a block and a half; at the corner with Allegheny stands mystery novelist Mary Roberts Rinehart's home from 1907 to 1911; here she wrote *The Circular Staircase*. Another writer inspired by this area was Marcia Davenport, whose 1940 best-seller, *The Valley of Decision*, tells the story of generations of iron makers, an elite at home in this neighborhood.

At the corner of Beech and Allegheny stands the extraordinary Calvary United Methodist Church, a Vrydaugh and Shepherd creation of 1892. The later Gothic purist Ralph Adams Cram might have observed that the architects here knew nothing of true Gothic, but one must admit that they "blundered into a picturesque scenery, not void of grandeur," to use Horace Walpole's phrase. The Methodists spared neither pains nor cost, and their lavishly adorned interior includes three Tiffany masterpieces, movingly depicting the Apocalypse, the Resurrection, and the Ascension.

A block north on Allegheny and North Avenues stands another church whose noble plainness makes Calvary look fretful and fluttery. The apse, visible from Buttercup Way, and facade, on West North Avenue, and bowed side wall on Allegheny itself—the foundation shifted early—all emanate repose, that most elusive and most desirable property of great architecture. There are no historical allusions here; the architect H. H. Richardson left the whole expression to elemental form and elemental materials, though the bricks are elegantly worked. Recognizing the genuine simplicity and natural quality of the 1886 structure, its neighbors dubbed Emmanuel Episcopal Church "the bake oven." Unsigned Tiffany windows grace the interior.

You will want a car for most of the rest of the tour, as the distances multiply.

Turning left off Allegheny Avenue onto West North we enter old Manchester, laid out in 1832, then merged in 1867 into Allegheny City. Isolated from its workplaces on the Ohio River by the construction of the Chateau Street Expressway, the neighborhood's decay accelerated in the early 1960s. Beginning in 1966, the History and Landmarks Foundation worked with the inhabitants to restore Manchester.

Their joint effort succeeded in creating the first historical district in the nation primarily for African Americans, and the first federally funded historic district program administered by community residents. The process contrasted with gentrification in its emphasis on the restoration of houses for low- to moderate-income residents, and in its programs to keep old-timers here.

Take West North to the end where it intersects with Chateau Street. Turn right, with another right after a few blocks on Liverpool. The big columned house on the right at 1423 may have originated in 1830 as the dwelling of James Anderson, Carnegie's inspiration for libraries (see above).

Beyond you see the 1300 block of Liverpool. Threats to its survival inspired, in the early 1960s, the first preservation organization in Allegheny County. Called "North Jerusalem" for the number of Jews living there originally, Liverpool had lost, but thanks to preservationists has now found again, its liveliness.

Frederick Sauer's 1892 Saint Joseph's Church—now the Original Church of God Deliverance Center—forms this street's backdrop; it too has fine stained glass windows. Turn right on Fulton, then left on Pennsylvania Avenue.

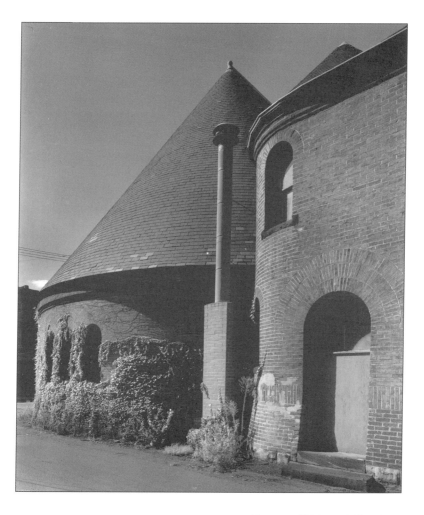

Emmanuel Episcopal Church

North Side stairs

Pennsylvania takes us out of Manchester to Brighton Road, where a left takes us, after a winding mile and a half, into a small commercial district where you will turn right on Woods Run; follow this curvy road nine-tenths of a mile, where two sharp right turns take you up the hill into Riverview Park, over 250 acres of mostly wild terrain. A slight jog left puts you on Riverview Drive. At the summit you come upon the gleaming Allegheny Observatory.

Martha Graham's autobiography is only the latest of many descriptions of industrial Pittsburgh's appalling gloom and pervasive materialism. Some books—Annie Dillard's *An American Childhood,* Elizabeth Moorhead's *Whirling Spindle,* Thomas Bell's *Out of This Furnace*—show how spirited souls grappled with this environment.

Nonmaterialistic pursuits varied. One of the most unexpected was the Allegheny Observatory. A group of businessmen, excited by the passage of Donati's comet in 1858, decided to pursue their romantic interest in the heavens by purchasing the third largest telescope in the country and building an observatory to house it. In 1867 they gave it all to the forerunner of the University of Pittsburgh. Many prominent industrialists maintained strong links with it.

Samuel Pierpont Langley, the observatory's first director, made the institution famous for the Allegheny System, a way of keeping time according to stars' positions. Railroads happily paid the observatory for the correct time. Langley left after twenty years to head the Smithsonian Institution. His successor, James Keeler, discovered that Saturn's rings were not solid but made up of particles—a notion Pittsburgh's atmosphere may have suggested. His successor was John Brashear.

Brashear was a magnetic figure, perhaps because he remained completely indifferent to any calculations but those of the stars and planets. He had been a mechanic, with little formal education, in a South Side mill. Telescopes were his avocation. That led him to begin grinding optical lenses.

William Thaw met Brashear through Langley and set him up on

the North Side with a shop, the Brashear Optical Works. There he produced lenses for astronomers abroad as well as in America, making a great contribution to science. (True to the observatory's tradition of correct measurements, he also established the standard for the length of the meter.)

Revered by all classes, he seemed irresistible to the rich. Henry Phipps sent him to Europe. Henry Clay Frick set up a program to realize Brashear's dream that "every boy and girl" might have "the privilege of seeing the beauties of the heavens" as he had. They also supplied the large sum necessary to build this luxurious and interesting building in 1912 for the observatory's three big telescopes.

Allegheny Observatory currently conducts another program of measurement, that of stellar parallaxes, or stars' distances from our sun. The Frick-funded public viewing program continues too; it is well worth making reservations, for a visit here can create the same excitement Donati's comet did in 1858.

Riverview Avenue east of the observatory—a left at the stop sign at the bottom of Observatory Drive—takes you to Perrysville Avenue, where you turn right. Continue on this a mile and four-tenths to the Federal Street Extension, which comes straight down a slope to Perrysville at a point where the latter turns right. That means you take a technical left turn to climb Federal, noticing the gingerbread Victorian house on the right-hand corner with Perrysville. The house is sited square with Federal, but the porch follows Perrysville's curve.

This is a long tour, and you may wish to proceed directly down Federal, where a view of downtown and Mount Washington, on a moody day, can bring to mind novelist Storm Jameson's comment that Pittsburgh "has a strange, awful, and at times overwhelming beauty."

But if you stick with the itinerary, you will have views just as splendid, and some neo-Gothic domestic architecture as well. Go left on Lafayette, then right on Osgood, and left on Marsonia. A quick right on Meadville takes you, after several blocks, to Catoma Street, where you turn left. This neighborhood is called Fineview, and here

you can see clearly why. Just beyond, at 416 on the left, stands Heath-
side Cottage, an 1850s delight. Go right on Warren to see two more
antebellum Gothic Revival structures, at 1521 and 1516, like Heath-
side solos in an otherwise architecturally undistinguished neighborhood. A left on Jay Street, where you can see the sandstone structure
better, leads you to Henderson Street. Take Henderson to the right,
and it will return you to Federal, which you follow to the left and
downhill.

10

TROY HILL, MILLVALE, ASPINWALL

This driving tour begins at Chestnut Street and Troy Hill Road and can easily be done as an extension of tour 9.

Not So Down to Earth

Pittsburghers' down-to-earth attitude makes sense, since most of the city's wealth came from the earth—coal, iron, oil, natural gas.

Some seemingly less earthy fortunes turn out on inspection to be likewise terrestrial in origin. The H. J. Heinz Company, for instance, had its beginnings in a Sharpsburg vegetable patch. But the Heinz story suggests that Pittsburgh was always doing more than merely digging and transforming products of the earth. Parts of this tour—and not only the obviously elevated ones—deal with efforts at transforming not things but thoughts.

The itinerary begins at Troy Hill Road and Chestnut, on the edge of Allegheny City's Dutchtown. The first sight, emblematic of much of what we'll see today, is both a reminder of the Old World's contribution to the new, and of matter's metamorphosis into spirit, or at least into spirits. As you begin climbing Troy Hill Road, you see on the left the Eberhardt and Ober Brewery. This 1880 red brick complex now serves multiple purposes, most prominently that of housing a thriving new brewery and restaurant. In addition, the North Side Civic Development Council established the Brewery Innovation Center here, an incubator where new businesses find a range of support services. At the top of the road, as it turns left, stands a festive green-and-white stick style house of 1877, bought by brewer John Ober. Note the fish-scale and diamond wood siding.

Turn left on Lowrie Street and left again on Kilkenbeck; go right on Goettmann. If Troy Hill rises above the Allegheny like an ocean liner above the sea, this stretch of Goettmann is the upper promenade. But farther down, with houses tightly packed on both sides, the meta-phor shifts, and the narrow street puts you in mind of an Italian hill town—insular, proud, possibly hostile.

Park toward the end of Goettmann, where, just left of Troy Hill Presbyterian Church, is a walkway that leads you to a wonderful view of the city; the nearby houses, with pink flamingos imprisoned in chain-link pens, are picturesque too. If you detect the scent of ketchup, it's from the Heinz plant below us, which we will visit pres-ently. Turn right here on Province, then right on Brabec, another street with a strong character. Gaps between its neat dwellings afford glimpses of Spring Hill. Were these in fact the medieval villages they look like, Spring Hill would be Troy Hill's hereditary enemy.

At the end of Brabec you will be forced right on Basin. A quick left on Goettmann will return you to Troy Hill Road off which, this time, you will turn right on Lowrie, noticing the horse's head over the beer distributor's door on the left. Before refrigeration and pasteuriza-tion, beer was kept cool in cellars or caves—the reason for the hillside or cavetop siting of early breweries. Horses—of which the Anheuser-Busch Clydesdales are the most memorable—advertised the swiftness of the brew's transport to the consumer. On the right side of Lowrie stand some restored post–Civil War houses.

Turn left on Froman Street, which you take to Harpster, where another left brings you shortly to the Shrine of Saint Anthony.

No one who has seen St. Anthony's chapel will be stingy with exclamations. It astonishes partly because of its sharp contrast with Troy Hill's generally modest, not to say austere, demeanor. The chapel, plain enough outside, within is so sumptuous that it would

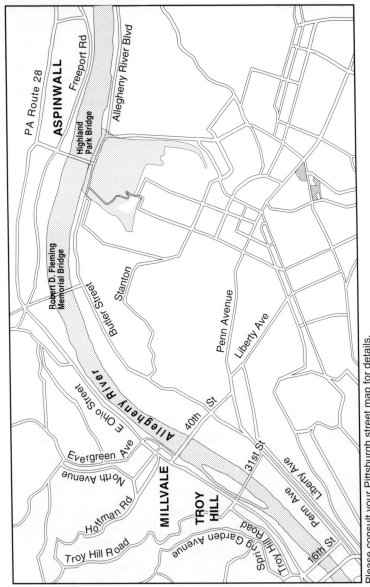

Please consult your Pittsburgh street map for details.

stand out even in baroque Salzburg. In Pittsburgh, it's staggering. Visiting hours are strictly limited; make sure you call ahead.

The Shrine of Saint Anthony was not a Pittsburgher's project, but that of a well-off Belgian priest, Suitbert Mollinger. He had studied in Padua, and perhaps at that time conceived his devotion to the great miracle-working saint who is buried there. As you enter Saint Anthony's, however, what first strikes you is not a reminder of the saint, but the colorful, lifelike stations of the cross. Carved in Bavaria, they dominate the interior, which had to be enlarged to hold them.

Nonetheless, they are but a teaser for the main feature: a holy array of over 4,500 relics of saints, including a first-class one of Saint Anthony, in reliquaries where silver and gilt intricacy is elaborated to the utmost.

Except in the Warhol Museum, with its captivating memorabilia, relics no longer enjoy the favor they once did. From a rationalist point of view, they are silly tokens of unjustifiable superstition. From the point of view of today's faithful, bits of bone and scraps of cloth deviate devotion from its right path—considering that God is a spirit, and not a tooth. But no rationalist has ever fully explained the phenomenon of relic-related miracles. As for the spiritually minded, why should they deny potency to fragments linked with great spirits?

Others, indifferent to all these considerations, may smile at the arcane harmony between Mollinger's pursuits and those of his contemporaries, the lords of Pittsburgh. In both cases they see accumulation beyond all reason, an obsessive materialism echoed in Andy Warhol's horde of stuff.

The builder and collector went swiftly to his reward. The day the enlarged chapel was dedicated, the Feast of Saint Anthony in 1892, Father Mollinger suffered a stroke; he died two days later.

To see a little more of Troy Hill, go left on Tinsbury Street and right on Hatteras, unmarked here. A left on Gardner leads back down Troy Hill Road, with more splendid views of the Allegheny River and the Golden Triangle. At the end stands a reminder of the German

House, Troy Hill Road

origins of this side of Allegheny City, the half-timbered seat of an old German choral society, the Teutonia Maennerchor, still singing, by the way.

Turn left on Chestnut toward the Sixteenth Street Bridge and cross East Ohio to Progress Street, where you turn left for the Heinz plant. Pull over and pause a moment in front of the employees' auditorium.

History has a deadly way of freezing and therefore justifying iniquity. Because capital did in fact succeed in subjugating labor in Homestead, Frick and Carnegie—the argument goes—had no rational alternative but to behave as they did. The logic of economics and therefore of history demanded the near-enslavement of their workers. This extreme interpretation has a diabolical attraction. If what happened had to happen, then what will be, will be—and there's no point in making a fuss to change it.

At least one turn-of-the-century industrial giant gave the lie to the view that capitalism and soul crushing had to coincide. Horrified by the violent railroad strikes of 1877, H. J. Heinz wanted, as he put it, "to humanize the business system." A good traveler, he had studied the paternalistic system in vogue in Germany—the land of his parents' birth—and he decided to adopt it here, with the goal of eliminating enmity between workers and bosses, capital and labor.

A pleasant workplace was basic to this effort. In 1884, he had built his vinegar works here on the Allegheny River and on the Pennsylvania Railroad's main line. Five years later, he expanded operations, establishing his principal plant in several neo-Romanesque buildings. These handsome structures, glazed pressed brick without, rich with stained glass and murals within, provided more than mere industrial efficiency. Heinz wanted to ensure the general well-being of his workers.

Employees—overwhelmingly female, unlike those of the entirely male metal-working industries—got regular manicures and medical treatment, enjoyed picnics and promenades in a special company wagonette, had access to a pool, a roof garden, piano music, and lectures. They were also offered courses in millinery, cooking, drawing, and the like.

Critics of paternalism call it a gentler and therefore more effective form of social control. They point out its lack of respect for individual autonomy—had the employees received higher wages, they would have had access to a broader field of action on their own, free of the company's watchful eye.

That eye was not always benevolent; Heinz fired at least one male employee who had neglected his family and taken up with another woman. (Heinz's moral energies were to find a perfect channel toward the end of his life in the Sunday School movement.) Despite this censorious undertone, paternalism worked. H. J. Heinz had no labor trouble, and no unions, for sixty-five years.

Heinz ably confronted another problem. Americans entertained a well-founded fear that packaged food products might be tainted. Careless processors had, in fact, poisoned many, and a fly-by-night image hovered over the industry. Heinz intended the solid grandeur of these buildings to dispel that. He also fought for the passage of a stringent pure food act in Congress.

From the outset, Heinz used quality as the best sales promotion. In prerefrigeration days, the American diet suffered from a blandness unimaginable today; no fruits and few vegetables were available for over half the year. Relishes relieved the monotony. Of these, horseradish was a favorite—also because it was believed to have medicinal qualities—but putting up the root was a knuckle-cutting, tear-inducing hardship for housewives. The stage was set for shysters to sell the stuff in brown or green bottles, padded with far-easier-to-prepare turnip. Heinz caused a relish revolution by using clear glass bottles; the horseradish you saw was the horseradish you got. He quickly outsold competitors.

Some advertising, and not the least effective, had little to do with quality or even the products, and everything to do with making a splash in America's consciousness. New York's first (1900) large elec-

Fire station, Troy Hill

Stations of the cross, St. Anthony's Chapel

tric sign was Heinz's forty-foot pickle outlined in twelve hundred blinking bulbs at Fifth Avenue and Twenty-third Street. (The pouring ketchup bottle recently installed on the side of the Heinz plant here, facing the Pittsburgh skyline, is a charming throwback to that low-tech era.) Andy Warhol's sculpture of a cardboard box of Heinz ketchup bottles, identical to the real thing, was an homage to Heinz's success in creating consumer culture icons.

Ketchup is indeed produced here, in nine-hundred-gallon batches for single-serving packets. Working at capacity, the plant can churn out twenty-one million such pouches a day. It also cooks up soup and baby food.

Tours of the Heinz plant, long a staple of a Pittsburgh education, are no longer offered. You may have noticed what looked like a Tudor mansion at East Ohio and Heinz Street; that was the 1913 Sarah Heinz settlement house, still serving the neighborhood as a community center.

Albert Kahn, the famous industrial architect, designed the fine building on the northwest corner of Progress and Heinz in 1930 to harmonize with the original 1890s structures, and he designed a couple more buildings within the complex. The tradition of commissioning outstanding architects continued in the 1950s when Skidmore, Owings, and Merrill produced a warehouse, a research building on the Allegheny shore (which we will pass), and the Vinegar Works visible from East Ohio Street—a Miesian masterpiece that looks somewhat frayed today, whose designer was Gordon Bunshaft. The Heinz family and foundation, in line with this tradition of successful patronage, recently funded the Carnegie's Heinz Architectural Center.

Turn right on unmarked Heinz Street, then left on River Avenue, where you see the research building. Enjoy the river views. Industry has so dominated this city's waterfront that you are rarely as close to the water in Pittsburgh as you are right here.

Turn right, just before the Thirty-first Street Bridge, at the Herr's Island Bridge. Once on the island, a left turn leads you to the rowing

Reliquary, St. Anthony's Chapel

club. Turn left into their parking lot and you will reach the gentle back channel of the Allegheny, lined with trees on the shore and rail tracks just behind.

Roberto Clemente Park downstream near the stadium offers many riverside pleasures—strolling, jogging, views. Boating is not one of them. Yet in nineteenth-century Pittsburgh, that was as popular a sport as baseball. But then mills and factories and railroads multiplied along the three rivers; even as they turned the air to miasma, they turned the flowing water into an open sewer. Now environmental cleansing, hastened by mills closing, has renewed the rivers' attraction; rowing is coming back, along with other forms of pleasure boating.

Herr's Island is in many ways an indication of the problems and possibilities of Pittsburgh's waterfront. Formerly occupied by a Pennsylvania Railroad holding pen for livestock, the island began its transformation in the late 1980s and early 1990s with a name change—Washington's Landing—and construction of a marina, rowing club, tennis courts, office buildings, and a sports factory. Discovery of hazardous waste—a constant problem along the rivers—delayed completion of some of this construction, which now includes a great deal of housing as well, with spectacular river and city views. The island is the point of departure for a twelve-mile linear park that will open the riverfront from here to Sandcastle in West Homestead.

Backtrack to River Avenue where you turn right, then quickly left on the Thirty-first Street Bridge, followed by an even quicker right on East Ohio Street, Route 28 North, for Millvale.

Take the Millvale exit and bear right with Evergreen. Then you are forced left at the old brick stockhouse. There is an even older stone house at 144 Evergreen, begun before 1826. Notice its Georgian entrance.

Continue on Evergreen—it becomes the Blue Belt—beyond the limits of Millvale for well over two miles. Turn right at the T intersection, followed by an immediate left on Rockridge. This takes you into Evergreen Hamlet.

This tour features three European ways of confronting problems—Roman Catholic devotion in Troy Hill, German social welfare programs at the Heinz plant, and Croatian art at a church we'll soon see in Millvale—and one American way: the suburb. Nonetheless, even as the other actors in this chapter were animated by idealism, so did idealism lie behind the foundation of Evergreen Hamlet.

By the middle of the nineteenth century, technological and industrial advances had changed American social psychology in important ways. For one thing, improved transportation, especially the railroad, meant the land had been tamed. Nature, no longer the haunt of unknown terrors, could be idealized and enjoyed. At the same time, industry was transforming the city, formerly synonymous with civilization, into a sink from which wise men wished to flee.

That wish fathered the suburb, of which Evergreen Hamlet was a very early example. In fact, its date—1851—gives it primacy over what is commonly considered the first romantic suburb in the country (Llewellyn Park, New Jersey, built in the mid 1850s). But Evergreen Hamlet never grew as its founders hoped.

Part of this experiment's interest is found in the character of its founders. No Thoreau-like recluses, they were solid men of business. But their hamlet's constitution explicitly invited those "who recognize no values but such as may be computed in dollars" not to join the group. Those who did join built four houses by 1852, Gothic Revival or Italianate, mostly in board and batten. Privacy was one of suburbia's original lures; in the summer, trees screen the houses from view.

Backtrack to Millvale, keeping alert, as Evergreen is poorly marked. At the city limits, you may want to stop at Regis Steedle Candies for a shake or sundae. Their antique sandwich menu features such Pittsburgh staples as jumbo and chipped ham. Continue on Evergreen (to the left of Steedle's) almost a mile to Butler, where you turn right.

Saint Anne's and a Methodist church flank Butler. Turn left on Grant, Millvale's main street, at the end of which you turn a sharp right just before the overpass of Route 28 South. Maryland Avenue takes you to Saint Nicholas Church, Frederick Sauer's pedestrian work for Millvale's Croatian Catholics.

The Russell Sage Foundation's Pittsburgh Survey of the early 1900s found Pittsburghers startlingly passive in the face of social problems. As far as workers went, fear of company reprisal justified a supine posture. Anyone looking aggressively for solutions tended to be outside this system of intimidation. On this tour, we have had two examples: a Belgian priest who imported holy relics and a powerful industrialist who imported German corporate paternalism.

Millvale provided another outsider a chance to enlist spirits on the side of action. Finding a bland chapel sheltering a dynamo of grace was a shock in Troy Hill; discovering that a Victorian manufacturing complex was an advanced laboratory for social experimentation was also a surprise. This banal yellow brick church may give you an equal jolt. Inside, it is covered with explosive revolutionary paintings, the work of Maxo Vanka, an immigrant from Croatia in the 1930s. Ask the priest or sacristan to turn on the lights; the switch is in the sacristy to the right of the altar.

Socially ambitious art rarely finds its way into churches. Here the juxtaposition of contemporary political and moral themes with traditional Christian iconography makes for visual schizophrenia, intensified by the uneasy overlay of expressionist, surrealist, and even pre-Raphaelite strains.

The most unusual scenes—done in true fresco, by the way, which means they were painted on still-damp fresh plaster, just as in the Sistine Chapel—are toward the front of the church. Notice, under the choir loft, the image of an angry Mary breaking a soldier's rifle and the crucified Christ bayonetted.

To the right and the left of this area, Vanka depicted two meals: on the left, the immigrants' table, blessed by Jesus; on the right, the cap-

Murals, St. Nicholas Croatian Church

Murals by Maxo Vanka, St. Nicholas Croatian Church

italist's. This latter created a furor and gave rise to a rumor that a prominent local banker tried to have it whitewashed over.

At right angles to these two scenes are images of maternal grief. On the left, Croatian mothers in the old country mourn a son killed in war; on the right, Croatian mothers here mourn a son killed in industry. The most distinctive of Vanka's visions dominates the wall just around the corner—a figure of Injustice seen as a sword-bearing, gas-masked woman, holding scales where a stack of gold coins outweigh bread, symbol of Christ. Vanka's consciousness-raising frescos date from 1937 to 1938 and 1941, but their message—not least for his strife-torn homeland—remains timely.

Continue up Maryland to the first stop sign, then go right, across Stanton Avenue and the creek to Grant. Go right to Route 28; go north toward Etna—which we don't visit—continuing to Sharpsburg, a town dominated by massive towered and domed Saint Mary's. Following locust-lined Main Street through the business district, you come on the H. J. Heinz Memorial Plaza, a heterogeneous monument featuring a statue of Guyasuta. (Heinz began his career here as a lad cultivating a vegetable garden in the Allegheny flood plain.)

In truth the statue was mass-produced, a glorified cigar store Indian, here named for a peaceable Native American acquaintance of George Washington, who hunted hereabouts. Originally Guyasuta dominated a fountain Heinz gave as he left Sharpsburg for Point Breeze, but the fountain got knocked down by drivers on more than one occasion. Now, bas relief panels show Heinz teaching Sunday School at Grace Methodist, a few blocks down West Canal Street on the left.

Continue along Main Street straight into Aspinwall, a pretty town just beyond the approaches to the Highland Park Bridge. Turn left at the light on Western, then right on Second Street, and left on Center, where, beyond the underpass, you see on the left a group of houses, more easily appreciated on foot. The entrance is opposite and uphill from 612. What is puzzling about this fantasy village is that the rest of architect Frederick Sauer's work—we saw his Saint Nicholas in Millvale—consisted mainly of dry, cookie-cutter churches. Here Sauer, working toward the end of his life in the 1920s and 1930s, showed he really wanted to produce sandcastles and dollhouses. He designed and built these himself. His methods, which included using salvaged materials and ornament, recall Gaudi; his results bring to mind both his native Heidelberg and Hollywood exotic.

Backtrack on Center to Freeport Road, where you turn left for Waterworks Mall, on Pittsburgh city property; the Aspinwall and Ross pumping stations stand as Beaux Arts reminders of how important this civic function was considered to be.

Return to Pittsburgh proper by the Highland Park Bridge.

11

SOUTH SIDE

This driving and walking tour begins with Station Square, located to the immediate right upon crossing the Smithfield Street Bridge from downtown. You may park in the lot east (upstream) of the Terminal Building, which means turning right once you have entered the complex.

Playing with History

As a city that has suffered convulsive changes, Pittsburgh must grapple with its history. Leaders of Pittsburgh's Renaissance dealt with it one way—by starting all over from scratch. They began their renewal by demolishing almost everything west of Stanwix Street.

The developers of Station Square, conversely, started with what they already had—the richly embellished rail terminal of the Pittsburgh and Lake Erie Railroad—and created the Station Square complex around it.

Big changes are in the works here on the Monongahela shore. Yet what Station Square has been is also significant. Without apologies to the better known "festival marketplaces" of the Rouse Corporation, Station Square styles itself a "festive marketplace." It's an amalgam of handsomely restored turn-of-the-century architecture, some imperfectly recycled historical artifacts, sundry commercial endeavors, and a couple of frankly ugly modern buildings. The curious thing is that its developer, far from being the slick operator you might expect, was a distinguished preservation group, the Pittsburgh History and Landmarks Foundation.

Americans' attitude toward history is ambivalent. Some simply deny its value; others make a fetish of its remnants. Between these extremes stand those who want to use the past to validate the future. That would appear to have been the Landmarks Foundation's choice when, in the mid 1970s, they boldly took on the challenge of converting the old train station into an office, commercial, and entertainment complex occupying fifty-two acres on the Monongahela shore opposite the Golden Triangle.

Their effort has borne fruit, so much so that Station Square is expanding. Salient features as they now appear are dominated by the terminal building itself. Notice from the parking lot, on its east or upstream facade, the relief of Locomotive 135 at the top.

As you approach the building from the east, you see a sculptured figure retrieved from some demolition keeping company with a pop dispenser; if that seems undignified, consider that the figure's sisters guard a garage over by the Sheraton. On the North Side, we saw a garden of architectural fragments planted by the Landmarks Foundation in their sojourn there; here, similar relics get exploited for their decorative value—which implies no disrespect, if you assume the stone lady likes Coke.

Entering the building you see a number of striking historical photographs. Beyond, the lavish waiting room of the old station now serves as the impressive Grand Concourse restaurant. You discern more of the character of this enterprise as you go out through the bar on the left, the Gandy Dancer Saloon.

Turning right outside, you come to the Bessemer Court Shops, which occupy old rail cars. A little farther on, an impressive ten-ton Bessemer convertor reigns. Other artifacts of interest dot the grounds, part of an Industrial Riverwalk, which should eventually link with the rest of the city's linear parkland.

Whatever its merits as a festive marketplace, this area has always been, and remains, a transportation nexus. Pittsburgh's light-rail cars (formerly trolleys) depart from Station Square and cross the Mon to

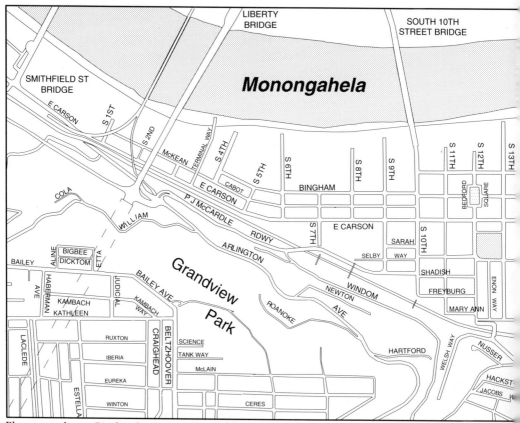

Please consult your Pittsburgh street map for details.

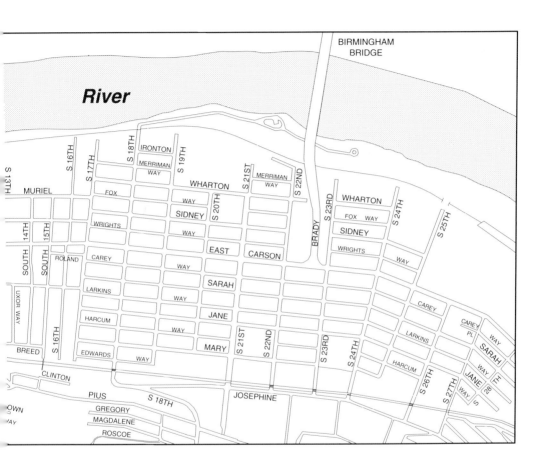

River

BIRMINGHAM
BRIDGE

IRONTON
MERRIMAN
WAY
S 13TH
S 16TH
S 17TH
S 18TH
S 19TH
MURIEL
FOX
WHARTON
S 21ST
MERRIMAN
WAY
S 22ND
WAY
S 20TH
S 23RD
WHARTON
SIDNEY
FOX WAY
S 24TH
WRIGHTS
WAY
SIDNEY
S 25TH
14TH
15TH
ROLAND
CAREY
EAST
CARSON
WRIGHTS
WAY
SOUTH
SOUTH
WAY
SARAH
LARKINS
WAY
JANE
CAREY
UXOR WAY
HARCUM
WAY
LARKINS
CAREY
PL
WAY
S 16TH
MARY
S 21ST
S 22ND
S 23RD
S 24TH
HARCUM
SARAH
BREED
EDWARDS
WAY
S 26TH
S 27TH
WAY
JANE
CLINTON
PIUS
S 18TH
JOSEPHINE
OWN
GREGORY
WAY
MAGDALENE
ROSCOE
BRADY

225

descend into the downtown subway system, or they go through the tunnel at the end of the Smithfield Street Bridge and into the South Hills.

Consider the bridge itself. This structure replaced an 1846 wire-suspension bridge built by John Roebling, an early local test of the wire rope Roebling invented, and which ultimately led to his commission to design the great Brooklyn Bridge. The Smithfield Street Bridge, dating from 1883, is distinguished by its now extremely rare football-shaped lenticular trusses. It has undergone a thorough rehabilitation, and its original brown, tan, and blue color scheme, as well as decorative fixtures, have been restored.

Pittsburgh's two remaining funiculars (the city's hills once supported twenty) depart from just south of Station Square's property. At the eastern end is the station for the oldest, the 1870 Monongahela Incline—a project which also benefited from John Roebling's wire cable. (Pittsburgh's extremely rooted and particular character is evident in the local terms for transportation. Funiculars are called inclines, the Liberty Tunnel under Mt. Washington is always referred to as "the Liberty Tubes," and Interstate 376 passing through town is always "the Parkway.")

Toward Station Square's western end, the Duquesne Incline, Pittsburgh's third, uses its original 1877 cars with their cherry-and-maple–paneled Eastlake interiors. The cable drum and wood-toothed drive gear, also original, will take you safely to the upper station, filled with memorabilia. Mt. Washington commuters, as well as tourists, habitually use the inclines.

Another form of transportation used by locals as well as visitors is the large Gateway Clipper fleet, moored a short distance downstream. Riverboats shuttle Pittsburghers to games at Three Rivers Stadium and tourists on excursions up and down the rivers. The fleet and Station Square's proximity to downtown have made it a prime target for the riverboat gambling industry. The History and Landmarks Foundation sold Station Square in 1994 to Promus Companies, Inc., of

Bessemer Court, Station Square

View of Smithfield Street Bridge from Station Square

Memphis and Forest City Enterprises of Cleveland, a partnership including one of the major players in the casino business.

Before the sale, Station Square had an approved master plan prepared principally by one of the designers of successful Battery Park City in Manhattan—Stan Eckstut of Ehrenkrantz, Eckstut, and Whitelaw. Maintaining Pittsburgh's informal mixed quality, the plan called for a residential village where the eastern parking lot now is, with streets on an angle for good river views.

West of Station Square and the Sheraton Hotel a terraced riverfront park connected with the mile-long industrial walk was planned. An office building and a recycling of the Lawrence Paint Company near the Duquesne Incline building for loft apartments would complete the expansion.

That plan remains in limbo as the Pennsylvania legislature debates the gambling question. Also holding up development here is yet another transportation project. The Wabash tunnel, between Station Square and the Fort Pitt Tunnel, is slated to reopen as a bus and high-occupancy vehicle route to the Parkway and airport, relieving the choked Fort Pitt Bridge. A new bridge across the Mon, from the new tunnel to downtown, will also be built.

Return to your car. Leaving Station Square, turn left or east on East Carson Street. On the left are a number of interesting industrial establishments. On the right, dominating a large area thanks to its squad of exotic domes, stands Saint John the Baptist Ukrainian Catholic Church, built between 1895 and 1917. First organized in 1890, this church underlined the importance in Pittsburgh of Byzantine rite Catholicism. Byzantine Catholics' liturgy follows that of ancient Constantinople, while organizationally they profess allegiance to the pope of Rome. Byzantines here have had their own bishop since 1907.

The pediment of the facade displays the essential South Side style; here a handsome Byzantine-style mosaic is surrounded by wood, a reminder of the Old World encased in the materials of the new. Within, a Roman baroque baldachino provides a counterpoint to the twentieth-century apse mural of Christ's baptism as though it happened in western Pennsylvania—Jesus at Ohiopyle.

Go left on Seventh Street, then right on Bingham, where you see on the right at Ninth a late-nineteenth-century industrial building, once a glass factory, now a Salvation Army center. Glass manufacturing in Pittsburgh began on the South Side in 1797, thanks to the coal that was simply chuted down Mt. Washington. Geographical position likewise helped Pittsburgh attain primacy in glass; difficult to transport over the mountains, from here it was easily shipped downriver to expanding western markets.

Out west, Pittsburgh window glass replaced oiled parchment and animal skins for keeping out the elements. But before long the local product was competing back east too, on a higher plane. Bakewell's tableware became the first American glass company to sell its product to a president for use in the White House (Monroe first in 1817, then Jackson in 1829). In fact, Benjamin Bakewell had lured skilled glassmakers here from Europe. Travelers marveled at his success all the same, since his work was carried on "amidst every discouragement incident to a want of taste and wealth."

Farther east, on the near left corner of Bingham and Ninth, stand the landmark Hemphill-Macintosh buildings. Just beyond is the 1915 fish-adorned Oliver Bathhouse, once intended for the populace's hygiene, now a swimming pool for their recreation. Turn right on Tenth Street and left on Carson. At 1005 stands another significant South Side church, Cleaves Temple C.M.E. Church, built in 1913 for the services of Ukrainian Presbyterians, recycled for Greek Catholics, and now used by Methodists.

Turn left on Twelfth and loop around the red brick South Side Market, an institution here since 1813. The present building, dating from 1893 and 1915, serves as a recreation center. The shops on the left keep the nineteenth-century ambiance alive; on the right, facing the market, is Café Allegro, a good restaurant. Club Café, a jazz

South Side

venue, is here, too. These places suggest the South Side's growing function as Pittsburgh's playground.

Continue on Twelfth south across Carson. Pull over a moment here if you can, then we'll turn left on Sarah Street. On your left you see a trompe l'oeil mural of old Birmingham, as this area was called until it became part of Pittsburgh in 1872. Birmingham had been a borough since 1826, the first in the county after Pittsburgh; glass and iron were its main industries. Its name suggested the area's industrial ambitions.

In fact, when Charles Dickens visited in 1842 he reported that "Pittsburg is like Birmingham in England; at least its townspeople say so. Setting aside the streets, the shops, the houses, waggons, factories, public buildings, and population, perhaps it may be. It certainly has a great quantity of smoke hanging about it."

Notice the tin pediment of the old Weilersbacher Hotel on South Twelfth before you turn left on Sarah. If Pittsburgh's identity seemed doubtful to Dickens, it got fixed as the century wore on. This neighborhood, a microcosm of the city as a whole, was originally settled by British Islanders and Germans. Immigration of Slavs began during the Civil War—first Poles, then Lithuanians, then Slovaks, then Ukrainians. The streets they created have remained stable in appearance and social makeup for generations now.

 Pittsburgh has enjoyed great success in meeting, channeling, and even initiating change. Yet the city's social fabric is conservative. An explanation may lie in the class structure. Civic leaders have made trenchant changes when they have deemed them necessary to the city's survival as an economic power; ordinary people have remained immobile. Pittsburghers have always been said to enjoy—if that's the word—a disproportionate chance of dying in Pittsburgh if they were born here; not for them the carefree, get-up-and-go that outsiders see as Americans' distinguishing trait. Why this immobility? Perhaps immigrants suffered such changes in leaving the European peasantry for the American proletariat that their appetite for upheaval was forever sated. Or perhaps the struggle here in the New World was so fierce that, surviving it, they wanted to enjoy the fruits in peace.

This social conservatism has kept Pittsburgh neighborhoods intact better than any preservation movement might have. Poverty too—the median family income here long was lower than in the rest of the city—is preservation's friend.

One of the surprising side effects of the intact quality of neighborhoods like this is that they make superb sets. Pittsburgh has become an increasingly popular backdrop for films. As a *New York Times* writer observed, not many businesses trace their origins to terror and psychotic murder, but that is the case of Pittsburgh's movie industry, which began in grand style with George Romero's *Night of the Living Dead* in 1967. *Silence of the Lambs* (1991) confirmed the article's headline that "In Pittsburgh, Horror Is a Thing of Beauty."

The next turn you'll be making is a jog left onto Seventeenth Street to continue then right on Sarah. Notice the sandstone and brick (and several other materials) house at 118 on the left of Seventeenth. After your right on Sarah, make a left on Eighteenth to proceed to South Side Riverfront Park, a key element in the linear park that will stretch from Herr's Island on the north shore of the Allegheny to Sandcastle upstream on the Monongahela in West Homestead.

Backtrack to Sarah and turn left, eastward. At Twentieth stands the 1893 South Side Presbyterian Church; glance up Twenty-first, to the right, to see the partly recycled 1899 Duquesne Brewery. A grand 1901 Lithuanian church, Saint Casimir's, stands at the corner of Twenty-second. Beyond, at Twenty-fourth, is the plain mid-Victorian Morse School, the focal point of a City Housing Authority seventy-unit apartment group.

Throughout this area, houses have been sheathed in various forms of siding, aluminum, Insulbrick, and Permastone. (Franklin Toker suggests that the South Side boasts the world's largest concentration of Koolvent aluminum awnings as well.) Siding arouses condemnation in gentrifiers' breasts, but they should recall that colonial-era builders committed the original sin here, disguising log houses' true structure with clapboards.

Cast a glance at the slopes from time to time. There structures just like those neatly aligned here on the flats appear to have been flung by a Cubist painter. Lacking the geometry of ordered tiers, they display a jaunty if somewhat haphazard air. Or are we in the presence of clinging desperation that only looks picturesque? No. A climb up any of the concrete stair-lined streets beyond the rail tracks suggests that hard-won stability has engendered serenity even here.

We're going in the opposite direction now. Turn left on Twenty-sixth and left again on East Carson. As you turn you see the site of an enormous steel mill that stood here as late as the 1990s. The Steel Valley Authority, a coalition of Mon Valley communities including Pittsburgh, worked valiantly to reopen the former Jones and Laughlin plant, idle from 1985. The effort, poignantly keeping alive hopes of an industrial resurrection, failed.

The area's slide into a service economy was confirmed yet again. But that had more to do with the tide of world economy than with any deficiency on the part of Pittsburghers. Didn't the Dow index pluck USX from its list in 1992 and replace it with Disney as more significant?

The site was recently spared another riverboat gambling scheme; South Side residents—old and new—put up a united front against it. Now the city is hoping to use these 130 acres for housing and commercial development, some public open space along the river, and an extension of the Pittsburgh Technology Center across the Mon.

Pittsburgh was never solely a manufacturing town. Its historical vocation has ranged from advancing the frontier of the West to advancing the frontier of knowledge. But there has been a constant in its activity, and that has been overwork. The early-twentieth-century Russell Sage Foundation Pittsburgh Survey indicted this city for the

South Side

South Side

"altogether incredible amount of overwork by everybody. . . . The general law of the region is protracted, unremitting toil."

A comment from almost a century earlier suggests the problem may be endemic. "The character of the people is that of enterprising and persevering industry; every man to his business is the prevailing maxim, therefore there is little time devoted to amusements or to the cultivation of refined social pleasures," wrote a traveler in 1817.

Despite the work ethic's stranglehold on Pittsburghers, it may be that Pittsburgh's most interesting future function is in the opposite of work, in entertainment. Here on the South Side, the neighborhood's Station Square and the inclines make splendid playgrounds. A walk down East Carson, especially on a weekend night, shows how lively clubs and restaurants are.

East Carson's popularity grew out of a combination of its fidelity to the past, as far as appearances go, and its willingness to adapt to the purposes of the present. The mostly Victorian buildings, with significant art deco punctuations, have kept their quality also thanks to the city's streetface program, which encourages correct renovation of facades. Carson Street has also been one of the National Trust for Historic Preservation's demonstration Main Streets.

Continue on Carson to Fourteenth—where you will be turning left—noticing (with all the other interesting commercial enterprises along the way) the Beehive café at 1327. Its name suggests industrious insects, but this is a place to lounge, drink coffee, and eat cake. Decoration includes an old Philco television set transformed into an aquarium.

Turn left on Fourteenth and left again on Sarah, then turn right on Fifteenth for Saint Adalbert's Church, a monumental 1889 structure built by Polish immigrants.

Turn right on Breed Street just after the church, then left on Twelfth; as it goes uphill, it runs left into Brosville Street. Turn left on Pius Street, which takes you by the mid-nineteenth-century German Catholic Saint Michael's Church. Its rectory features two frozen-custard-style metal domes. Here, during Lent, parishioners present *Veronica's Veil,* a large-scale Passion play that combines entertainment and edification in the truest South Side spirit.

Take Pius east and turn right on South Eighteenth, then right again after several long blocks on Monastery Avenue, which leads to the 1853 Saint Paul of the Cross Monastery, like Saint Michael's an institution of the Passionist Fathers; the two were formerly connected by a hillside garden. The church's interior is impressive; the view of Pittsburgh even more so.

12

This tour, mostly driven, begins on the South Side at the foot of Mt.
Washington on the McArdle Roadway. Coming from downtown, McArdle
is the immediate right, before the tunnel, upon crossing the Liberty Bridge.

Views

The South Side's most distinctive feature is not a historic building nor a nightspot nor even the winning waterfront. What dominates this, and other parts of Pittsburgh as well, is the looming
mass of Mt. Washington. This long, steep hill, over four hundred feet
high, tightly bounds some five miles of the Monongahela's shore. In
winter, stripped of its green, the escarpment darkens the horizon omi-
nously.

Yet Pittsburgh owes much to Mt. Washington. It was, in all proba-
bility, from here that George Washington designated the site for the
fort that gave the town birth. Later, its coal gave local entrepreneurs
their edge in manufacturing. Now, views from its summit dramatize the
city's possibilities in tourism.

Take McArdle Roadway, passing under the Monongahela Incline,
up to Grandview Avenue, where you turn left, admiring as you turn a
restored Queen Anne house on the curve. Stop shortly beyond to see
the interior of the 1896 church of Saint Mary of the Mount; try the side
door if the front is closed. Freshly restored stained-glass windows
illustrate the life of Christ.

Cross Grandview for the Gallagher Overlook, where a plaque out-
lines the significance of Coal Hill, as Mt. Washington was called until

239

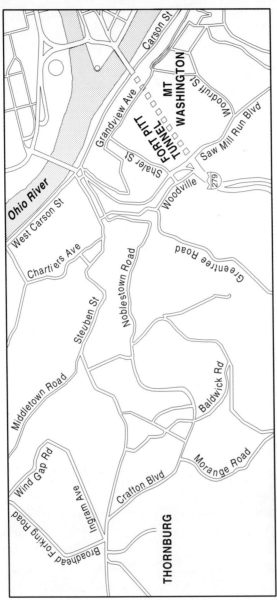

Please consult your Pittsburgh street map for details.

1851; the name change is an early instance of verbal gentrification. Coal, mined here from the time of Fort Pitt, was so abundant that settlers claimed Pittsburgh bees produced bituminous honey. Washington had grasped the military importance of the site, but what was to make Pittsburgh great was underneath it, the coal that powered industry.

Some good buildings stand along this stretch, including several more Queen Anne houses; there is also a dignified little library at 315. But Mt. Washington's architecture mainly looks a little haphazard, a surprise, considering that the view is one of the grandest in America. The explanation lies in the fact that when most Pittsburgh houses were built, smoke engulfed both downtown and the industrial riverbanks, hiding hillside views. What's more, many of the glories of the Golden Triangle date from the 1970s and 1980s; only now has the skyline really packed a punch.

Continue driving along Grandview to the Monongahela Incline station, where you're forced right on Wyoming Street. Make a sharp right after a couple of blocks onto Virginia Avenue; you will drive several blocks through an unimpressive residential area. Yet on this back slope of Mt. Washington, at Bigham Street, nestles Chatham Village, one of America's most significant experiments in housing.

As the director of the Pittsburgh Housing Association in the 1920s summed it up, the city had "rotten bad housing." He felt "a very real inferiority complex" inhibited Pittsburghers from addressing this and other urban problems. Finally, in the classic Pittsburgh way, reform efforts came—from above. The business leaders who ran the Buhl Foundation decided to demonstrate that capitalism could provide low-cost housing, and make a profit to boot.

The Bigham Street site, previously thought too hilly for such a project, turned out to be felicitous. The 216 units, built in 1932 and 1936, fit on seventeen acres, while thirty acres more remain woods or playground space. Planners Clarence Stein and Henry Wright clustered the houses—designed by Ingham and Boyd—around green spaces landscaped by Ralph Griswold and Theodore Kohankie.

241

Mt.
Washington,
Thornburg,
Fort
Pitt
Tunnel

Griswold later served as Point State Park's landscape architect. The atmosphere is that of a particularly well-kept village, unpretentious, cozy, and harmonious.

Despite the excellent relation to its site and the pleasant scale and detailing of its architecture, Chatham Village had detractors. Jane Jacobs found the enclave's harmony an aspect of its antiurban exclusiveness. Prospective tenants were carefully screened so that Chatham Villagers never need "be concerned lest a socially undesirable family move next door." Such scrutiny did produce homogeneity, and links with the larger neighborhood weakened accordingly. In fact, Chatham's builders had hoped to fill it with clerical or skilled manual workers, but screening and taste gave it a population of white-collar and junior executive families.

It did succeed in providing attractive yet inexpensive rental housing profitably; the occupancy rate was always close to 100 percent. (Chatham Village has been a cooperative since 1960.) Curiously, the private sector never sought to replicate it, in Pittsburgh or elsewhere.

Follow the road on the left (Bigham) along the outer edge of the complex and park at its social center, the 1844 Bigham House, now called Chatham Hall. In pre–Civil War times this dwelling served escaping slaves as a stop on the underground railway. Take a walk through the village, noting the various towerlets and pavilions, not to mention the deftly placed and extremely elegant garages. The solid yet gentle Georgian aesthetic of Chatham Village, along with its exemplary site planning, compensate mightily for its insufficient social integration.

Return to your car to continue the outer loop, exiting by turning right on Virginia. Go left on Bigham, then left again on Grandview. Here you will find a number of restaurants where the panorama has priority. Among the least pretentious are the Grandview Saloon, or, for real simplicity, the café next door. Just beyond is the Duquesne Incline station, with its transportation memorabilia.

You will be forced left at Republic Street after a few blocks. Take

View from Grandview Avenue, Mount Washington

Chatham Village

the second right onto Greenleaf Street, which becomes the Duquesne Heights Greenway as it takes you to the West End Circle. With caution—this can be a very congested area—go to the right, crossing over to the near left-hand lane. After the underpass, make a left onto unmarked West Carson. You are following, for now, signs to McKees Rocks. Admire the great arch and restrained decoration of the early 1930s West End Bridge.

After more than half a mile on West Carson, turn left (it's the first one) at the light through the handsome Corliss Street Tunnel. Proceed to Chartiers Avenue and turn left at the stoplight. Go left on Lorenz Avenue at another light, and right on Rue Grande Vue—where you then keep left—for the West End Overlook.

Here you find what the *rue*'s name promises, a head-on view of Pittsburgh, with the Allegheny's visibly muddier waters mixing with the Monongahela's to form the Ohio River. Although there is too much parking lot in the middle ground near the stadium and Science Center, this vista prompts grand reflections on the city.

Guidebooks, like cookbooks, are thinly camouflaged moral treatises. Telling people what to look at is a little like telling them what truth is, what is important, and how it relates to them. Here, from the West End Overlook, as from no place else, you can grasp the importance of rivers to Pittsburgh. We have been so engaged with particular places and their significance in this guide that we have only fleetingly touched on what Pittsburgh is as a whole. Yet few cities constitute so distinctive a whole, with such a strong sense of place.

Rootlessness, disorientation, and uncertain identity are problems afflicting America now more than ever. Pittsburgh's historically high specific gravity, its quiddity, has alleviated those problems here. Pittsburghers usually have a good idea who they are and where they are.

Yet the new service industry—unlike manufacturing, which, to borrow a term from outdoor sculpture, is site-specific—glories in mobility. The great mills grounded Pittsburghers, giving them both orientation and identity. Strip malls and chain stores cannot do that;

they will never transform space into place, into an environment whose distinctive character helps establish the identity of those dwelling there.

Seeing
Pittsburgh

In most American cities, featureless as they often are, sports teams generate civic images. Will that be Pittsburgh's case? The fiery furnaces are spent. Can the Pirates' and Steelers' and Penguins' black and gold substitute for the overwhelming dynamics of the world's most intense industrial activity, to give the town a new face?

From this vantage, it is interesting to consider the relation of sports to the rivers in Pittsburgh. For the first century of the city's history, recreation and rivers were closely connected. This link was strongest with the very popular rowing associations of the latter part of the nineteenth century. But industry, needing the flat shores for its plants, the running water for its processes and wastes, broke that bond. The stadium enjoys no relation to the three rivers except in its name.

Now the community has taken steps toward reclaiming the rivers, both for recreation in boating and for the civic image, as in Point State Park and the new Allegheny riverfront park downtown. These efforts bode well.

What makes for a good sense of place? Even in the industrial era, as in the military and commercial ones, Pittsburgh's strength grew out of its site, out of the geographical and geological peculiarities of its location. Can the *genius loci,* the spirit of place that made Pittsburgh a success in imperial, commercial, and industrial ages, again, in an environmental and ecological age, give the town glory?

That depends on Pittsburghers. The need to rediscover the city's identity and refurbish its image coincides with the need to restore an industry-ravaged land. Something like that began with Pittsburgh's Renaissance in the 1940s and 1950s.

Pittsburgh papers occasionally host debates in the letters columns about what to call the city, now that the smoke has cleared. Topographical considerations—City of Trees or City of Hills or City of

Chatham Village

West End Overlook

Rivers—tend to win out. Few want the town known as Liver Transplant Capital of the World.

That is as it should be, for topography, specifically the way the three dimensions are strongly marked, distinguishes daily experience here. The verticals of closely spaced and obdurate slopes contrast with the flowing horizontals of the rivers—and depth gets pinched by both. Unless you're in a boat, you're always running into something in Pittsburgh.

The difficult topography led to giant engineering projects from the beginning of the city's history. Their success may explain why Pittsburghers so readily adopt a can-do approach to problems; in their daily round they are repeatedly shown how blasting tunnels and building bridges makes life better.

This setting, while encouraging technological optimism, sometimes makes the cityscape claustrophobic. The rivers' return to the community will alter that. As the unchanging hills bound Pittsburgh's horizon, closing and hardening it, the rivers soften and open prospects.

Its topography is both what is truest about Pittsburgh and what sets it apart. Places like the West End Overlook, Grandview Avenue, and Chatham Village exploit Pittsburgh's peculiar landscape; the city now, in search for identity, should follow their example on a larger scale.

Former Mayor Sophie Masloff was quoted as saying that "Pittsburgh's no place for pretensions." If this means that putting on airs doesn't suit the place, she's right. But if the phrase is intended to curb aspirations, she's wrong. Pittsburgh has always richly rewarded high ambition. As the 1878 "Hymn of Pittsburgh" has it, "My father was mighty Vulcan. . . . I think great thoughts strong-winged with steel, / I coin vast iron acts, / And weld the impalpable dream of Seers / Into utile lyric facts."

Daniel Burnham's credo, "Make no little plans. . . . They have no magic to stir men's blood," applies to Pittsburgh as well as to Chicago or Washington. Pittsburgh's most successful mayor, the eminently practical David Lawrence, talked of recapturing Pittsburgh's "old-time zip": "Pittsburgh will need more than good will to keep its pace; it will need proficiency, imagination, a certain recklessness that shocks and stirs the hardheaded men of business and of politics. It is not enough to be industrious; there must be a flair, a touch of genius."

Pittsburgh's thirty-five miles of waterfront are now, thanks to manufacturing's withdrawal, nearly all ready for recycling. A nonprofit coalition of civic and environmental groups, Friends of the Riverfront, has begun to turn nearly twelve of them into the Three Rivers Heritage Trail, a linear park for bikers, strollers, and joggers linking Herr's Island on the Allegheny to Sandcastle on the Monongahela. Four miles are completed along the North Shore. This trail will eventually hook up with the Mon Valley's Steel Industry Heritage Trail, and these ultimately with trails to Ohiopyle, Pennsylvania, and Washington, D.C. Pittsburgh's present mayor, Tom Murphy, was one of the earliest proponents of this idea.

Now the city planning department has commissioned UDA Architects (with Heinz and Mellon foundation support) to research a comprehensive riverfront development plan. This plan should guide such issues as building height along the riverfront (the new jail was in sore need of such guidance) and consistency in the shoreline's appearance. Happily for Pittsburgh, the plan is necessary because of an imminent burst of riverfront development—including housing on the North and South Sides, on Herr's Island, and high above the Monongahela at Nine Mile Run in Squirrel Hill.

The trail, with its interpretive markers at historic sites and housing near the water, will respond in the simplest ways to Pittsburgh's identity and image problems. Returning the rivers to the community, the trail will heal the breach industry wrought between Pittsburgh and nature. Ready accessibility to the shore will permit city dwellers once again to engage with their geography, for recreation and for orientation.

Nothing, since the smoke has gone, follows through in Pittsburgh. Smoke pervaded not only the atmosphere but also the city's psyche because it had a sacramental quality; the material element, particles in the air, symbolized a spiritual fact—industry, people at work. Pittsburgh's rivers alone have a chance of serving as the same sort of comprehensive—and far healthier—symbol. Unifying distant neighborhoods, accessible rivers will provide a secure sense of place, an immediate answer to the question, "Why am I in Pittsburgh?"

251

Mt.
Washington,
Thornburg,
Fort
Pitt
Tunnel

Backtrack on Rue Grande Vue to Lorenz, where you turn left; turn left again on Steuben Street, which you take back to the West End Circle. Don't take the immediate right turn off of Steuben. Follow the bend and make the next right-hand turn onto Route 60 North toward Crafton. You do not want to turn onto Route 51, Saw Mill Run Boulevard.

This portion of Route 60 North is South Main Street, which features LaVerne's Diner on the left and a mural across the way. We are entering Temperanceville, so named for its founders' antipathy to liquor. As the large tavern bearing the neighborhood's name attests, spirits won in the end. Veer to the right on South Main—to the left is Noblestown Road—to take a look at West End United Methodist Church, built between 1887 and 1889; its architect was Frank E. Alden, one of the Carnegie Institute's designers.

Backtrack a few yards to Noblestown Road (the continuation of Route 60 North). Now distances stretch. Take Noblestown until it turns sharply left, where you continue going straight onto what is now Crafton Boulevard. You're in Crafton, a village founded in 1873. After passing the elementary school, turn right on Noble Avenue. Notice 51 on the left; now an architects' studio, it is a log house veneered in brick and stone.

Turn left on unmarked Crennell Avenue half a block after the light. Pass under the railroad bridge. Just after a set of lights, Crennell curves to West Crafton and to the 1906 Saint Philip's Church, the work of William P. Ginther, who had done the Immaculate Heart of Mary on

LaVerne's Diner, Route 60

Polish Hill a couple of years earlier. He takes a freehand approach to Gothic here; the interior has no supporting columns. Tudor buildings complete the ecclesiastical complex.

Shortly beyond Saint Philip's, turn left at the T intersection onto West Steuben, following the signs for Route 60 North. Immediately after Chartiers Creek Bridge on the edge of town take a sharp left onto Cornell; you will see a discreet wood sign for Thornburg. Founded in 1899, this parklike suburb shares with other attractions on this tour a happy relation with its site, in the woods above Chartiers Creek. You're on Cornell. Glance up at the white-columned house at 1080 Stanford; the cobblestone at 1137 on the left side is more characteristic of this shingle and stone neighborhood. Turn right on Hamilton Road, with its stucco school, then turn around after the tennis court. Go left on Dartmouth, right on Harvard, right on Yale, left on Cornell and out.

Backtrack across the bridge and retrace your route. That means staying on West Steuben until you turn right on West Crafton (at Saint Philip's). Follow the brick road as it becomes Crennell. Go under the bridge, around the traffic circle, right on Noble, then left on Crafton Boulevard. A couple of blocks beyond the elementary school, turn right on Baldwick Road, following the signs for the Blue Belt. Go left on Noblestown at the junction for Route 50 East; here site planning lapses. Go right on Poplar Street, at the junction for 121 South, then follow signs for 279 North, which you take to return to downtown Pittsburgh.

One of Pittsburgh's peculiar glories, related to its distinctive site, is that when you get here, you know it. You don't just seep in, you arrive. The grand finale of this tour, one of the most dramatic urban experiences in America or anywhere, is passage through the Fort Pitt tunnel.

APPENDIX

Telephone Numbers of Sites and Attractions

1. POINT STATE PARK AND GATEWAY CENTER

Blockhouse: 471–1764
Fort Pitt Museum: 281–9284

2. THE OUTER TRIANGLE (DOWNTOWN)

Benedum Center for the Performing Arts and Byham Theater: 456–6666
First Lutheran Church: 471–8125
Heinz Hall: 392–4800
Pittsburgh Filmmakers at the Harris Theater: 471–9700, 681–5449

3. THE INNER TRIANGLE (DOWNTOWN)

First Presbyterian Church: 531–1035
Smithfield United Church: 281–1811
Trinity Cathedral: 232–6404

4. THE HILL, OAKLAND, SCHENLEY PARK

Bellefield Presbyterian Church: 687–3222
The Carnegie: 622–3141
Carnegie Mellon University: 268–2000
Epiphany Church: 471–0654
First Baptist Church: 621–0500
Heinz Chapel (University of Pittsburgh): 624–8960
Henry Clay Frick Fine Arts Building (University of Pittsburgh): 648–2400

255

Nationality Rooms (University of Pittsburgh): 624–6000
Phipps Conservatory: 622–6914
Pittsburgh Playhouse (Point Park College): 621–4445

Saint Benedict the Moor Roman Catholic Church: 281–3141
Saint Nicholas Greek Orthodox Cathedral: 682–3866
Saint Paul's Cathedral: 621–4951
Soldiers and Sailors Memorial Hall: 621–4253
Stephen Foster Memorial (University of Pittsburgh): 624–4100

5. SHADYSIDE, EAST LIBERTY, HIGHLAND PARK

Calvary Episcopal Church: 661–0120
Church of the Ascension: 621–4361
East Liberty Presbyterian Church: 441–3800
Holy Spirit Catholic Church: 687–1220
Pittsburgh Zoo: 665–3640
Regent Theatre: 362–6664
Rodef Shalom Temple: 621–6566
Sacred Heart Church: 661–0187
Shadyside Presbyterian Church: 682–4300
Third Presbyterian Church: 661–4710

6. SQUIRREL HILL, POINT BREEZE, HOMEWOOD, EDGEWOOD

Chatham College: 365–1100
Clayton: 371–0606
Holy Rosary Church: 731–3020
Homewood A.M.E. Zion Church: 371–6521
Pittsburgh Center for the Arts: 361–0873
Pittsburgh Civic Garden Center: 441–4442

7. HAZELWOOD, HOMESTEAD, BRADDOCK

Carnegie Library of Braddock: 351–5357
Carnegie Library of Homestead: 462–3444

Church of the Good Shepherd (Hazelwood): 421–8497
Saint Gregory the Theologian Russian Orthodox Church: 461–2426
Saint Michael's Church (Munhall): 461–5725

8. THE STRIP, LAWRENCEVILLE, BLOOMFIELD

Allegheny Cemetery: 682–1624
First United Methodist Church of Pittsburgh: 681–4222
Immaculate Heart of Mary Church: 621–5170
Pittsburgh Brewing Company: 682–7400
Saint Augustine Church: 682–0929
Saint Stanislaus Kostka Church: 471–4767
Senator John Heinz Pittsburgh Regional History Center: 454–6000
Stephen Foster House / American Wind Symphony: 681–8866

9. NORTH SIDE

Allegeny Landing Water Taxi (Three Rivers Charter Service): 363–2628
Allegheny Observatory: 321–2400
Andy Warhol Museum: 237–8300
Calvary United Methodist Church: 323–1070
Carnegie Science Center: 237–3400
Emmanuel Episcopal Church: 231–0454
Mattress Factory: 231–3169
National Aviary: 323–7234
Original Church of God Deliverance Center (formerly Saint Joseph's
    Church): 321–6211
Pittsburgh Children's Festival: 321–5520
Pittsburgh Children's Museum: 322–5058
Pittsburgh Public Theater: 323–8200

10. TROY HILL, MILLVALE, ASPINWALL

Saint Anthony's Chapel: 323–9504
Saint Nicholas Croatian Church of Millvale: 821–3438

11. SOUTH SIDE

Cleaves Temple C.M.E. Church: 481–0535

Prince of Peace Parish (Saint Adalbert's, Saint Casimir's, Saint Michael's):
   431–0168

Saint John the Baptist Ukrainian Catholic Church: 481–5022

Saint Paul of the Cross Monastery: 381–1188

South Side Presbyterian Church: 431–0118

12. MT. WASHINGTON, THORNBURG, FORT PITT TUNNEL

Friends of the Riverfront: 488–0212

Saint Mary of the Mount Church: 381–0212

Saint Philip's Church: 922–6300

West End United Methodist Church: 921–1432

NOTES

1. WHAT'S THE POINT?: POINT STATE PARK AND GATEWAY CENTER

Birth of the city: The main sources for this chapter are: Baldwin, *Pittsburgh;* O'Meara, *Guns at the Forks;* Alberts, *The Shaping of the Point;* Lorant, *Pittsburgh;* and Kidney, *Landmark Architecture: Pittsburgh and Allegheny County.*

5   Washington, "I spent some time": Baldwin, *Pittsburgh,* p. 15.

6   Indian raiding parties: Baldwin, *Pittsburgh,* p. 44.

6   Forbes, "a most diabolical work": O'Meara, *Guns at the Forks,* p. 195.

8   Forbes to Pitt, "I have used the freedom": Baldwin, *Pittsburgh,* p. 54.

9   Blockhouse preservation. Alberts, *Shaping of the Point,* pp. 167–73.

9   Pitt, "maintain His Majesty's subjects": O'Meara, *Guns at the Forks,* p. 218.

11   Bouquet, "a trading place": O'Meara, *Guns at the Forks,* p. 248.

11   Wright, "abandon it": Secrest, *Frank Lloyd Wright,* p. 462.

13   Mellon influences Pennsylvania Railroad: Alberts, *Shaping of the Point,* pp. 132–33.

14   Wright's plan for Point: Alberts, *Shaping of the Point,* pp. 95–96.

16–18   Lawrence to Equitable Life: Lorant, *Pittsburgh,* pp. 428.

18   Le Corbusier on cities: *Looking at City Planning,* pp. 110, 18, 108.

18   Sheathing on Gateway towers: Toker, *Pittsburgh,* p. 26.

20   Corporate concentration: Lorant, *Pittsburgh,* p. 374.

2. URBAN MAGNETISM: THE OUTER TRIANGLE

25   Boat building: Baldwin, *Keelboat Age,* pp. 161, 173; Baldwin, *Pittsburgh,* p. 131; Buck and Buck, *Planting of Civilization,* p. 247.

30   Toker on courthouse: *Pittsburgh,* pp. 73–76.

32   Richardson, "If they honor me": O'Gorman, *H. H. Richardson,* pp. 49–50.

34   Toker on Frick buildings: *Pittsburgh,* p. 70.

34   Burnham, "the most beautiful": Hines, *Burnham of Chicago,* p. 302.

36   U.S. Steel to USX: Hoerr, *And the Wolf Finally Came,* p. 521.

40   1877 railroad strike: Lorant, *Pittsburgh,* pp. 156–58.

3. THE INS AND OUTS OF PLANNING: THE INNER TRIANGLE

Downtown planning. The best overall account of the downtown planning
process is Barnett, "Designing Downtown Pittsburgh."

51   Sir Henry Wotton, "both for the natural imbecility": Clark, *The Gothic
Revival,* p. 14, quoting Wotton's *Elements of Architecture.*

53   Goldberger on PPG Place: Davis, *Remaking Cities,* p. 27.

53   "Tomb of the Unknown Bowler": Attributed to Peter Leo, columnist for the
Pittsburgh Post-Gazette.

56   Toker on Bartberger: *Pittsburgh,* p. 40.

59   Smithfield Church spire: Toker in Tarr, ed., *Pittsburgh-Sheffield Sister
Cities,* p. 6.

4. THE CIVIC PSYCHE: THE HILL, OAKLAND, SCHENLEY PARK

71   Pittsburgh's African-American community: Penetrating studies of the settlement and mobility of African-Americans in Pittsburgh can be found in
Bodnar et al., *Lives of Their Own;* and Tarr, "Community and Mobility."

71   Black poverty rates in Pittsburgh: Jones, "Jobs, Prosperity Elusive for
City's Black Families," pp. D7, D11.

72–74   August Wilson on the Hill: Brantley, "The World That Created August
Wilson," p. 5; "The plays' settings": ibid., p. 5.

73–74   "From the deep and the near": *Joe Turner's Come and Gone,* preface; "leftovers": *Ma Rainey's Black Bottom,* p. 57; "carved in the manner": *The
Piano Lesson,* preface, setting; "Now I can look at you": *Joe Turner's Come
and Gone,* p. 71; "It is hard to define": *Ma Rainey's Black Bottom,* p. xvi;
"to reconnect": *Joe Turner's Come and Gone,* preface.

75   "Hell with the lid taken off": Attributed to James Parton, *The Atlantic Monthly*, 1868.

81   Roosevelt, "if Andrew Carnegie": Wall, *Andrew Carnegie*, p. 985.

81   *Blackwood's*, "Push and screw": Wall, *Andrew Carnegie*, p. 836.

81   Carnegie, "It has never been": Lorant, *Pittsburgh*, p. 203; Moorhead, "a barren and unlovely place": *Whirling Spindle*, pp. 262–63.

85   Helen Frick and Germans: Alberts, *Pitt*, pp. 353–54.

86–89   Cathedral of Learning: The main source for this section on building the Cathedral is Alberts, *Pitt*.

87   Bowman and R. B. Mellon: Alberts, *Pitt*, p. 84.

87   Bowman, "singing upward": Alberts, *Pitt*, p. 85.

88   Bowman, "If the youth": Alberts, *Pitt*, p. 90.

88   Bowman, "Draw a room": Alberts, *Pitt*, p. 97.

88   Toker on Cathedral: *Pittsburgh*, p. 85.

89   Klauder, "The whole structure": Alberts, *Pitt*, p. 108.

99   Carnegie, "It is really astonishing": Brashear, *A Man Who Loved the Stars*, p. 158.

99   Moorhead, "Carnegie Tech was instituted": *Pittsburgh Portraits*, p. 89.

99   Funari on immigrant values: Alberts, *Pitt*, p. viii.

104   Parks as "elevation": Hays, ed., *City at the Point*, p. 239.

5. PRESBYTERIANS AND OTHER PRIMATES: SHADYSIDE, EAST LIBERTY, HIGHLAND PARK

109   Downing, "Nature and domestic life": Andrew Jackson Downing, *The Horticulturist* III (1848): 10; qtd. in Jackson, *Crabgrass Frontier*, p. 64.

111   Hunt house, Loring: "Architectural Tour de Force," pp. 88–95.

111   Pittsburgh's "narrow virtue": Francis G. Couvares in Hays, ed., *City at the Point*, p. 278.

111   "Luxury is a sin": James Parton, "Pittsburgh," *Atlantic Monthly* (Jan. 1868), qtd. in Couvares, *The Remaking of Pittsburgh*, p. 34.

112   Founding of Shadyside Presbyterian: Belfour, *Centennial History of the Shadyside Presbyterian Church*.

115   Dillard on Shadyside Presbyterian: *An American Childhood*, "it might have been," p. 36; "long since encrusted," p. 192; "from the moment their mothers," p. 92.

116   Weber and Stearns: Spencer, *The Spencers of Amberson Avenue*, p. xviii.

117   Moorhead, "bewilderment and terror": *Whirling Spindle*, p. 223; "They never took," p. 227.

119   Cram, "bold, dominating": *My Life in Architecture*, p. 33.

120   Prewar articles on Pittsburgh: From Lubove, *Twentieth Century Pittsburgh*, quoting Duffus, "Is Pittsburgh Civilized?," p. 537, and Macdonald, "Pittsburgh," pp. 51, 57, 56.

120   Andrew Mellon, "every man wants": Russell, "Paul Mellon's Quiet Tradition of Generosity," p. 17.

120   "Mellon Fire Escape": Toker, *Pittsburgh*, p. 210.

121   Cram, "almost passionate": *My Life in Architecture*, p. 253.

121   Cram on clients' taste for Gothic: *My Life in Architecture*, p. 96.

121   Cram on Mellon specifications: *My Life in Architecture*, p. 255.

121   East Liberty traffic patterns: Hazo, *The Pittsburgh That Starts Within You*, p. 18.

124   Baywood as Civic Arena site: Weber, *Don't Call Me Boss*, pp. 266–88.

6. THE VARIETIES OF DOMESTIC EXPERIENCE: SQUIRREL HILL, POINT BREEZE, HOMEWOOD, EDGEWOOD

125   "Aggressive conservation": UDA press release.

127   Willa Cather in Pittsburgh: Moorhead, *These Too Were Here*, pp. 45–62.

127   Cather, "the most beautiful girl": Moorhead, *These Too Were Here*, p. 46.

127   Cather, "in that rich world": Moorhead, *These Too Were Here*, p. 51.

129   Rachel Carson at Chatham College: Gartner, *Rachel Carson*.

129–30   *Time*, "emotional and inaccurate": November 1962 issue quoted in Brooks, *House of Life*, p. 297.

130   Toker on Frank House: *Pittsburgh*, p. 256.

130   Carnegie in Point Breeze: Wall, *Andrew Carnegie*, p. 146.

132   Dillard on Point Breeze: *An American Childhood*, pp. 75–76.

132–36 Henry Clay Frick at Clayton: The best account of Clayton is Hellerstedt et al., *Clayton*. Henry Clay Frick's life and character are amply and perceptively handled in Wall, *Andrew Carnegie*.

132   Schwab on Frick, "absolutely cold-blooded": Hessen, *Steel Titan*, p. 106.

138   George Westinghouse: The only full-length biography of Westinghouse is Prout, *A Life of George Westinghouse*. Haniel Long gives a poetical account of life at Solitude in *Pittsburgh Memoranda*, pp. 42–44.

139   Cram, "particular associations": *My Life in Architecture*, p. 241.

139   Wideman, *Damballah*, p. 158.

140–43 Jane Grey Swisshelm: Larsen, ed., *Crusader and Feminist*.

142   Moorhead on Swisshelm: *Whirling Spindle*, p. 243.

7. CAPITALISM TRIUMPHS, FOR A WHILE: HAZELWOOD, HOMESTEAD, BRADDOCK

148–50 Homestead Strike: I am indebted for this account to Wall, *Andrew Carnegie*, and to Burgoyne, *The Homestead Strike of 1892* and its afterword by David P. Demarest.

150   "Before 1892": Bodnar et al., *Lives of Their Own*, p. 17.

150–51 Wall, Homestead after strike: *Andrew Carnegie*, p. 580.

151   *The Pittsburgh Survey* on Homestead: Fitch, *The Steel Workers*, p. 297.

151   "These men with spirit dead": Wall, *Andrew Carnegie*, p. 580.

152   Carnegie libraries: Wall, *Andrew Carnegie*, p. 816.

152   Toker on Homestead churches: *Pittsburgh*, p. 272.

152–53 Black steel workers. This important history is told vividly in *Struggles in Steel*, a documentary film about African-American steelworkers, written and directed by Tony Buba and Raymond Henderson.

153   Eastern European steel workers: Hays, ed. *City at the Point*, p. 130.

153   Eastern European churches: Roy Lubove quoting Margaret Byington in Hays, ed., *City at the Point*, pp. 299–300.

155   Duquesne household purchasing power, 1980–1986: Hoerr, *And the Wolf Finally Came*, p. 571; Pittsburgh vs. Philadelphia workers' incomes: *Pittsburgh Post-Gazette*, April 22, 1991.

155   Hoerr, "The mill towns": *And the Wolf Finally Came*, p. 11.

156   Wall, Carnegie's experience in bridge building: *Andrew Carnegie*, p. 275.

159   Spencer, "Six months residence": Wall, *Andrew Carnegie*, p. 386.

161   Schwab, "I disagreed": Hessen, *Steel Titan*, p. xv.

161   Bell, *Out of This Furnace*, pp. 343, 34.

8. FROM CRADLE TO GRAVE: THE STRIP, LAWRENCEVILLE, BLOOMFIELD

167–68 Polish settlement in Pittsburgh: This account owes much to Bodnar et al., *Lives of Their Own.*

167   Immigrant reactions to Pittsburgh, "An excellent place," "Pittsburgh is by no means": Lorant, *Pittsburgh*, pp. 50, 79.

172   Sources on Stephen Foster include: Elkus, ed., *Famous Men and Women of Pittsburgh;* and Moorhead, *Whirling Spindle.*

173   Dickens on Arsenal: *American Notes*, p. 183.

176–77 Downing on cemeteries: *Rural Essays*, p. 155.

177   Kidney on cemeteries: *Allegheny Cemetery*, p. 4.

9. SOLOS: THE NORTH SIDE

179   Toker on Allegheny Landing: *Pittsburgh*, p. 157.

179   Wall on Henry Phipps: *Andrew Carnegie*, p. 241.

182–83 Andy Warhol: Sources on Warhol include Ratcliff, *Andy Warhol;* and Gangewere, "Talking to Mark Francis."

184   Warhol, "People's fantasies": Ratcliff, *Andy Warhol*, p. 108.

188   Cather, "Double Birthday," in Demarest, ed., *From These Hills*, p. 150.

196   Stein, "There is something": Quoted from the last of Stein's autobiographies in Hobhouse, *Everybody Who Was Anybody*, p. 1.

196–97 Cassatt meets Stein: Mellow, *Charmed Circle*, p. 14.

197   Graham, "completely bleak," "Pittsburgh was dark": *Blood Memory*, pp. 18, 30.

197   Walpole, "blundered": Quoted in Clark, *The Gothic Revival*, p. 18.

201   Brashear, *A Man Who Loved the Stars*, p. 143.

202   Jameson, "has a strange": Quoted in Alberts, *Pitt*, p. 232.

10. NOT SO DOWN TO EARTH: TROY HILL, MILLVALE, ASPINWALL

209–10 H. J. Heinz: Much of this account is derived from Alberts, *The Good Provider*.

216   Evergreen Hamlet: Lowry, "Hamlet Out of Hiding."

221   Frederick Sauer houses: Van Trump, *Life and Architecture in Pittsburgh*, p. 26.

11. PLAYING WITH HISTORY: SOUTH SIDE

230   Glass manufacturing in Pittsburgh: Innes, *Pittsburgh Glass, 1787–1891*, p. 28.

230   "Amidst every discouragement": Elkus, *Famous Men and Women of Pittsburgh*, p. 3.

232   Dickens, "Pittsburg is like Birmingham": *American Notes*, p. 183.

233   Pittsburgh and horror films. Hinds, "In Pittsburgh Horror Is a Thing of Beauty," p. A12.

237   Pittsburgh Survey, "altogether incredible": Kellogg, ed., *The Pittsburgh District*, p. 4.

237   Pittsburgh work ethic, "The character": Lorant, *Pittsburgh*, p. 78.

12. VIEWS: MOUNT WASHINGTON, THORNBURG, FORT PITT TUNNEL

241   1920s "rotten bad housing": Lubove, *Twentieth-Century Pittsburgh*, p. 66.

242   Chatham Village criticisms: Lubove, *Twentieth-Century Pittsburgh*, pp. 70, 64.

249   "Hymn of Pittsburgh" by Richard Realf: Pittsburgh Survey, *The Pittsburgh District*, 1914.

249   Burnham, "Make no little plans": Hines, *Burnham of Chicago*, p. 74.

250   Lawrence on Pittsburgh, "old-time-zip": Lorant, *Pittsburgh*, pp. 390, 447.

250   Mayor Murphy and rivers: Murphy, "Will Future Pittsburgh Be Defined by Its Rivers?"

BIBLIOGRAPHY

Adams, Henry et al. *John La Farge*. New York: Abbeville Press, 1987.

Alberts, Robert C. *The Good Provider: H. J. Heinz and His 57 Varieties*. Boston: Little, Brown & Co., 1973.

——. *Pitt: The Story of the University of Pittsburgh, 1787–1987*. Pittsburgh: University of Pittsburgh Press, 1987.

——. *The Shaping of the Point: Pittsburgh's Renaissance Park*. Pittsburgh: University of Pittsburgh Press, 1980.

Baldwin, Leland D. *The Keelboat Age on Western Waters*. 1941; rpt. Pittsburgh: University of Pittsburgh Press, 1969.

——. *Pittsburgh: The Story of a City*. 1937; rpt. Pittsburgh: University of Pittsburgh Press, 1970.

Barnett, Jonathan. "Designing Downtown Pittsburgh." *Architectural Record* (Jan. 1982): 90–107.

Belfour, Stanton. *Centennial History of the Shadyside Presbyterian Church*. Pittsburgh: The Shadyside Presbyterian Church, 1966.

Bell, Thomas. *Out of This Furnace*. 1941; rpt. Pittsburgh: University of Pittsburgh Press, 1976.

Bodnar, John. *Steelton: Immigration and Industrialization, 1870–1940*. Pittsburgh: University of Pittsburgh Press, 1977.

Bodnar, John, Roger Simon, Michael P. Weber. *Lives of Their Own: Blacks, Italians and Poles in Pittsburgh, 1900–1960*. Urbana: University of Illinois Press, 1982.

Brantley, Ben. "The World That Created August Wilson." *New York Times*, 5 February 1995.

Brashear, John A. *A Man Who Loved the Stars: The Autobiography of John A. Brashear*. Pittsburgh: University of Pittsburgh Press, 1988.

Brooks, Paul. *House of Life: Rachel Carson at Work*. Boston: Houghton Mifflin Company, 1972.

Buba, Tony, and Raymond Henderson. *Struggles in Steel*. Braddock Films, 1996.

267

Buck, Solon J., and Elizabeth Hawthorn Buck. *The Planting of Civilization in Western Pennsylvania.* Pittsburgh: University of Pittsburgh Press, 1939.

Burgoyne, Arthur G. *The Homestead Strike of 1892.* Afterword by David P. Demarest. 1893; rpt. Pittsburgh: University of Pittsburgh Press, 1979.

Cather, Willa. *Collected Short Fiction.* Ed. Virginia Faulkner. Lincoln: University of Nebraska Press, 1970.

——. *The Kingdom of Art: Willa Cather's First Principles and Critical Statements, 1893–1896.* Ed. Bernice Slote. Lincoln: University of Nebraska Press, 1966.

——. *The World and the Parish: Willa Cather's Articles and Reviews, 1893–1902.* Ed. William M. Curtin. Lincoln: University of Nebraska Press, 1970.

Clark, Kenneth. *The Gothic Revival.* 1928; rpt. London: John Murray, 1973.

Cleveland, H. W. S. *Landscape Architecture.* Ed. Roy Lubove. 1873; rpt. Pittsburgh: University of Pittsburgh Press, 1965.

Couvares, Francis G. *The Remaking of Pittsburgh: Class and Culture in an Industrializing City, 1877–1919.* Albany: SUNY Press, 1984.

Cram, Ralph Adams. *My Life in Architecture.* Boston: Little, Brown and Co., 1936.

Davenport, Marcia. *The Valley of Decision.* 1942; rpt. Pittsburgh: University of Pittsburgh Press, 1989.

Davis, Barbara, ed. *Remaking Cities: Proceedings of the 1988 International Conference in Pittsburgh.* Pittsburgh: University of Pittsburgh Press, 1989.

Demarest, David P. Jr., ed., *From These Hills, From These Valleys: Selected Fiction About Western Pennsylvania.* Pittsburgh: University of Pittsburgh Press, 1976.

Dickens, Charles. *American Notes.* New York: Charles Scribners Sons, 1900.

Dillard, Annie. *An American Childhood.* New York: Harper & Row, 1987.

Downing, Andrew Jackson. *Rural Essays.* Ed. George W. Curtis. New York: Da Capo Press, 1974.

Duffus, R. L. "Is Pittsburgh Civilized?" *Harpers,* 16 Oct. 1930.

Elkus, Leonore R., ed. *Famous Men and Women of Pittsburgh.* Pittsburgh: Pittsburgh History and Landmarks Foundation, 1981.

Fein, Albert. *Frederick Law Olmsted and the American Environmental Tradition.* New York: George Brazillier, 1972.

Fitch, John. *The Steel Workers.* 1910; rpt. Pittsburgh: University of Pittsburgh Press, 1989.

Gangewere, R. Jay. "The Three Rivers Heritage Trail." *Carnegie Magazine* 60, no. 8 (March/April 1991): 20–30.

——. "Talking to Mark Francis." *Carnegie Magazine* 60, no. 4 (July/August 1990): 12–21.

Gartner, Carol B. *Rachel Carson.* New York: F. Ungar Publishing Co., 1985.

Gay, Vernon, and Marilyn Evert. *Discovering Pittsburgh's Sculpture.* Pittsburgh: University of Pittsburgh Press, 1983.

Gleason, Judith. *Agotime.* New York: Grossman Publishers, 1970.

Graham, Martha. *Blood Memory.* New York: Doubleday, 1989.

Hays, Samuel P., ed. *City at the Point: Essays on the Social History of Pittsburgh.* Pittsburgh: University of Pittsburgh Press, 1990.

Hazo, Samuel. *The Pittsburgh That Starts Within You.* Pittsburgh: Byblos, 1986.

Hellerstedt, Kahren Jones et al. *Clayton: The Pittsburgh Home of Henry Clay Frick, Art and Funishings.* Pittsburgh: The Helen Clay Frick Foundation, 1988.

Hessen, Robert. *Steel Titan: The Life of Charles M. Schwab.* 1975; rpt. Pittsburgh: University of Pittsburgh Press, 1990.

Hinds, Michael de Courcy. "In Pittsburgh Horror Is a Thing of Beauty." *New York Times,* 7 February 1992.

Hines, Thomas S. *Burnham of Chicago.* New York: Oxford University Press, 1974.

Hitchcock, Henry Russell. *The Architecture of H. H. Richardson and His Times.* 1936; rpt. Boston: MIT Press, 1966.

Hobhouse, Janet. *Everybody Who Was Anybody.* New York: G. P. Putnam's Sons, 1975.

Hoerr, John P. *And the Wolf Finally Came: The Decline of the American Steel Industry.* Pittsburgh: University of Pittsburgh Press, 1988.

Innes, Lowell. *Pittsburgh Glass, 1797–1891: A History and Guide for Collectors.* Boston: Houghton Mifflin Company, 1976.

Jackson, Kenneth T. *Crabgrass Frontier.* New York: Oxford University Press, 1985.

Jacobs, Jane. *The Death and Life of Great American Cities.* New York: Random House, 1961.

Jones, R. Lamont Jr. "Jobs, Prosperity Elusive for City's Black Families." *Pittsburgh Post-Gazette,* 29 June 1995.

Kellogg, Paul U., ed. *The Pittsburgh District: Civic Frontage.* 1914; rpt. New York: Arno Press, 1974.

Kidney, Walter C. *Allegheny Cemetery.* Pittsburgh: Pittsburgh History and Landmarks Foundation, 1992.

——. *Landmark Architecture: Pittsburgh and Allegheny County.* Pittsburgh: Pittsburgh History and Landmarks Foundation, 1985.

Kidney, Walter C., James Van Trump, and Arthur Ziegler, Jr. *Landmark Architecture of Allegheny County, Pa.* Pittsburgh: Pittsburgh History and Landmarks Foundation, 1967.

Larsen, Arthur, J., ed. *Crusader and Feminist: Letters of Jane Grey Swisshelm.* St. Paul: Minnesota Historical Society, 1934.

Le Corbusier. *Looking at City Planning*. New York: Grossman Publishers, 1971.

Long, Haniel. *Pittsburgh Memoranda*. 1939; rpt. Pittsburgh: University of Pittsburgh Press, 1990.

Lorant, Stefan. *Pittsburgh: The Story of an American City*. Lenox, Mass.: Authors Edition, Inc., 1977.

Loring, John. "Architectural Tour de Force: A Surprising Approach to Aluminum." *Architectural Digest* 34, no. 2 (March 1977): 88–95.

Lowry, Patricia. "Hamlet Out of Hiding." *Pittsburgh Press,* 13 Jan. 1991.

Lubove, Roy. *Twentieth-Century Pittsburgh: Volume One: Government, Business and Environmental Change*. Pittsburgh: University of Pittsburgh Press, 1969.

Macdonald, Dwight. "Pittsburgh: What a City Shouldn't Be." *Forum,* 10 Aug. 1938.

Mellow, James R. *Charmed Circle: Gertrude Stein and Company*. New York: Praeger, 1974.

Moorhead, Elizabeth. *Pittsburgh Portraits*. Pittsburgh: The Beechwood Press, 1955.

——. *These Too Were Here*. Pittsburgh: University of Pittsburgh Press, 1950.

——. *Whirling Spindle*. Pittsburgh: University of Pittsburgh Press, 1942.

Muccigrosso, Robert. *The Mind and Art of Ralph Adams Cram*. Washington, D.C.: University Press of America, 1979.

Murphy, Tom. "Will Future Pittsburgh Be Defined By Its Rivers?" *Executive Report* (Jan. 1990): 7.

O'Brien, Sharon. *Willa Cather*. New York: Oxford University Press, 1987.

O'Gorman, James F. *H. H. Richardson: Architectural Forms for an American Society*. Chicago: University of Chicago Press, 1987.

Oliver, Richard. *Bertram Grosvenor Goodhue*. New York: The Architectural History Foundation, 1983.

O'Meara, Walter. *Guns at the Forks*. 1965; rpt. Pittsburgh: University of Pittsburgh Press, 1979.

The Pittsburgh Survey. *The Pittsburgh District: Civic Frontage,* ed. Paul U. Kellogg. 1914; rpt. New York: Arno Press, 1974.

Prout, Henry G. *A Life of George Westinghouse*. New York: The American Society of Mechanical Engineers, 1921.

Ratcliff, Carter. *Andy Warhol*. New York: Abbeville Press, 1985.

Russell, John. "Paul Mellon's Quiet Tradition of Generosity." *Pittsburgh Post-Gazette,* 21 Mar. 1991, pp. 15, 17.

Secrest, Maryle. *Frank Lloyd Wright*. New York: Alfred A. Knopf, 1992.

Spencer, Ethel. *The Spencers of Amberson Avenue: A Turn-of-the-Century Memoir*. Pittsburgh: University of Pittsburgh Press, 1983.

Stanton, Phoebe. *Pugin*. New York: Viking Press, 1971.

Tarr, Joel A. "Community and Mobility." In Hays, ed., *City at the Point*.

——. *Pittsburgh-Sheffield Sister Cities*. Pittsburgh: Carnegie Mellon University Press, 1986.

Tarr, Joel A., and Shelby Stewman. "Four Decades of Public-Private Partnerships in Pittsburgh." In Foster R. Scott and Renee A. Berger, *Public-Private Partnerships in American Communities: Several Case Studies*. Lexington, Mass.: D. C. Heath & Company, 1982.

Toker, Franklin. *Pittsburgh: An Urban Portrait*. University Park, Pa.: Pennsylvania State University Press, 1986.

Van Trump, James D., *Life and Architecture in Pittsburgh*. Pittsburgh: Pittsburgh History and Landmarks Foundation, 1983.

——. *1300–1335 Liverpool Street*. Pittsburgh: Pittsburgh History and Landmarks Foundation.

Wall, Joseph Frazier. *Andrew Carnegie*. 1970; rpt. Pittsburgh: University of Pittsburgh Press, 1989.

Warhol, Andy. *The Philosophy of Andy Warhol from A to B and Back Again*. New York: Harcourt, Brace, Jovanovich, 1975.

Weber, Michael P. *Don't Call Me Boss: David L. Lawrence, Pittsburgh's Renaissance Mayor*. Pittsburgh: University of Pittsburgh Press, 1988.

Wideman, John Edgar. *Damballah*. New York: Vintage Books, 1988.

Wilson, August. *Joe Turner's Come and Gone*. New York: New American Library, 1988.

——. *Ma Rainey's Black Bottom*. New York: New American Library, 1985.

——. *The Piano Lesson*. New York: New American Library, 1990.

——. *Three Plays*. Pittsburgh: University of Pittsburgh Press, 1992.

WQED-TV. *Wylie Avenue Days*. Produced by Doug Bolin and Christopher Moore. QED Communications, 1991.

ACKNOWLEDGMENTS

I owe thanks, first of all, to Franklin Toker, whose witty and perceptive *Pittsburgh: An Urban Portrait* was my faithful guide to the city. Next, my gratitude goes to this book's godfather, Keith Recker. His enterprising spirit and tact got the project off the ground; he and his family provided generous assistance of every sort. Equally firm in his backing was my noble friend Bill Gleason. The late and much-lamented Ric Witt also gave me and this undertaking invaluable support. Jocelyn Cerul's constancy as a traveling companion is matched only by her grace and good spirit as a friend. Ian Birnie, Albert Filoni, Mark McCormick, Arch Pelley, Terry Sharkey, and Regis McManus all shared helpful insights, and Kirk Ralston coruscated usefully. Tony Mauro offered warm Italian hospitality, and a scrupulous and constructive reading of the text to boot. When Kristin Kovacic was this project's Alpha, she could not have foreseen that destiny wanted her to be its Omega as well, updating and immeasurably improving the final text. Helpful in this phase were Richard O. Price, a tireless fellow traveler, and Kirk and Mary Jeanne Weixel, cheerful fact checkers. My friend John Rahaim not only offered quantities of precious Pittsburgh information, he also gave a framework for understanding cities generally. He and Darrell Packer went far beyond the call of duty in helping us with maps. At the University of Pittsburgh Press, Fred Hetzel provided this book substantial financial aid; Peter Oresick gave it even more impressive moral support. Beth Detwiler grappled valiantly with a project as complex as her city. Other helpful Pittsburghers included Inez Plunkett, Cathy Plunkett, Shamshir Taibjee,

273

and Rob Zellers. Filip Bogaert moved several aspects of the project forward, as did Stephen Berwind. Michael and Jean Holowaty, Cesare Petrillo, and Robert Holley, Sr., clarified Pittsburgh arcana for me. Friends who calmed rough waters include Degna Marconi, Constance Moore, Maud Gleason, Alan Schultz, and Roberto Daniele.

INDEX

Page references in italics indicate photographs.

34–35; mother of, 130; paradoxical nature of, 80, 85; as philanthropist, 75, 80–81, 84, 87, 133, 152, 161, 188, 198; psychology of, 133; relationship of with Henry Clay Frick, 33–34, 132–33, 147–48; views of on education, 79, 96, 99–100; views of on Pennsylvania Railroad, 40, 133

Carnegie (Serra), 82, *83*

Carnegie, Tom, 130

Carnegie Hall (Braddock), *158*

Carnegie Institute, 80, 82, 84, 127, 152, 183, 251; aesthetic relationship of with the Cathedral of Learning, 89; and Andy Warhol Museum, 182–83; beginnings of, 75, 80; and Hall of Architecture, 82, 84; and Heinz Architectural Center, 82, 84, 213; library of, 84–85; Music Hall of, 84; and Scaife Gallery, 82, 130; sculpture hall of, 82; and Wyckoff Hall of Arctic Life, 82. *See also* Carnegie Science Center

Carnegie Institute of Technology (Carnegie Tech), 79, 96, 99

Carnegie International, 81

Carnegie libraries: Allegheny City, 187–88; Duquesne, 152; Library Street (Braddock), 152, *158*, 159, 161; Tenth Ave. (Homestead), 152; Wylie Ave. (Hill District), 74

Carnegie Mellon University, 182; and Baker Hall, 100; beginnings of, 79, 96, 99; buildings of, 100; College of Fine Arts of, 100, 103; as designed by Hornbostel, 100, 105; drama department of, 103; Graduate School of Industrial Administration of, 99, 103; golf course of, 104, 145; and Hamerschlag Hall, 100; and Hunt book collection, 100, 111; Hunt Library at, 100; and the Intelligent Workplace (Hartkopf), 103; Kresge Theater at, 100; Margaret Morrison Carnegie Hall at, 103; new arts center of, 103; parking garage of, 103; and Pittsburgh Technology Center, 95, 144, 234; and Robotics Institute, 175; School for Computer Science at, 99; School of Applied Design at, 100; Software Engineering Institute at, 79; student center of, 103; Tokyo business office of, 99

Carnegie–Point Park library, 55, 57

Carnegie Science Center, 15, 187, 194–96

Carnegie Steel's Pittsburgh works, 153

Carrie blast furnaces, 153, 155

Carson, Rachel, 129–30

Cassatt, Alexander, 42, 196

Cassatt, Mary, 42, 196–97

Cathedral of Learning (University of Pittsburgh), 51, 82, 86–89, *90*, 100, 120, 144–45

Cathedral of Saint John the Divine (Manhattan), 121

Cather, Willa, 72, 117, 127–28, 129, 135, 188

cemeteries, Victorian, 175, 177

Center Avenue (Aspinwall), 220–21

Central Catholic High School, 107–08

Centre Avenue (Hill District), 71

Chabon, Michael, 95

Chalfant, Henry, 18–19

Chandler, Theophilus Parsons, Jr., 62, 118

Chateau Street Expressway, 198

Chatham College, 129

Chatham Hall, 242

Chatham Village, 241–42, *244*, *247*, 249

Chautauqua Ice Company, 162–63

Chevron Corporation, 39

Chicago World's Fair (1893), 33, 56, 75, 96, 100

Childs (Frick), Adelaide, 133–35

Chiodo's, 148

Chislett, John, 55, 175, 192

Christian Science church (Berkeley, California), 118

Church of the Ascension, 108, 147

Church of the Good Shepherd, 147

Circular Staircase, The (Rinehart), 197

City of the Apocalypse (Willett), 118

City Banana Company, 165

City Beautiful movement, 76, 86, 89, 91; beginnings of, 33, 75; ideas about, 44, 76–77, 79, 82, 87

Factory, the (Manhattan), 182
Fairplay, Nicholas, 103
Falconer, William, 96
Fallingwater (Wright), 14, 59
Farmer's Choice, 166
Fathy, Hassan, 39, 53
Federal Courts Building, 40
Federal Reserve (Grant St.), 40
Federal Street, 184, 191–92
Federal Street Extension, 202
Fences (Wilson), 72–73
Fickes Hall, 130
Fidelity Trust Building, 56
Fifth Avenue, 49, 57, 69, 112
Fifth Avenue Place, 20, 47, 49
Fineview, 202–03
First Avenue, 24–25
First Baptist Church, 76
First Church of Christ, Scientist, 76
First Lutheran Church, 39
First Presbyterian Church, 62, 118
Firstside, 24
First United Methodist Church of Pittsburgh, 170
Fjelde, Paul, 103–04
Forbes, General John, 6, 8–9, 11–12, 112. *See also* Forbes Road
Forbes Avenue, 57
Forbes Field, 85–86, 195
Forbes Road, 6, 8–9, 42, 145
Forest City Enterprises, 229
Forest Devil (Snelson), 60
Fort Duquesne, 5–6, 8–9, 11, 112
Fort Duquesne Bridge, 16
Fortieth Street Bridge, 175
Fort Pitt, 9–11, 145. *See also* Blockhouse, the; Fort Pitt Museum; Music Bastion
Fort Pitt Boulevard, 25
Fort Pitt Bridge, 229
Fort Pitt Commons, 27
Fort Pitt Museum, 5–6, *7*, 8–9
Fort Prince George, 5
Foster, Stephen, 172–73, 177
Foster, William, 172
Four Gateway Center, 20
Fourth Avenue, 53, 55–56

Fragonard, Jean Honore, 136
Francis, Mark, 183
Frank House, 130
French, Daniel Chester, 103, 188
French and Indian War, 6, 8
Frick (Childs), Adelaide, 133–35
Frick, Helen Clay, 85, 132–36
Frick, Henry Clay, 12, 35, 116, 136, 138, 143; as art collector, 81–82; assassination attempt on, 134–35; as businessman, 133–34, 147–50, 161, 209; and Clayton (home), 132–36, 175; buildings commissioned by, 56, 59–60, 79, 123; as philanthropist, 202; psychology of, 132–36, 138; relationship of with Carnegie, 33–34, 132–33, 147–48
Frick, Henry Clay, Jr., 134
Frick, Martha, 132, 134–35
Frick Art Museum, 130, 136, *137*
Frick Building, 32–36, 39, 40, 56, 92
Frick Collection (Manhattan), 136
Frick family, 130
Frick Park, 143
Friendship (neighborhood), 170
Friendship Avenue, 170
Friendship School, 170
Friends of the Riverfront, 250
Fulton, the, 181
Fulton, Robert, 173
Funari, John, 99

Gallagher Overlook, 239
Garden Theater, 191
Garner, Erroll, 74
Gateway Center, 16–20, *21*, 22–24, 179
Gateway Plaza, 16, *17*, 18–20
Gaudi, Antonio, 221
General Nutrition Corporation, 172
George Westinghouse Bridge, 156
Gibson, Josh, 177
Ginther, William P., 168, 251, 253
Gluckman, Richard, 182
Goettmann Street, 205
Goldberger, Paul, 53
Golden Triangle, 15–16, 27–28, 46–47, 69, 194, 241

Olmsted, Frederick Law, Jr., 27
One Mellon Bank Center, 35–36, *37*, 59
Original Church of God Deliverance Center, 198
Osterling, Frederick: and Armstrong Cork Factory, 165; and Arrot Building, 55; and building at Smithfield St. and Third Ave., 57; and church on South Aiken Ave., 116; and Clayton, 134–35; and County Mortuary, 29; Isabella Street studio of, 181; and no. 1133 Penn Avenue, 162; and Schwab house, 161; and Times Building, 56; and Union Trust Arcade, 35, 181
Out of This Furnace (Bell), 161, 201
Oxford Centre, 28
Oyster House, 49

Panther Hollow Bridge, 96
Park Place School, 140
Passionist Fathers, 238
Pat's Place, 73
Paulowna Street, 168
Peabody and Stearns (architects), 123
Pei, I. M., 71
Penn Avenue, 43–44, 121, 136, 162, 172–73
Penn Avenue Place, 47, 49
Penn family, 62
Pennsylvania College for Women, 129
Pennsylvania Macaroni, 166
Pennsylvania Railroad, 156, 215; and the Blockhouse, 9; construction of station for, 42; criticized by Pittsburghers, 40; and Edgewood, 140; former switching yards of, 163; and Pittsburgh Renaissance, 13; and Shadyside, 109; strike of (1877), 40, 42, 133, 209
Pennsylvania Station, 40, *41*, 42, 56, 196
People's Savings Bank, 55
Phipps, Henry, 96, 179, 181, 194, 196, 202
Phipps Conservatory, 96, *97*
Piano Lesson, The (Wilson), 72–74
Piazza Lavoro (Smyth), 178
Picasso Museum (Paris), 183

Pinkerton guards, 149–50
Pittsburgh: and Allegheny City, 178, 184; aluminum industry in, 60–61, 167; Anglo-Saxons in, 112; attitude of toward education, 99; automobiles in, 109, 121; beginnings of, 3, 5–6, 8–11, 16; blacks in, 67, 69, 71–74, 152–53, 198; boat building industry in, 25; bottling industry in, 165; Britons in, 232; brutalist architecture in, 76; Byzantine rite Catholicism in, 229; and coal, 241; Central and Eastern Europeans in, 73, 152–53, 159; character of, ix–xi, xv, 3, 105, 107, 120, 127, 167, 197, 201–02, 226, 232–33, 245–46, 249–51, 253; and coke, 133, 145, 147; and cork industry, 165; downtown of (Golden Triangle), 27–28, 46–47, 66; funiculars in, 226; future of, 246, 249, 250–51; as a gateway to the West, 24–25; Germans in, 170, 173, 232; glass industry in, 230; Great Fire of (1845), 24; housing reform, 241; immigrants and immigration in, 73, 99, 109, 112, 116, 153, 162, 167, 177; industrial economy of, x–xi, 12–14, 20, 39, 145, 155–56, 159, 162, 245; and Islam, 74; Italians in, 92, 95, 168, 170; Jews in, 73–74, 107, 128, 198; labor history of, 20, 33–34, 36, 40, 42, 115, 133–34, 148–53, 155, 159, 209–10, 219, 234–36; Lithuanians in, 232; maps of, xii–xiii, 2, 26, 48, 68, 106, 126, 146, 164, 180, 206, 224–25, 240; neighborhood commercial centers in, 116; parks in, 194; Poles in, 167–68, 170, 232; and pollution, ix–x, 3, 11, 13, 16, 18, 138, 215, 232, 251; Presbyterianism in, 112, 115, 117, 120, 127, 135; produce trade in, 163; railroads in, 13, 40, 42, 75, 109, 133, 140, 147, 156, 159, 163, 166; Renaissance of, 11–16, 18, 60, 69, 138, 184, 222, 246; riverboats in, 226; riverfront development plan for, 250; Scots and Scotch-Irish in, 112, 115, 120, 167; service economy in, xi, 14, 20, 39, 234, 245; Slovaks in,